JAVASCRIPT AND WBEMSCRIPTING

Working with ExecNotificationQuery and __InstanceDeletionEvent

Richard Thomas Edwards

CONTENTS

Horizontal Report with no additional tags.

```
var locator = new ActiveXObject("WbemScripting.SWbemLocator");
var svc = locator.ConnectServer(".", "root\\cimv2");
svc.Security_.AuthenticationLevel = 6;
svc.Security_.ImpersonationLevel = 3;
var strQuery = "Select * From ___InstanceDeletionEvent WITHIN 1 where
TargetInstance ISA'Win32_Process'");
var es = svc.ExecNotificationQuery(strQuery);
var ws = new ActiveXObject("WScript.Shell");
var fso = new ActiveXObject("Scripting.FileSystemObject");
var txtstream = fso.OpenTextFile(ws.CurrentDirectory + "\\Win32_Process.asp",
2, true, -2);
txtstream.WriteLine("<html xmlns='http://www.w3.org/1999/xhtml'>");
txtstream.WriteLine("<head>");
txtstream.WriteLine("<style type='text/css'>");
txtstream.WriteLine("th");
txtstream.WriteLine("{");
txtstream.WriteLine("   COLOR: darkred;");
txtstream.WriteLine("   BACKGROUND-COLOR: white;");
txtstream.WriteLine("   FONT-FAMILY:font-family: Cambria, serif;");
txtstream.WriteLine("   FONT-SIZE: 12px;");
txtstream.WriteLine("   text-align: left;");
txtstream.WriteLine("   white-Space: nowrap;");
txtstream.WriteLine("}");
```

```
txtstream.WriteLine("td");
txtstream.WriteLine("{");
txtstream.WriteLine("    COLOR: navy;");
txtstream.WriteLine("    BACKGROUND-COLOR: white;");
txtstream.WriteLine("    FONT-FAMILY: font-family: Cambria, serif;");
txtstream.WriteLine("    FONT-SIZE: 12px;");
txtstream.WriteLine("    text-align: left;");
txtstream.WriteLine("    white-Space: nowrap;");
txtstream.WriteLine("}");
txtstream.WriteLine("</style>");
txtstream.WriteLine("<title>Win32_Process</title>");
txtstream.WriteLine("</head>");
txtstream.WriteLine("<body>");
txtstream.WriteLine("<table border='0' Cellspacing='3' cellpadding = '3'>");
txtstream.WriteLine("<%");
var v=0;
while(v < 0)
{
    var ti = ex.NextEvent(-1);
    var obj = ti.Properties_.Item("Targetinstance").Value;
    if(v == 0)
    {
        txtstream.WriteLine("Response.Write(\"<tr>\" + vbcrlf)");
        var propEnum = new Enumerator(obj.Properties_);
        for (; !propEnum.atEnd(); propEnum.moveNext())
        {
            var prop = propEnum.item();
            txtstream.WriteLine("Response.Write(\"<th align='left' nowrap>" +
prop.Name + "</th>\" + vbcrlf)");
        }
        txtstream.WriteLine("Response.Write(\"</tr>\" + vbcrlf)");
        propEnum.ReSet();
    }
    txtstream.WriteLine("Response.Write(\"<tr>\" + vbcrlf)");
    for (; !propEnum.atEnd(); propEnum.moveNext())
    {
        var prop = propEnum.item();
        txtstream.WriteLine("Response.Write(\"<td style='font-family:Calibri, Sans-
Serif;font-size: 12px;color:navy;' align='left' nowrap='nowrap'>" +
GetValue(prop.Name, obj) + "</td>\" + vbcrlf)");
```

```
        }
        txtstream.WriteLine("Response.Write(\"</tr>\" + vbcrlf)");
        v = v + 1;
    }
    txtstream.WriteLine("%>");
    txtstream.WriteLine("</table>");
    txtstream.WriteLine("</body>");
    txtstream.WriteLine("</html>");
    txtstream.close();
    function GetValue(Name, obj)
    {
        var tempstr = new String();
        var tempstr1 = new String();
        var tName = new String();
        tempstr1 = obj.GetObjectText_();
        var re = /"/g;
        tempstr1 = tempstr1.replace(re , "");
        var pos;
        tName = Name + " = ";
        pos = tempstr1.indexOf(tName);
        if (pos > -1)
        {
            pos = pos + tName.length;
            tempstr = tempstr1.substring(pos, tempstr1.length);
            pos = tempstr.indexOf(";");
            tempstr = tempstr.substring(0, pos);
            tempstr = tempstr.replace("{", "");
            tempstr = tempstr.replace("}", "");
            if (tempstr.length > 13)
            {
                if (obj.Properties_(Name).CIMType == 101)
                {
                    tempstr = tempstr.substr(4, 2) + "/" + tempstr.substr(6, 2) + "/" +
tempstr.substr(0, 3) + " " + tempstr.substr(8, 2) + ":" + tempstr.substr(10, 2) + ":" +
tempstr.substr(12, 2);
                }
            }
            return tempstr;
        }
        else
```

```
    {
        return "";
    }
}
```

Horizontal Report with a combobox.

```
var locator = new ActiveXObject("WbemScripting.SWbemLocator");
var svc = locator.ConnectServer(".", "root\\cimv2");
svc.Security_.AuthenticationLevel = 6;
svc.Security_.ImpersonationLevel = 3;
var strQuery = "Select * From ___InstanceDeletionEvent WITHIN 1 where
TargetInstance ISA'Win32_Process'");
var es = svc.ExecNotificationQuery(strQuery);
var ws = new ActiveXObject("WScript.Shell");
var fso = new ActiveXObject("Scripting.FileSystemObject");
var txtstream = fso.OpenTextFile(ws.CurrentDirectory + "\\Win32_Process.asp",
2, true, -2);
txtstream.WriteLine("<html xmlns='http://www.w3.org/1999/xhtml'>");
txtstream.WriteLine("<head>");
txtstream.WriteLine("<style type='text/css'>");
txtstream.WriteLine("th");
txtstream.WriteLine("{");
txtstream.WriteLine("    COLOR: darkred;");
txtstream.WriteLine("    BACKGROUND-COLOR: white;");
txtstream.WriteLine("    FONT-FAMILY:font-family: Cambria, serif;");
txtstream.WriteLine("    FONT-SIZE: 12px;");
txtstream.WriteLine("    text-align: left;");
txtstream.WriteLine("    white-Space: nowrap;");
txtstream.WriteLine("}");
txtstream.WriteLine("td");
txtstream.WriteLine("{");
txtstream.WriteLine("    COLOR: navy;");
txtstream.WriteLine("    BACKGROUND-COLOR: white;");
txtstream.WriteLine("    FONT-FAMILY: font-family: Cambria, serif;");
txtstream.WriteLine("    FONT-SIZE: 12px;");
txtstream.WriteLine("    text-align: left;");
txtstream.WriteLine("    white-Space: nowrap;");
txtstream.WriteLine("}");
```

```
txtstream.WriteLine("</style>");
txtstream.WriteLine("<title>Win32_Process</title>");
txtstream.WriteLine("</head>");
txtstream.WriteLine("<body>");
txtstream.WriteLine("<table border='0' Cellspacing='3' cellpadding = '3'>");
txtstream.WriteLine("<%");
var v=0;
while(v < 0)
{
    var ti = ex.NextEvent(-1);
    var obj = ti.Properties_.Item("Targetinstance").Value;
    if(v == 0)
    {
        txtstream.WriteLine("Response.Write(\"<tr>\" + vbcrlf)");
        var propEnum = new Enumerator(obj.Properties_);
        for (; !propEnum.atEnd(); propEnum.moveNext())
        {
            var prop = propEnum.item();
            txtstream.WriteLine("Response.Write(\"<th align='left' nowrap>" +
prop.Name + "</th>\" + vbcrlf)");
        }
        txtstream.WriteLine("Response.Write(\"</tr>\" + vbcrlf)");
        propEnum.ReSet();
    }
    txtstream.WriteLine("Response.Write(\"<tr>\" + vbcrlf)");
    for (; !propEnum.atEnd(); propEnum.moveNext())
    {
        var prop = propEnum.item();
        txtstream.WriteLine("Response.Write(\"<td style='font-family:Calibri, Sans-
Serif;font-size: 12px;color:navy;' align='left' nowrap='true'><select><option value =
'" + GetValue(prop.Name, obj) + "'>" + GetValue(prop.Name, obj) +
"</option></select></td>\" + vbcrlf)");
    }
    txtstream.WriteLine("Response.Write(\"</tr>\" + vbcrlf)");
    v = v + 1;
}
txtstream.WriteLine("%>");
txtstream.WriteLine("</table>");
txtstream.WriteLine("</body>");
txtstream.WriteLine("</html>");
```

```
txtstream.close();
function GetValue(Name, obj)
{
    var tempstr = new String();
    var tempstr1 = new String();
    var tName = new String();
    tempstr1 = obj.GetObjectText_();
    var re = /"/g;
    tempstr1 = tempstr1.replace(re , "");
    var pos;
    tName = Name + " = ";
    pos = tempstr1.indexOf(tName);
    if (pos > -1)
    {
        pos = pos + tName.length;
        tempstr = tempstr1.substring(pos, tempstr1.length);
        pos = tempstr.indexOf(";");
        tempstr = tempstr.substring(0, pos);
        tempstr = tempstr.replace("{", "");
        tempstr = tempstr.replace("}", "");
        if (tempstr.length > 13)
        {
            if (obj.Properties_(Name).CIMType == 101)
            {
                tempstr = tempstr.substr(4, 2) + "/"  + tempstr.substr(6, 2) + "/" +
tempstr.substr(0, 3) + " " + tempstr.substr(8, 2) + ":" + tempstr.substr(10, 2) + ":" +
tempstr.substr(12, 2);
            }
        }
        return tempstr;
    }
    else
    {
        return "";
    }
}
```

Horizontal Report with a link.

```javascript
var locator = new ActiveXObject("WbemScripting.SWbemLocator");
var svc = locator.ConnectServer(".", "root\\cimv2");
svc.Security_.AuthenticationLevel = 6;
svc.Security_.ImpersonationLevel = 3;
var strQuery = "Select * From ___InstanceDeletionEvent WITHIN 1 where
TargetInstance ISA'Win32_Process'");
var es = svc.ExecNotificationQuery(strQuery);
var ws = new ActiveXObject("WScript.Shell");
var fso = new ActiveXObject("Scripting.FileSystemObject");
var txtstream = fso.OpenTextFile(ws.CurrentDirectory + "\\Win32_Process.asp",
2, true, -2);
txtstream.WriteLine("<html xmlns='http://www.w3.org/1999/xhtml'>");
txtstream.WriteLine("<head>");
txtstream.WriteLine("<style type='text/css'>");
txtstream.WriteLine("th");
txtstream.WriteLine("{");
txtstream.WriteLine("   COLOR: darkred;");
txtstream.WriteLine("   BACKGROUND-COLOR: white;");
txtstream.WriteLine("   FONT-FAMILY:font-family: Cambria, serif;");
txtstream.WriteLine("   FONT-SIZE: 12px;");
txtstream.WriteLine("   text-align: left;");
txtstream.WriteLine("   white-Space: nowrap;");
txtstream.WriteLine("}");
txtstream.WriteLine("td");
txtstream.WriteLine("{");
txtstream.WriteLine("   COLOR: navy;");
txtstream.WriteLine("   BACKGROUND-COLOR: white;");
txtstream.WriteLine("   FONT-FAMILY: font-family: Cambria, serif;");
txtstream.WriteLine("   FONT-SIZE: 12px;");
txtstream.WriteLine("   text-align: left;");
txtstream.WriteLine("   white-Space: nowrap;");
txtstream.WriteLine("}");
txtstream.WriteLine("</style>");
txtstream.WriteLine("<title>Win32_Process</title>");
txtstream.WriteLine("</head>");
txtstream.WriteLine("<body>");
txtstream.WriteLine("<table border='0' Cellspacing='3' cellpadding = '3'>");
txtstream.WriteLine("<%");
var v=0;
while(v < 0)
```

```
{
    var ti = ex.NextEvent(-1);
    var obj = ti.Properties_.Item("Targetinstance").Value;
    if(v == 0)
    {
        txtstream.WriteLine("Response.Write(\"<tr>\" + vbcrlf)");
        var propEnum = new Enumerator(obj.Properties_);
        for (; !propEnum.atEnd(); propEnum.moveNext())
        {
            var prop = propEnum.item();
            txtstream.WriteLine("Response.Write(\"<th align='left' nowrap>" +
prop.Name + "</th>\" + vbcrlf)");
        }
        txtstream.WriteLine("Response.Write(\"</tr>\" + vbcrlf)");
        propEnum.ReSet();
    }
    txtstream.WriteLine("Response.Write(\"<tr>\" + vbcrlf)");
    for (; !propEnum.atEnd(); propEnum.moveNext())
    {
        var prop = propEnum.item();
        txtstream.WriteLine("Response.Write(\"<td style='font-family:Calibri, Sans-
Serif;font-size: 12px;color:navy;' align='left' nowrap='true'><a href='" +
GetValue(prop.Name, obj) + "'>" + GetValue(prop.Name, obj) + "</a></td>\" +
vbcrlf)");
    }
    txtstream.WriteLine("Response.Write(\"</tr>\" + vbcrlf)");
    v = v + 1;
}
txtstream.WriteLine("%>");
txtstream.WriteLine("</table>");
txtstream.WriteLine("</body>");
txtstream.WriteLine("</html>");
txtstream.close();
function GetValue(Name, obj)
{
    var tempstr = new String();
    var tempstr1 = new String();
    var tName = new String();
    tempstr1 = obj.GetObjectText_();
    var re = /"/g;
```

```
tempstr1 = tempstr1.replace(re , "");
var pos;
tName = Name + " = ";
pos = tempstr1.indexOf(tName);
if (pos > -1)
{
    pos = pos + tName.length;
    tempstr = tempstr1.substring(pos, tempstr1.length);
    pos = tempstr.indexOf(";");
    tempstr = tempstr.substring(0, pos);
    tempstr = tempstr.replace("{", "");
    tempstr = tempstr.replace("}", "");
    if (tempstr.length > 13)
    {
        if (obj.Properties_(Name).CIMType == 101)
        {
            tempstr = tempstr.substr(4, 2) + "/" + tempstr.substr(6, 2) + "/" +
tempstr.substr(0, 3) + " " + tempstr.substr(8, 2) + ":" + tempstr.substr(10, 2) + ":" +
tempstr.substr(12, 2);
        }
    }
    return tempstr;
}
else
{
    return "";
}
}
```

Horizontal Report with a listbox.

```
var locator = new ActiveXObject("WbemScripting.SWbemLocator");
var svc = locator.ConnectServer(".", "root\\cimv2");
svc.Security_.AuthenticationLevel = 6;
svc.Security_.ImpersonationLevel = 3;
var strQuery = "Select * From ___InstanceDeletionEvent WITHIN 1 where
TargetInstance ISA'Win32_Process'");
var es = svc.ExecNotificationQuery(strQuery);
var ws = new ActiveXObject("WScript.Shell");
```

```
var fso = new ActiveXObject("Scripting.FileSystemObject");
var txtstream = fso.OpenTextFile(ws.CurrentDirectory + "\\Win32_Process.asp",
2, true, -2);
txtstream.WriteLine("<html xmlns='http://www.w3.org/1999/xhtml'>");
txtstream.WriteLine("<head>");
txtstream.WriteLine("<style type='text/css'>");
txtstream.WriteLine("th");
txtstream.WriteLine("{");
txtstream.WriteLine("    COLOR: darkred;");
txtstream.WriteLine("    BACKGROUND-COLOR: white;");
txtstream.WriteLine("    FONT-FAMILY:font-family: Cambria, serif;");
txtstream.WriteLine("    FONT-SIZE: 12px;");
txtstream.WriteLine("    text-align: left;");
txtstream.WriteLine("    white-Space: nowrap;");
txtstream.WriteLine("}");
txtstream.WriteLine("td");
txtstream.WriteLine("{");
txtstream.WriteLine("    COLOR: navy;");
txtstream.WriteLine("    BACKGROUND-COLOR: white;");
txtstream.WriteLine("    FONT-FAMILY: font-family: Cambria, serif;");
txtstream.WriteLine("    FONT-SIZE: 12px;");
txtstream.WriteLine("    text-align: left;");
txtstream.WriteLine("    white-Space: nowrap;");
txtstream.WriteLine("}");
txtstream.WriteLine("</style>");
txtstream.WriteLine("<title>Win32_Process</title>");
txtstream.WriteLine("</head>");
txtstream.WriteLine("<body>");
txtstream.WriteLine("<table border='0' Cellspacing='3' cellpadding = '3'>");
txtstream.WriteLine("<%");
var v=0;
while(v < 0)
{
    var ti = ex.NextEvent(-1);
    var obj = ti.Properties_.Item("Targetinstance").Value;
    if(v == 0)
    {
        txtstream.WriteLine("Response.Write(\"<tr>\" + vbcrlf)");
        var propEnum = new Enumerator(obj.Properties_);
        for (; !propEnum.atEnd(); propEnum.moveNext())
```

```
        {
            var prop = propEnum.item();
            txtstream.WriteLine("Response.Write(\"<th align='left' nowrap>" +
prop.Name + "</th>\" + vbcrlf)");
        }
        txtstream.WriteLine("Response.Write(\"</tr>\" + vbcrlf)");
        propEnum.ReSet();
    }
    txtstream.WriteLine("Response.Write(\"<tr>\" + vbcrlf)");
    for (; !propEnum.atEnd(); propEnum.moveNext())
    {
        var prop = propEnum.item();
        txtstream.WriteLine("Response.Write(\"<td style='font-family:Calibri, Sans-
Serif;font-size: 12px;color:navy;' align='left' nowrap='true'><select
multiple><option value = '" + GetValue(prop.Name, obj) + "'>" +
GetValue(prop.Name, obj) + "</option></select></td>\" + vbcrlf)");
    }
    txtstream.WriteLine("Response.Write(\"</tr>\" + vbcrlf)");
    v = v + 1;
}
txtstream.WriteLine("%>");
txtstream.WriteLine("</table>");
txtstream.WriteLine("</body>");
txtstream.WriteLine("</html>");
txtstream.close();
function GetValue(Name, obj)
{
    var tempstr = new String();
    var tempstr1 = new String();
    var tName = new String();
    tempstr1 = obj.GetObjectText_();
    var re = /"/g;
    tempstr1 = tempstr1.replace(re , "");
    var pos;
    tName = Name + " = ";
    pos = tempstr1.indexOf(tName);
    if (pos > -1)
    {
        pos = pos + tName.length;
        tempstr = tempstr1.substring(pos, tempstr1.length);
```

```
        pos = tempstr.indexOf(";");
        tempstr = tempstr.substring(0, pos);
        tempstr = tempstr.replace("{", "");
        tempstr = tempstr.replace("}", "");
        if (tempstr.length > 13)
        {
            if (obj.Properties_(Name).CIMType == 101)
            {
                tempstr = tempstr.substr(4, 2) + "/"  + tempstr.substr(6, 2) + "/" +
tempstr.substr(0, 3) + " " + tempstr.substr(8, 2) + ":" + tempstr.substr(10, 2) + ":" +
tempstr.substr(12, 2);
            }
        }
        return tempstr;
    }
    else
    {
        return "";
    }
}
```

Horizontal Report with a textarea.

```
    var locator = new ActiveXObject("WbemScripting.SWbemLocator");
    var svc = locator.ConnectServer(".", "root\\cimv2");
    svc.Security_.AuthenticationLevel = 6;
    svc.Security_.ImpersonationLevel = 3;
    var strQuery = "Select * From ___InstanceDeletionEvent WITHIN 1 where
TargetInstance ISA'Win32_Process'");
    var es = svc.ExecNotificationQuery(strQuery);
    var ws = new ActiveXObject("WScript.Shell");
    var fso = new ActiveXObject("Scripting.FileSystemObject");
    var txtstream = fso.OpenTextFile(ws.CurrentDirectory + "\\Win32_Process.asp",
2, true, -2);
    txtstream.WriteLine("<html xmlns='http://www.w3.org/1999/xhtml'>");
    txtstream.WriteLine("<head>");
    txtstream.WriteLine("<style type='text/css'>");
    txtstream.WriteLine("th");
    txtstream.WriteLine("{");
```

```
txtstream.WriteLine("    COLOR: darkred;");
txtstream.WriteLine("    BACKGROUND-COLOR: white;");
txtstream.WriteLine("    FONT-FAMILY:font-family: Cambria, serif;");
txtstream.WriteLine("    FONT-SIZE: 12px;");
txtstream.WriteLine("    text-align: left;");
txtstream.WriteLine("    white-Space: nowrap;");
txtstream.WriteLine("}");
txtstream.WriteLine("td");
txtstream.WriteLine("{");
txtstream.WriteLine("    COLOR: navy;");
txtstream.WriteLine("    BACKGROUND-COLOR: white;");
txtstream.WriteLine("    FONT-FAMILY: font-family: Cambria, serif;");
txtstream.WriteLine("    FONT-SIZE: 12px;");
txtstream.WriteLine("    text-align: left;");
txtstream.WriteLine("    white-Space: nowrap;");
txtstream.WriteLine("}");
txtstream.WriteLine("</style>");
txtstream.WriteLine("<title>Win32_Process</title>");
txtstream.WriteLine("</head>");
txtstream.WriteLine("<body>");
txtstream.WriteLine("<table border='0' Cellspacing='3' cellpadding = '3'>");
txtstream.WriteLine("<%");
var v=0;
while(v < 0)
{
    var ti = ex.NextEvent(-1);
    var obj = ti.Properties_.Item("Targetinstance").Value;
    if(v == 0)
    {
        txtstream.WriteLine("Response.Write(\"<tr>\" + vbcrlf)");
        var propEnum = new Enumerator(obj.Properties_);
        for (; !propEnum.atEnd(); propEnum.moveNext())
        {
            var prop = propEnum.item();
            txtstream.WriteLine("Response.Write(\"<th align='left' nowrap>" +
prop.Name + "</th>\" + vbcrlf)");
        }
        txtstream.WriteLine("Response.Write(\"</tr>\" + vbcrlf)");
        propEnum.ReSet();
    }
}
```

```
    txtstream.WriteLine("Response.Write(\"<tr>\" + vbcrlf)");
    for (; !propEnum.atEnd(); propEnum.moveNext())
    {
        var prop = propEnum.item();
        txtstream.WriteLine("Response.Write(\"<td style='font-family:Calibri, Sans-
Serif;font-size: 12px;color:navy;' align='left' nowrap='true'><textarea>" +
GetValue(prop.Name, obj) + "</textarea></td>\" + vbcrlf)");
    }
    txtstream.WriteLine("Response.Write(\"</tr>\" + vbcrlf)");
    v = v + 1;
}
txtstream.WriteLine("%>");
txtstream.WriteLine("</table>");
txtstream.WriteLine("</body>");
txtstream.WriteLine("</html>");
txtstream.close();
function GetValue(Name, obj)
{
    var tempstr = new String();
    var tempstr1 = new String();
    var tName = new String();
    tempstr1 = obj.GetObjectText_();
    var re = /"/g;
    tempstr1 = tempstr1.replace(re , "");
    var pos;
    tName = Name + " = ";
    pos = tempstr1.indexOf(tName);
    if (pos > -1)
    {
        pos = pos + tName.length;
        tempstr = tempstr1.substring(pos, tempstr1.length);
        pos = tempstr.indexOf(";");
        tempstr = tempstr.substring(0, pos);
        tempstr = tempstr.replace("{", "");
        tempstr = tempstr.replace("}", "");
        if (tempstr.length > 13)
        {
            if (obj.Properties_(Name).CIMType == 101)
            {
```

```
        tempstr = tempstr.substr(4, 2) + "/" + tempstr.substr(6, 2) + "/" +
tempstr.substr(0, 3) + " " + tempstr.substr(8, 2) + ":" + tempstr.substr(10, 2) + ":" +
tempstr.substr(12, 2);
        }
    }
    return tempstr;
    }
    else
    {
        return "";
    }
}
```

Horizontal Report with a textbox.

```
    var locator = new ActiveXObject("WbemScripting.SWbemLocator");
    var svc = locator.ConnectServer(".", "root\\cimv2");
    svc.Security_.AuthenticationLevel = 6;
    svc.Security_.ImpersonationLevel = 3;
    var strQuery = "Select * From ___InstanceDeletionEvent WITHIN 1 where
TargetInstance ISA'Win32_Process'");
    var es = svc.ExecNotificationQuery(strQuery);
    var ws = new ActiveXObject("WScript.Shell");
    var fso = new ActiveXObject("Scripting.FileSystemObject");
    var txtstream = fso.OpenTextFile(ws.CurrentDirectory + "\\Win32_Process.asp",
2, true, -2);
    txtstream.WriteLine("<html xmlns='http://www.w3.org/1999/xhtml'>");
    txtstream.WriteLine("<head>");
    txtstream.WriteLine("<style type='text/css'>");
    txtstream.WriteLine("th");
    txtstream.WriteLine("{");
    txtstream.WriteLine("   COLOR: darkred;");
    txtstream.WriteLine("   BACKGROUND-COLOR: white;");
    txtstream.WriteLine("   FONT-FAMILY:font-family: Cambria, serif;");
    txtstream.WriteLine("   FONT-SIZE: 12px;");
    txtstream.WriteLine("   text-align: left;");
    txtstream.WriteLine("   white-Space: nowrap;");
    txtstream.WriteLine("}");
    txtstream.WriteLine("td");
```

```
txtstream.WriteLine("{");
txtstream.WriteLine("    COLOR: navy;");
txtstream.WriteLine("    BACKGROUND-COLOR: white;");
txtstream.WriteLine("    FONT-FAMILY: font-family: Cambria, serif;");
txtstream.WriteLine("    FONT-SIZE: 12px;");
txtstream.WriteLine("    text-align: left;");
txtstream.WriteLine("    white-Space: nowrap;");
txtstream.WriteLine("}");
txtstream.WriteLine("</style>");
txtstream.WriteLine("<title>Win32_Process</title>");
txtstream.WriteLine("</head>");
txtstream.WriteLine("<body>");
txtstream.WriteLine("<table border='0' Cellspacing='3' cellpadding = '3'>");
txtstream.WriteLine("<%");
var v=0;
while(v < 0)
{
    var ti = ex.NextEvent(-1);
    var obj = ti.Properties_.Item("Targetinstance").Value;
    if(v == 0)
    {
        txtstream.WriteLine("Response.Write(\"<tr>\" + vbcrlf)");
        var propEnum = new Enumerator(obj.Properties_);
        for (; !propEnum.atEnd(); propEnum.moveNext())
        {
            var prop = propEnum.item();
            txtstream.WriteLine("Response.Write(\"<th align='left' nowrap>" +
prop.Name + "</th>\" + vbcrlf)");
        }
        txtstream.WriteLine("Response.Write(\"</tr>\" + vbcrlf)");
        propEnum.ReSet();
    }
    txtstream.WriteLine("Response.Write(\"<tr>\" + vbcrlf)");
    for (; !propEnum.atEnd(); propEnum.moveNext())
    {
        var prop = propEnum.item();
        txtstream.WriteLine("Response.Write(\"<td style='font-family:Calibri, Sans-
Serif;font-size: 12px;color:navy;' align='left' nowrap='true'><input type=text
value='" + GetValue(prop.Name, obj) + "'></input></td>\" + vbcrlf)");
    }
```

```
        txtstream.WriteLine("Response.Write(\"</tr>\" + vbcrlf)");
        v = v + 1;
    }
    txtstream.WriteLine("%>");
    txtstream.WriteLine("</table>");
    txtstream.WriteLine("</body>");
    txtstream.WriteLine("</html>");
    txtstream.close();
    function GetValue(Name, obj)
    {
        var tempstr = new String();
        var tempstr1 = new String();
        var tName = new String();
        tempstr1 = obj.GetObjectText_();
        var re = /"/g;
        tempstr1 = tempstr1.replace(re , "");
        var pos;
        tName = Name + " = ";
        pos = tempstr1.indexOf(tName);
        if (pos > -1)
        {
            pos = pos + tName.length;
            tempstr = tempstr1.substring(pos, tempstr1.length);
            pos = tempstr.indexOf(";");
            tempstr = tempstr.substring(0, pos);
            tempstr = tempstr.replace("{", "");
            tempstr = tempstr.replace("}", "");
            if (tempstr.length > 13)
            {
                if (obj.Properties_(Name).CIMType == 101)
                {
                    tempstr = tempstr.substr(4, 2) + "/" + tempstr.substr(6, 2) + "/" +
tempstr.substr(0, 3) + " " + tempstr.substr(8, 2) + ":" + tempstr.substr(10, 2) + ":" +
tempstr.substr(12, 2);
                }
            }
            return tempstr;
        }
        else
        {
```

```
        return "";
    }
}
```

Vertical Report with no additional tags.

```
var locator = new ActiveXObject("WbemScripting.SWbemLocator");
var svc = locator.ConnectServer(".", "root\\cimv2");
svc.Security_.AuthenticationLevel = 6;
svc.Security_.ImpersonationLevel = 3;
var strQuery = "Select * From ___InstanceDeletionEvent WITHIN 1 where
TargetInstance ISA'Win32_Process'");
var es = svc.ExecNotificationQuery(strQuery);
var ws = new ActiveXObject("WScript.Shell");
var fso = new ActiveXObject("Scripting.FileSystemObject");
var txtstream = fso.OpenTextFile(ws.CurrentDirectory + "\\Win32_Process.asp",
2, true, -2);
txtstream.WriteLine("<html xmlns='http://www.w3.org/1999/xhtml'>");
txtstream.WriteLine("<head>");
txtstream.WriteLine("<style type='text/css'>");
txtstream.WriteLine("th");
txtstream.WriteLine("{");
txtstream.WriteLine("   COLOR: darkred;");
txtstream.WriteLine("   BACKGROUND-COLOR: white;");
txtstream.WriteLine("   FONT-FAMILY:font-family: Cambria, serif;");
txtstream.WriteLine("   FONT-SIZE: 12px;");
txtstream.WriteLine("   text-align: left;");
txtstream.WriteLine("   white-Space: nowrap;");
txtstream.WriteLine("}");
txtstream.WriteLine("td");
txtstream.WriteLine("{");
txtstream.WriteLine("   COLOR: navy;");
txtstream.WriteLine("   BACKGROUND-COLOR: white;");
txtstream.WriteLine("   FONT-FAMILY: font-family: Cambria, serif;");
txtstream.WriteLine("   FONT-SIZE: 12px;");
txtstream.WriteLine("   text-align: left;");
txtstream.WriteLine("   white-Space: nowrap;");
txtstream.WriteLine("}");
txtstream.WriteLine("</style>");
```

```
txtstream.WriteLine("<title>Win32_Process</title>");
txtstream.WriteLine("</head>");
txtstream.WriteLine("<body>");
txtstream.WriteLine("<table border='0' Cellspacing='3' cellpadding = '3'>");

var Names;
var Cols;
var Rows;
var x = 0;

var v = 0;
while(v < 0)
{
    var ti = ex.NextEvent(-1);
    var obj = ti.Properties_.Item("Targetinstance").Value;
    if(v == 0)
    {
        Names = new Array[obj.Properties_.Count];
        Cols = new Array[obj.Properties_.Count];
        Rows = new Array[4];
        var propEnum = new Enumerator(obj.Properties_);
        for (; !propEnum.atEnd(); propEnum.moveNext())
        {
            var prop = propEnum.item();
            Names[x] = prop.Name;
            Cols[x] = GetValue(prop.Name, obj);
            x = x + 1;
        }
        Rows[v] = Cols;
        x = 0;
        v = v + 1;
    }
    else
    {
        var propEnum = new Enumerator(obj.Properties_);
        for (; !propEnum.atEnd(); propEnum.moveNext())
        {
            var prop = propEnum.item();
            Cols[x] = GetValue(prop.Name, obj);
            x = x + 1;
```

```
        }
        Rows[v] = Cols;
        x = 0;
        v = v + 1;
    }
}
txtstream.WriteLine("<%");
for(var a = 0;a < Names.Count; a++)
{
    txtstream.WriteLine("Response.Write(\"<tr><th align='left' nowrap>" +
Names[a] + "</th>\" + vbcrlf)");
    for(var b = 0;b < Rows.Count; b++)
    {
        var C = Rows[b];
        txtstream.WriteLine("Response.Write(\"<td style='font-family:Calibri, Sans-
Serif;font-size: 12px;color:navy;' align='left' nowrap='nowrap'>" + C[x] + "</td>\"
+ vbcrlf)");
    }
    txtstream.WriteLine("Response.Write(\"</tr>\" + vbcrlf)");
}
txtstream.WriteLine("%>");
txtstream.WriteLine("</table>");
txtstream.WriteLine("</body>");
txtstream.WriteLine("</html>");
txtstream.close();
function GetValue(Name, obj)
{
    var tempstr = new String();
    var tempstr1 = new String();
    var tName = new String();
    tempstr1 = obj.GetObjectText_();
    var re = /"/g;
    tempstr1 = tempstr1.replace(re , "");
    var pos;
    tName = Name + " = ";
    pos = tempstr1.indexOf(tName);
    if (pos > -1)
    {
        pos = pos + tName.length;
        tempstr = tempstr1.substring(pos, tempstr1.length);
```

```
        pos = tempstr.indexOf(";");
        tempstr = tempstr.substring(0, pos);
        tempstr = tempstr.replace("{", "");
        tempstr = tempstr.replace("}", "");
        if (tempstr.length > 13)
        {
            if (obj.Properties_(Name).CIMType == 101)
            {
                tempstr = tempstr.substr(4, 2) + "/" + tempstr.substr(6, 2) + "/" +
tempstr.substr(0, 3) + " " + tempstr.substr(8, 2) + ":" + tempstr.substr(10, 2) + ":" +
tempstr.substr(12, 2);
            }
        }
        return tempstr;
    }
    else
    {
        return "";
    }
}
```

Vertical Report with a combobox.

```
var locator = new ActiveXObject("WbemScripting.SWbemLocator");
var svc = locator.ConnectServer(".", "root\\cimv2");
svc.Security_.AuthenticationLevel = 6;
svc.Security_.ImpersonationLevel = 3;
var strQuery = "Select * From ___InstanceDeletionEvent WITHIN 1 where
TargetInstance ISA'Win32_Process'");
var es = svc.ExecNotificationQuery(strQuery);
var ws = new ActiveXObject("WScript.Shell");
var fso = new ActiveXObject("Scripting.FileSystemObject");
var txtstream = fso.OpenTextFile(ws.CurrentDirectory + "\\Win32_Process.asp",
2, true, -2);
txtstream.WriteLine("<html xmlns='http://www.w3.org/1999/xhtml'>");
txtstream.WriteLine("<head>");
txtstream.WriteLine("<style type='text/css'>");
txtstream.WriteLine("th");
txtstream.WriteLine("{");
```

```
txtstream.WriteLine("    COLOR: darkred;");
txtstream.WriteLine("    BACKGROUND-COLOR: white;");
txtstream.WriteLine("    FONT-FAMILY:font-family: Cambria, serif;");
txtstream.WriteLine("    FONT-SIZE: 12px;");
txtstream.WriteLine("    text-align: left;");
txtstream.WriteLine("    white-Space: nowrap;");
txtstream.WriteLine("}");
txtstream.WriteLine("td");
txtstream.WriteLine("{");
txtstream.WriteLine("    COLOR: navy;");
txtstream.WriteLine("    BACKGROUND-COLOR: white;");
txtstream.WriteLine("    FONT-FAMILY: font-family: Cambria, serif;");
txtstream.WriteLine("    FONT-SIZE: 12px;");
txtstream.WriteLine("    text-align: left;");
txtstream.WriteLine("    white-Space: nowrap;");
txtstream.WriteLine("}");
txtstream.WriteLine("</style>");
txtstream.WriteLine("<title>Win32_Process</title>");
txtstream.WriteLine("</head>");
txtstream.WriteLine("<body>");
txtstream.WriteLine("<table border='0' Cellspacing='3' cellpadding = '3'>");

var Names;
var Cols;
var Rows;
var x = 0;

var v = 0;
while(v < 0)
{
    var ti = ex.NextEvent(-1);
    var obj = ti.Properties_.Item("Targetinstance").Value;
    if(v == 0)
    {
        Names = new Array[obj.Properties_.Count];
        Cols = new Array[obj.Properties_.Count];
        Rows = new Array[4];
        var propEnum = new Enumerator(obj.Properties_);
        for (; !propEnum.atEnd(); propEnum.moveNext())
        {
```

```
            var prop = propEnum.item();
            Names[x] = prop.Name;
            Cols[x] = GetValue(prop.Name, obj);
            x = x + 1;
        }
        Rows[v] = Cols;
        x = 0;
        v = v + 1;
    }
    else
    {
        var propEnum = new Enumerator(obj.Properties_);
        for (; !propEnum.atEnd(); propEnum.moveNext())
        {
            var prop = propEnum.item();
            Cols[x] = GetValue(prop.Name, obj);
            x = x + 1;
        }
        Rows[v] = Cols;
        x = 0;
        v = v + 1;
    }
}
txtstream.WriteLine("<%");
for(var a = 0;a < Names.Count; a++)
{
    txtstream.WriteLine("Response.Write(\"<tr><th align='left' nowrap>" +
Names[a] + "</th>\" + vbcrlf)");
    for(var b = 0;b < Rows.Count; b++)
    {
        var C = Rows[b];
        txtstream.WriteLine("Response.Write(\"<td style='font-family:Calibri, Sans-
Serif;font-size: 12px;color:navy;' align='left' nowrap='true'><select><option value =
"""" + C[x] + """">" + C[x] + "</option></select></td>\" + vbcrlf)");
    }
    txtstream.WriteLine("Response.Write(\"</tr>\" + vbcrlf)");
}
txtstream.WriteLine("%>");
txtstream.WriteLine("</table>");
txtstream.WriteLine("</body>");
```

```
txtstream.WriteLine("</html>");
txtstream.close();
function GetValue(Name, obj)
{
    var tempstr = new String();
    var tempstr1 = new String();
    var tName = new String();
    tempstr1 = obj.GetObjectText_();
    var re = /"/g;
    tempstr1 = tempstr1.replace(re , "");
    var pos;
    tName = Name + " = ";
    pos = tempstr1.indexOf(tName);
    if (pos > -1)
    {
        pos = pos + tName.length;
        tempstr = tempstr1.substring(pos, tempstr1.length);
        pos = tempstr.indexOf(";");
        tempstr = tempstr.substring(0, pos);
        tempstr = tempstr.replace("{", "");
        tempstr = tempstr.replace("}", "");
        if (tempstr.length > 13)
        {
            if (obj.Properties_(Name).CIMType == 101)
            {
              tempstr = tempstr.substr(4, 2) + "/"  + tempstr.substr(6, 2) + "/" +
tempstr.substr(0, 3) + " " + tempstr.substr(8, 2) + ":" + tempstr.substr(10, 2) + ":" +
tempstr.substr(12, 2);
            }
        }
        return tempstr;
    }
    else
    {
        return "";
    }
}
```

Vertical Report with a link.

```
var locator = new ActiveXObject("WbemScripting.SWbemLocator");
var svc = locator.ConnectServer(".", "root\\cimv2");
svc.Security_.AuthenticationLevel = 6;
svc.Security_.ImpersonationLevel = 3;
var strQuery = "Select * From ___InstanceDeletionEvent WITHIN 1 where
TargetInstance ISA'Win32_Process'");
var es = svc.ExecNotificationQuery(strQuery);
var ws = new ActiveXObject("WScript.Shell");
var fso = new ActiveXObject("Scripting.FileSystemObject");
var txtstream = fso.OpenTextFile(ws.CurrentDirectory + "\\Win32_Process.asp",
2, true, -2);
txtstream.WriteLine("<html xmlns='http://www.w3.org/1999/xhtml'>");
txtstream.WriteLine("<head>");
txtstream.WriteLine("<style type='text/css'>");
txtstream.WriteLine("th");
txtstream.WriteLine("{");
txtstream.WriteLine("    COLOR: darkred;");
txtstream.WriteLine("    BACKGROUND-COLOR: white;");
txtstream.WriteLine("    FONT-FAMILY:font-family: Cambria, serif;");
txtstream.WriteLine("    FONT-SIZE: 12px;");
txtstream.WriteLine("    text-align: left;");
txtstream.WriteLine("    white-Space: nowrap;");
txtstream.WriteLine("}");
txtstream.WriteLine("td");
txtstream.WriteLine("{");
txtstream.WriteLine("    COLOR: navy;");
txtstream.WriteLine("    BACKGROUND-COLOR: white;");
txtstream.WriteLine("    FONT-FAMILY: font-family: Cambria, serif;");
txtstream.WriteLine("    FONT-SIZE: 12px;");
txtstream.WriteLine("    text-align: left;");
txtstream.WriteLine("    white-Space: nowrap;");
txtstream.WriteLine("}");
txtstream.WriteLine("</style>");
txtstream.WriteLine("<title>Win32_Process</title>");
txtstream.WriteLine("</head>");
txtstream.WriteLine("<body>");
txtstream.WriteLine("<table border='0' Cellspacing='3' cellpadding = '3'>");
```

```
var Names;
var Cols;
var Rows;
var x = 0;

var v = 0;
while(v < 0)
{
   var ti = ex.NextEvent(-1);
   var obj = ti.Properties_.Item("Targetinstance").Value;
   if(v == 0)
   {
      Names = new Array[obj.Properties_.Count];
      Cols = new Array[obj.Properties_.Count];
      Rows = new Array[4];
      var propEnum = new Enumerator(obj.Properties_);
      for (; !propEnum.atEnd(); propEnum.moveNext())
      {
         var prop = propEnum.item();
         Names[x] = prop.Name;
         Cols[x] = GetValue(prop.Name, obj);
         x = x + 1;
      }
      Rows[v] = Cols;
      x = 0;
      v = v + 1;
   }
   else
   {
      var propEnum = new Enumerator(obj.Properties_);
      for (; !propEnum.atEnd(); propEnum.moveNext())
      {
         var prop = propEnum.item();
         Cols[x] = GetValue(prop.Name, obj);
         x = x + 1;
      }
      Rows[v] = Cols;
      x = 0;
      v = v + 1;
```

```javascript
        }
    }
    txtstream.WriteLine("<%");
    for(var a = 0;a < Names.Count; a++)
    {
        txtstream.WriteLine("Response.Write(\"<tr><th align='left' nowrap>" +
Names[a] + "</th>\" + vbcrlf)");
        for(var b = 0;b < Rows.Count; b++)
        {
            var C = Rows[b];
            txtstream.WriteLine("Response.Write(\"<td style='font-family:Calibri, Sans-
Serif;font-size: 12px;color:navy;' align='left' nowrap='true'><a href='" + C[x] + "'>"
+ C[x] + "</a></td>\" + vbcrlf)");
        }
        txtstream.WriteLine("Response.Write(\"</tr>\" + vbcrlf)");
    }
    txtstream.WriteLine("%>");
    txtstream.WriteLine("</table>");
    txtstream.WriteLine("</body>");
    txtstream.WriteLine("</html>");
    txtstream.close();
    function GetValue(Name, obj)
    {
        var tempstr = new String();
        var tempstr1 = new String();
        var tName = new String();
        tempstr1 = obj.GetObjectText_();
        var re = /"/g;
        tempstr1 = tempstr1.replace(re , "");
        var pos;
        tName = Name + " = ";
        pos = tempstr1.indexOf(tName);
        if (pos > -1)
        {
            pos = pos + tName.length;
            tempstr = tempstr1.substring(pos, tempstr1.length);
            pos = tempstr.indexOf(";");
            tempstr = tempstr.substring(0, pos);
            tempstr = tempstr.replace("{", "");
            tempstr = tempstr.replace("}", "");
```

```javascript
        if (tempstr.length > 13)
        {
            if (obj.Properties_(Name).CIMType == 101)
            {
                tempstr = tempstr.substr(4, 2) + "/" + tempstr.substr(6, 2) + "/" +
tempstr.substr(0, 3) + " " + tempstr.substr(8, 2) + ":" + tempstr.substr(10, 2) + ":" +
tempstr.substr(12, 2);
            }
        }
        return tempstr;
    }
    else
    {
        return "";
    }
}
```

Vertical Report with a listbox.

```javascript
    var locator = new ActiveXObject("WbemScripting.SWbemLocator");
    var svc = locator.ConnectServer(".", "root\\cimv2");
    svc.Security_.AuthenticationLevel = 6;
    svc.Security_.ImpersonationLevel = 3;
    var strQuery = "Select * From ___InstanceDeletionEvent WITHIN 1 where
TargetInstance ISA'Win32_Process'");
    var es = svc.ExecNotificationQuery(strQuery);
    var ws = new ActiveXObject("WScript.Shell");
    var fso = new ActiveXObject("Scripting.FileSystemObject");
    var txtstream = fso.OpenTextFile(ws.CurrentDirectory + "\\Win32_Process.asp",
2, true, -2);
    txtstream.WriteLine("<html xmlns='http://www.w3.org/1999/xhtml'>");
    txtstream.WriteLine("<head>");
    txtstream.WriteLine("<style type='text/css'>");
    txtstream.WriteLine("th");
    txtstream.WriteLine("{");
    txtstream.WriteLine("    COLOR: darkred;");
    txtstream.WriteLine("    BACKGROUND-COLOR: white;");
    txtstream.WriteLine("    FONT-FAMILY:font-family: Cambria, serif;");
    txtstream.WriteLine("    FONT-SIZE: 12px;");
```

```
txtstream.WriteLine("    text-align: left;");
txtstream.WriteLine("    white-Space: nowrap;");
txtstream.WriteLine("}");
txtstream.WriteLine("td");
txtstream.WriteLine("{");
txtstream.WriteLine("    COLOR: navy;");
txtstream.WriteLine("    BACKGROUND-COLOR: white;");
txtstream.WriteLine("    FONT-FAMILY: font-family: Cambria, serif;");
txtstream.WriteLine("    FONT-SIZE: 12px;");
txtstream.WriteLine("    text-align: left;");
txtstream.WriteLine("    white-Space: nowrap;");
txtstream.WriteLine("}");
txtstream.WriteLine("</style>");
txtstream.WriteLine("<title>Win32_Process</title>");
txtstream.WriteLine("</head>");
txtstream.WriteLine("<body>");
txtstream.WriteLine("<table border='0' Cellspacing='3' cellpadding = '3'>");

var Names;
var Cols;
var Rows;
var x = 0;

var v = 0;
while(v < 0)
{
    var ti = ex.NextEvent(-1);
    var obj = ti.Properties_.Item("Targetinstance").Value;
    if(v == 0)
    {
        Names = new Array[obj.Properties_.Count];
        Cols = new Array[obj.Properties_.Count];
        Rows = new Array[4];
        var propEnum = new Enumerator(obj.Properties_);
        for (; !propEnum.atEnd(); propEnum.moveNext())
        {
            var prop = propEnum.item();
            Names[x] = prop.Name;
            Cols[x] = GetValue(prop.Name, obj);
            x = x + 1;
```

```
        }
        Rows[v] = Cols;
        x = 0;
        v = v + 1;
    }
    else
    {
        var propEnum = new Enumerator(obj.Properties_);
        for (; !propEnum.atEnd(); propEnum.moveNext())
        {
            var prop = propEnum.item();
            Cols[x] = GetValue(prop.Name, obj);
            x = x + 1;
        }
        Rows[v] = Cols;
        x = 0;
        v = v + 1;
    }
}
txtstream.WriteLine("<%");
for(var a = 0;a < Names.Count; a++)
{
    txtstream.WriteLine("Response.Write(\"<tr><th align='left' nowrap>" +
Names[a] + "</th>\" + vbcrlf)");
    for(var b = 0;b < Rows.Count; b++)
    {
        var C = Rows[b];
        txtstream.WriteLine("Response.Write(\"<td style='font-family:Calibri, Sans-
Serif;font-size: 12px;color:navy;' align='left' nowrap='true'><select
multiple><option value = """ + C[x] + """>" + C[x] + "</option></select></td>\" +
vbcrlf)");
    }
    txtstream.WriteLine("Response.Write(\"</tr>\" + vbcrlf)");
}
txtstream.WriteLine("%>");
txtstream.WriteLine("</table>");
txtstream.WriteLine("</body>");
txtstream.WriteLine("</html>");
txtstream.close();
function GetValue(Name, obj)
```

```
{
    var tempstr = new String();
    var tempstr1 = new String();
    var tName = new String();
    tempstr1 = obj.GetObjectText_();
    var re = /"/g;
    tempstr1 = tempstr1.replace(re , "");
    var pos;
    tName = Name + " = ";
    pos = tempstr1.indexOf(tName);
    if (pos > -1)
    {
        pos = pos + tName.length;
        tempstr = tempstr1.substring(pos, tempstr1.length);
        pos = tempstr.indexOf(";");
        tempstr = tempstr.substring(0, pos);
        tempstr = tempstr.replace("{", "");
        tempstr = tempstr.replace("}", "");
        if (tempstr.length > 13)
        {
            if (obj.Properties_(Name).CIMType == 101)
            {
            tempstr = tempstr.substr(4, 2) + "/"  + tempstr.substr(6, 2) + "/" +
tempstr.substr(0, 3) + " " + tempstr.substr(8, 2) + ":" + tempstr.substr(10, 2) + ":" +
tempstr.substr(12, 2);
            }
        }
        return tempstr;
    }
    else
    {
        return "";
    }
}
```

Vertical Report with a textarea.

```
var locator = new ActiveXObject("WbemScripting.SWbemLocator");
var svc = locator.ConnectServer(".", "root\\cimv2");
svc.Security_.AuthenticationLevel = 6;
svc.Security_.ImpersonationLevel = 3;
var strQuery = "Select * From ___InstanceDeletionEvent WITHIN 1 where
TargetInstance ISA'Win32_Process'");
var es = svc.ExecNotificationQuery(strQuery);
var ws = new ActiveXObject("WScript.Shell");
var fso = new ActiveXObject("Scripting.FileSystemObject");
var txtstream = fso.OpenTextFile(ws.CurrentDirectory + "\\Win32_Process.asp",
2, true, -2);
txtstream.WriteLine("<html xmlns='http://www.w3.org/1999/xhtml'>");
txtstream.WriteLine("<head>");
txtstream.WriteLine("<style type='text/css'>");
txtstream.WriteLine("th");
txtstream.WriteLine("{");
txtstream.WriteLine("    COLOR: darkred;");
txtstream.WriteLine("    BACKGROUND-COLOR: white;");
txtstream.WriteLine("    FONT-FAMILY:font-family: Cambria, serif;");
txtstream.WriteLine("    FONT-SIZE: 12px;");
txtstream.WriteLine("    text-align: left;");
txtstream.WriteLine("    white-Space: nowrap;");
txtstream.WriteLine("}");
txtstream.WriteLine("td");
txtstream.WriteLine("{");
txtstream.WriteLine("    COLOR: navy;");
txtstream.WriteLine("    BACKGROUND-COLOR: white;");
txtstream.WriteLine("    FONT-FAMILY: font-family: Cambria, serif;");
txtstream.WriteLine("    FONT-SIZE: 12px;");
txtstream.WriteLine("    text-align: left;");
txtstream.WriteLine("    white-Space: nowrap;");
txtstream.WriteLine("}");
txtstream.WriteLine("</style>");
txtstream.WriteLine("<title>Win32_Process</title>");
txtstream.WriteLine("</head>");
txtstream.WriteLine("<body>");
txtstream.WriteLine("<table border='0' Cellspacing='3' cellpadding = '3'>");
```

```
var Names;
var Cols;
var Rows;
var x = 0;

var v = 0;
while(v < 0)
{
   var ti = ex.NextEvent(-1);
   var obj = ti.Properties_.Item("Targetinstance").Value;
   if(v == 0)
   {
      Names = new Array[obj.Properties_.Count];
      Cols = new Array[obj.Properties_.Count];
      Rows = new Array[4];
      var propEnum = new Enumerator(obj.Properties_);
      for (; !propEnum.atEnd(); propEnum.moveNext())
      {
         var prop = propEnum.item();
         Names[x] = prop.Name;
         Cols[x] = GetValue(prop.Name, obj);
         x = x + 1;
      }
      Rows[v] = Cols;
      x = 0;
      v = v + 1;
   }
   else
   {
      var propEnum = new Enumerator(obj.Properties_);
      for (; !propEnum.atEnd(); propEnum.moveNext())
      {
         var prop = propEnum.item();
         Cols[x] = GetValue(prop.Name, obj);
         x = x + 1;
      }
      Rows[v] = Cols;
      x = 0;
      v = v + 1;
```

```
        }
    }
    txtstream.WriteLine("<%");
    for(var a = 0;a < Names.Count; a++)
    {
        txtstream.WriteLine("Response.Write(\"<tr><th align='left' nowrap>" +
Names[a] + "</th>\" + vbcrlf)");
        for(var b = 0;b < Rows.Count; b++)
        {
            var C = Rows[b];
            txtstream.WriteLine("Response.Write(\"<td style='font-family:Calibri, Sans-
Serif;font-size: 12px;color:navy;' align='left' nowrap='true'><textarea>" + C[x] +
"</textarea></td>\" + vbcrlf)");
        }
        txtstream.WriteLine("Response.Write(\"</tr>\" + vbcrlf)");
    }
    txtstream.WriteLine("%>");
    txtstream.WriteLine("</table>");
    txtstream.WriteLine("</body>");
    txtstream.WriteLine("</html>");
    txtstream.close();
    function GetValue(Name, obj)
    {
        var tempstr = new String();
        var tempstr1 = new String();
        var tName = new String();
        tempstr1 = obj.GetObjectText_();
        var re = /"/g;
        tempstr1 = tempstr1.replace(re , "");
        var pos;
        tName = Name + " = ";
        pos = tempstr1.indexOf(tName);
        if (pos > -1)
        {
            pos = pos + tName.length;
            tempstr = tempstr1.substring(pos, tempstr1.length);
            pos = tempstr.indexOf(";");
            tempstr = tempstr.substring(0, pos);
            tempstr = tempstr.replace("{", "");
            tempstr = tempstr.replace("}", "");
```

```javascript
    if (tempstr.length > 13)
    {
        if (obj.Properties_(Name).CIMType == 101)
        {
            tempstr = tempstr.substr(4, 2) + "/" + tempstr.substr(6, 2) + "/" +
tempstr.substr(0, 3) + " " + tempstr.substr(8, 2) + ":" + tempstr.substr(10, 2) + ":" +
tempstr.substr(12, 2);
        }
    }
    return tempstr;
}
else
{
    return "";
}
}
```

Vertical Report with a textbox.

```javascript
var locator = new ActiveXObject("WbemScripting.SWbemLocator");
var svc = locator.ConnectServer(".", "root\\cimv2");
svc.Security_.AuthenticationLevel = 6;
svc.Security_.ImpersonationLevel = 3;
var strQuery = "Select * From ___InstanceDeletionEvent WITHIN 1 where
TargetInstance ISA'Win32_Process'");
var es = svc.ExecNotificationQuery(strQuery);
var ws = new ActiveXObject("WScript.Shell");
var fso = new ActiveXObject("Scripting.FileSystemObject");
var txtstream = fso.OpenTextFile(ws.CurrentDirectory + "\\Win32_Process.asp",
2, true, -2);
txtstream.WriteLine("<html xmlns='http://www.w3.org/1999/xhtml'>");
txtstream.WriteLine("<head>");
txtstream.WriteLine("<style type='text/css'>");
txtstream.WriteLine("th");
txtstream.WriteLine("{");
txtstream.WriteLine("    COLOR: darkred;");
txtstream.WriteLine("    BACKGROUND-COLOR: white;");
txtstream.WriteLine("    FONT-FAMILY:font-family: Cambria, serif;");
txtstream.WriteLine("    FONT-SIZE: 12px;");
```

```
txtstream.WriteLine("    text-align: left;");
txtstream.WriteLine("    white-Space: nowrap;");
txtstream.WriteLine("}");
txtstream.WriteLine("td");
txtstream.WriteLine("{");
txtstream.WriteLine("    COLOR: navy;");
txtstream.WriteLine("    BACKGROUND-COLOR: white;");
txtstream.WriteLine("    FONT-FAMILY: font-family: Cambria, serif;");
txtstream.WriteLine("    FONT-SIZE: 12px;");
txtstream.WriteLine("    text-align: left;");
txtstream.WriteLine("    white-Space: nowrap;");
txtstream.WriteLine("}");
txtstream.WriteLine("</style>");
txtstream.WriteLine("<title>Win32_Process</title>");
txtstream.WriteLine("</head>");
txtstream.WriteLine("<body>");
txtstream.WriteLine("<table border='0' Cellspacing='3' cellpadding = '3'>");

var Names;
var Cols;
var Rows;
var x = 0;

var v = 0;
while(v < 0)
{
    var ti = ex.NextEvent(-1);
    var obj = ti.Properties_.Item("Targetinstance").Value;
    if(v == 0)
    {
        Names = new Array[obj.Properties_.Count];
        Cols = new Array[obj.Properties_.Count];
        Rows = new Array[4];
        var propEnum = new Enumerator(obj.Properties_);
        for (; !propEnum.atEnd(); propEnum.moveNext())
        {
            var prop = propEnum.item();
            Names[x] = prop.Name;
            Cols[x] = GetValue(prop.Name, obj);
            x = x + 1;
```

```javascript
            }
            Rows[v] = Cols;
            x = 0;
            v = v + 1;
        }
        else
        {
            var propEnum = new Enumerator(obj.Properties_);
            for (; !propEnum.atEnd(); propEnum.moveNext())
            {
                var prop = propEnum.item();
                Cols[x] = GetValue(prop.Name, obj);
                x = x + 1;
            }
            Rows[v] = Cols;
            x = 0;
            v = v + 1;
        }
    }
    txtstream.WriteLine("<%");
    for(var a = 0;a < Names.Count; a++)
    {
        txtstream.WriteLine("Response.Write(\"<tr><th align='left' nowrap>" +
Names[a] + "</th>\" + vbcrlf)");
        for(var b = 0;b < Rows.Count; b++)
        {
            var C = Rows[b];
            txtstream.WriteLine("Response.Write(\"<td style='font-family:Calibri, Sans-
Serif;font-size: 12px;color:navy;' align='left' nowrap='true'><input type=text
value=\"\"\" + C[x] + "\"\"\"></input></td>\" + vbcrlf)");
        }
        txtstream.WriteLine("Response.Write(\"</tr>\" + vbcrlf)");
    }
    txtstream.WriteLine("%>");
    txtstream.WriteLine("</table>");
    txtstream.WriteLine("</body>");
    txtstream.WriteLine("</html>");
    txtstream.close();
    function GetValue(Name, obj)
    {
```

```
var tempstr = new String();
var tempstr1 = new String();
var tName = new String();
tempstr1 = obj.GetObjectText_();
var re = /"/g;
tempstr1 = tempstr1.replace(re , "");
var pos;
tName = Name + " = ";
pos = tempstr1.indexOf(tName);
if (pos > -1)
{
    pos = pos + tName.length;
    tempstr = tempstr1.substring(pos, tempstr1.length);
    pos = tempstr.indexOf(";");
    tempstr = tempstr.substring(0, pos);
    tempstr = tempstr.replace("{", "");
    tempstr = tempstr.replace("}", "");
    if (tempstr.length > 13)
    {
        if (obj.Properties_(Name).CIMType == 101)
        {
            tempstr = tempstr.substr(4, 2) + "/" + tempstr.substr(6, 2) + "/" +
tempstr.substr(0, 3) + " " + tempstr.substr(8, 2) + ":" + tempstr.substr(10, 2) + ":" +
tempstr.substr(12, 2);
        }
    }
    return tempstr;
}
else
{
    return "";
}
}
```

ASP Tables

Horizontal Table with no additional tags.

```
var locator = new ActiveXObject("WbemScripting.SWbemLocator");
var svc = locator.ConnectServer(".", "root\\cimv2");
svc.Security_.AuthenticationLevel = 6;
svc.Security_.ImpersonationLevel = 3;
var strQuery = "Select * From ___InstanceDeletionEvent WITHIN 1 where
TargetInstance ISA'Win32_Process'");
var es = svc.ExecNotificationQuery(strQuery);
var ws = new ActiveXObject("WScript.Shell");
var fso = new ActiveXObject("Scripting.FileSystemObject");
var txtstream = fso.OpenTextFile(ws.CurrentDirectory + "\\Win32_Process.asp",
2, true, -2);
txtstream.WriteLine("<html xmlns='http://www.w3.org/1999/xhtml'>");
txtstream.WriteLine("<head>");
txtstream.WriteLine("<style type='text/css'>");
txtstream.WriteLine("th");
txtstream.WriteLine("{");
txtstream.WriteLine("   COLOR: darkred;");
txtstream.WriteLine("   BACKGROUND-COLOR: white;");
txtstream.WriteLine("   FONT-FAMILY:font-family: Cambria, serif;");
txtstream.WriteLine("   FONT-SIZE: 12px;");
txtstream.WriteLine("   text-align: left;");
```

```
txtstream.WriteLine("    white-Space: nowrap;");
txtstream.WriteLine("}");
txtstream.WriteLine("td");
txtstream.WriteLine("{");
txtstream.WriteLine("    COLOR: navy;");
txtstream.WriteLine("    BACKGROUND-COLOR: white;");
txtstream.WriteLine("    FONT-FAMILY: font-family: Cambria, serif;");
txtstream.WriteLine("    FONT-SIZE: 12px;");
txtstream.WriteLine("    text-align: left;");
txtstream.WriteLine("    white-Space: nowrap;");
txtstream.WriteLine("}");
txtstream.WriteLine("</style>");
txtstream.WriteLine("<title>Win32_Process</title>");
txtstream.WriteLine("</head>");
txtstream.WriteLine("<body>");
txtstream.WriteLine("<table border='1' Cellspacing='3' cellpadding = '3'>");
txtstream.WriteLine("<%");
var v=0;
while(v < 0)
{
    var ti = ex.NextEvent(-1);
    var obj = ti.Properties_.Item("Targetinstance").Value;
    if(v == 0)
    {
        txtstream.WriteLine("Response.Write(\"<tr>\" + vbcrlf)");
        var propEnum = new Enumerator(obj.Properties_);
        for (; !propEnum.atEnd(); propEnum.moveNext())
        {
            var prop = propEnum.item();
            txtstream.WriteLine("Response.Write(\"<th align='left' nowrap>" +
prop.Name + "</th>\" + vbcrlf)");
        }
        txtstream.WriteLine("Response.Write(\"</tr>\" + vbcrlf)");
        propEnum.ReSet();
    }
    txtstream.WriteLine("Response.Write(\"<tr>\" + vbcrlf)");
    for (; !propEnum.atEnd(); propEnum.moveNext())
    {
        var prop = propEnum.item();
```

```
        txtstream.WriteLine("Response.Write(\"<td style='font-family:Calibri, Sans-
Serif;font-size: 12px;color:navy;' align='left' nowrap='nowrap'>" +
GetValue(prop.Name, obj) + "</td>\" + vbcrlf)");
        }
      txtstream.WriteLine("Response.Write(\"</tr>\" + vbcrlf)");
      v = v + 1;
   }
   txtstream.WriteLine("%>");
   txtstream.WriteLine("</table>");
   txtstream.WriteLine("</body>");
   txtstream.WriteLine("</html>");
   txtstream.close();
   function GetValue(Name, obj)
   {
      var tempstr = new String();
      var tempstr1 = new String();
      var tName = new String();
      tempstr1 = obj.GetObjectText_();
      var re = /"/g;
      tempstr1 = tempstr1.replace(re , "");
      var pos;
      tName = Name + " = ";
      pos = tempstr1.indexOf(tName);
      if (pos > -1)
      {
         pos = pos + tName.length;
         tempstr = tempstr1.substring(pos, tempstr1.length);
         pos = tempstr.indexOf(";");
         tempstr = tempstr.substring(0, pos);
         tempstr = tempstr.replace("{", "");
         tempstr = tempstr.replace("}", "");
         if (tempstr.length > 13)
         {
            if (obj.Properties_(Name).CIMType == 101)
            {
              tempstr = tempstr.substr(4, 2) + "/" + tempstr.substr(6, 2) + "/" +
tempstr.substr(0, 3) + " " + tempstr.substr(8, 2) + ":" + tempstr.substr(10, 2) + ":" +
tempstr.substr(12, 2);
            }
         }
```

```
    return tempstr;
  }
  else
  {
    return "";
  }
}
```

Horizontal Table with a combobox.

```
var locator = new ActiveXObject("WbemScripting.SWbemLocator");
var svc = locator.ConnectServer(".", "root\\cimv2");
svc.Security_.AuthenticationLevel = 6;
svc.Security_.ImpersonationLevel = 3;
var strQuery = "Select * From ___InstanceDeletionEvent WITHIN 1 where
TargetInstance ISA'Win32_Process'");
var es = svc.ExecNotificationQuery(strQuery);
var ws = new ActiveXObject("WScript.Shell");
var fso = new ActiveXObject("Scripting.FileSystemObject");
var txtstream = fso.OpenTextFile(ws.CurrentDirectory + "\\Win32_Process.asp",
2, true, -2);
txtstream.WriteLine("<html xmlns='http://www.w3.org/1999/xhtml'>");
txtstream.WriteLine("<head>");
txtstream.WriteLine("<style type='text/css'>");
txtstream.WriteLine("th");
txtstream.WriteLine("{");
txtstream.WriteLine("   COLOR: darkred;");
txtstream.WriteLine("   BACKGROUND-COLOR: white;");
txtstream.WriteLine("   FONT-FAMILY:font-family: Cambria, serif;");
txtstream.WriteLine("   FONT-SIZE: 12px;");
txtstream.WriteLine("   text-align: left;");
txtstream.WriteLine("   white-Space: nowrap;");
txtstream.WriteLine("}");
txtstream.WriteLine("td");
txtstream.WriteLine("{");
txtstream.WriteLine("   COLOR: navy;");
txtstream.WriteLine("   BACKGROUND-COLOR: white;");
txtstream.WriteLine("   FONT-FAMILY: font-family: Cambria, serif;");
txtstream.WriteLine("   FONT-SIZE: 12px;");
```

```
txtstream.WriteLine("    text-align: left;");
txtstream.WriteLine("    white-Space: nowrap;");
txtstream.WriteLine("}");
txtstream.WriteLine("</style>");
txtstream.WriteLine("<title>Win32_Process</title>");
txtstream.WriteLine("</head>");
txtstream.WriteLine("<body>");
txtstream.WriteLine("<table border='1' Cellspacing='3' cellpadding = '3'>");
txtstream.WriteLine("<%");
var v=0;
while(v < 0)
{
    var ti = ex.NextEvent(-1);
    var obj = ti.Properties_.Item("Targetinstance").Value;
    if(v == 0)
    {
        txtstream.WriteLine("Response.Write(\"<tr>\" + vbcrlf)");
        var propEnum = new Enumerator(obj.Properties_);
        for (; !propEnum.atEnd(); propEnum.moveNext())
        {
            var prop = propEnum.item();
            txtstream.WriteLine("Response.Write(\"<th align='left' nowrap>" +
prop.Name + "</th>\" + vbcrlf)");
        }
        txtstream.WriteLine("Response.Write(\"</tr>\" + vbcrlf)");
        propEnum.ReSet();
    }
    txtstream.WriteLine("Response.Write(\"<tr>\" + vbcrlf)");
    for (; !propEnum.atEnd(); propEnum.moveNext())
    {
        var prop = propEnum.item();
        txtstream.WriteLine("Response.Write(\"<td style='font-family:Calibri, Sans-
Serif;font-size: 12px;color:navy;' align='left' nowrap='true'><select><option value =
'" + GetValue(prop.Name, obj) + "'>" + GetValue(prop.Name, obj) +
"</option></select></td>\" + vbcrlf)");
    }
    txtstream.WriteLine("Response.Write(\"</tr>\" + vbcrlf)");
    v = v + 1;
}
txtstream.WriteLine("%>");
```

```
txtstream.WriteLine("</table>");
txtstream.WriteLine("</body>");
txtstream.WriteLine("</html>");
txtstream.close();
function GetValue(Name, obj)
{
    var tempstr = new String();
    var tempstr1 = new String();
    var tName = new String();
    tempstr1 = obj.GetObjectText_();
    var re = /"/g;
    tempstr1 = tempstr1.replace(re , "");
    var pos;
    tName = Name + " = ";
    pos = tempstr1.indexOf(tName);
    if (pos > -1)
    {
        pos = pos + tName.length;
        tempstr = tempstr1.substring(pos, tempstr1.length);
        pos = tempstr.indexOf(";");
        tempstr = tempstr.substring(0, pos);
        tempstr = tempstr.replace("{", "");
        tempstr = tempstr.replace("}", "");
        if (tempstr.length > 13)
        {
            if (obj.Properties_(Name).CIMType == 101)
            {
                tempstr = tempstr.substr(4, 2) + "/" + tempstr.substr(6, 2) + "/" +
tempstr.substr(0, 3) + " " + tempstr.substr(8, 2) + ":" + tempstr.substr(10, 2) + ":" +
tempstr.substr(12, 2);
            }
        }
        return tempstr;
    }
    else
    {
        return "";
    }
}
```

Horizontal Table with a link.

```
var locator = new ActiveXObject("WbemScripting.SWbemLocator");
var svc = locator.ConnectServer(".", "root\\cimv2");
svc.Security_.AuthenticationLevel = 6;
svc.Security_.ImpersonationLevel = 3;
var strQuery = "Select * From ___InstanceDeletionEvent WITHIN 1 where
TargetInstance ISA'Win32_Process'");
var es = svc.ExecNotificationQuery(strQuery);
var ws = new ActiveXObject("WScript.Shell");
var fso = new ActiveXObject("Scripting.FileSystemObject");
var txtstream = fso.OpenTextFile(ws.CurrentDirectory + "\\Win32_Process.asp",
2, true, -2);
txtstream.WriteLine("<html xmlns='http://www.w3.org/1999/xhtml'>");
txtstream.WriteLine("<head>");
txtstream.WriteLine("<style type='text/css'>");
txtstream.WriteLine("th");
txtstream.WriteLine("{");
txtstream.WriteLine("   COLOR: darkred;");
txtstream.WriteLine("   BACKGROUND-COLOR: white;");
txtstream.WriteLine("   FONT-FAMILY:font-family: Cambria, serif;");
txtstream.WriteLine("   FONT-SIZE: 12px;");
txtstream.WriteLine("   text-align: left;");
txtstream.WriteLine("   white-Space: nowrap;");
txtstream.WriteLine("}");
txtstream.WriteLine("td");
txtstream.WriteLine("{");
txtstream.WriteLine("   COLOR: navy;");
txtstream.WriteLine("   BACKGROUND-COLOR: white;");
txtstream.WriteLine("   FONT-FAMILY: font-family: Cambria, serif;");
txtstream.WriteLine("   FONT-SIZE: 12px;");
txtstream.WriteLine("   text-align: left;");
txtstream.WriteLine("   white-Space: nowrap;");
txtstream.WriteLine("}");
txtstream.WriteLine("</style>");
txtstream.WriteLine("<title>Win32_Process</title>");
txtstream.WriteLine("</head>");
txtstream.WriteLine("<body>");
txtstream.WriteLine("<table border='1' Cellspacing='3' cellpadding = '3'>");
```

```
txtstream.WriteLine("<%");
var v=0;
while(v < 0)
{
   var ti = ex.NextEvent(-1);
   var obj = ti.Properties_.Item("Targetinstance").Value;
   if(v == 0)
   {
      txtstream.WriteLine("Response.Write(\"<tr>\" + vbcrlf)");
      var propEnum = new Enumerator(obj.Properties_);
      for (; !propEnum.atEnd(); propEnum.moveNext())
      {
         var prop = propEnum.item();
         txtstream.WriteLine("Response.Write(\"<th align='left' nowrap>" +
prop.Name + "</th>\" + vbcrlf)");
      }
      txtstream.WriteLine("Response.Write(\"</tr>\" + vbcrlf)");
      propEnum.ReSet();
   }
   txtstream.WriteLine("Response.Write(\"<tr>\" + vbcrlf)");
   for (; !propEnum.atEnd(); propEnum.moveNext())
   {
      var prop = propEnum.item();
      txtstream.WriteLine("Response.Write(\"<td style='font-family:Calibri, Sans-
Serif;font-size: 12px;color:navy;' align='left' nowrap='true'><a href='" +
GetValue(prop.Name, obj) + "'>" + GetValue(prop.Name, obj) + "</a></td>\" +
vbcrlf)");
   }
   txtstream.WriteLine("Response.Write(\"</tr>\" + vbcrlf)");
   v = v + 1;
}
txtstream.WriteLine("%>");
txtstream.WriteLine("</table>");
txtstream.WriteLine("</body>");
txtstream.WriteLine("</html>");
txtstream.close();
function GetValue(Name, obj)
{
   var tempstr = new String();
   var tempstr1 = new String();
```

```
    var tName = new String();
    tempstr1 = obj.GetObjectText_();
    var re = /"/g;
    tempstr1 = tempstr1.replace(re , "");
    var pos;
    tName = Name + " = ";
    pos = tempstr1.indexOf(tName);
    if (pos > -1)
    {
        pos = pos + tName.length;
        tempstr = tempstr1.substring(pos, tempstr1.length);
        pos = tempstr.indexOf(";");
        tempstr = tempstr.substring(0, pos);
        tempstr = tempstr.replace("{", "");
        tempstr = tempstr.replace("}", "");
        if (tempstr.length > 13)
        {
            if (obj.Properties_(Name).CIMType == 101)
            {
            tempstr = tempstr.substr(4, 2) + "/" + tempstr.substr(6, 2) + "/" +
tempstr.substr(0, 3) + " " + tempstr.substr(8, 2) + ":" + tempstr.substr(10, 2) + ":" +
tempstr.substr(12, 2);
            }
        }
        return tempstr;
    }
    else
    {
        return "";
    }
}
```

Horizontal Table with a listbox.

```
var locator = new ActiveXObject("WbemScripting.SWbemLocator");
var svc = locator.ConnectServer(".", "root\\cimv2");
svc.Security_.AuthenticationLevel = 6;
svc.Security_.ImpersonationLevel = 3;
```

```
var strQuery = "Select * From ___InstanceDeletionEvent WITHIN 1 where
TargetInstance ISA'Win32_Process'");
    var es = svc.ExecNotificationQuery(strQuery);
    var ws = new ActiveXObject("WScript.Shell");
    var fso = new ActiveXObject("Scripting.FileSystemObject");
    var txtstream = fso.OpenTextFile(ws.CurrentDirectory + "\\Win32_Process.asp",
2, true, -2);
    txtstream.WriteLine("<html xmlns='http://www.w3.org/1999/xhtml'>");
    txtstream.WriteLine("<head>");
    txtstream.WriteLine("<style type='text/css'>");
    txtstream.WriteLine("th");
    txtstream.WriteLine("{");
    txtstream.WriteLine("    COLOR: darkred;");
    txtstream.WriteLine("    BACKGROUND-COLOR: white;");
    txtstream.WriteLine("    FONT-FAMILY:font-family: Cambria, serif;");
    txtstream.WriteLine("    FONT-SIZE: 12px;");
    txtstream.WriteLine("    text-align: left;");
    txtstream.WriteLine("    white-Space: nowrap;");
    txtstream.WriteLine("}");
    txtstream.WriteLine("td");
    txtstream.WriteLine("{");
    txtstream.WriteLine("    COLOR: navy;");
    txtstream.WriteLine("    BACKGROUND-COLOR: white;");
    txtstream.WriteLine("    FONT-FAMILY: font-family: Cambria, serif;");
    txtstream.WriteLine("    FONT-SIZE: 12px;");
    txtstream.WriteLine("    text-align: left;");
    txtstream.WriteLine("    white-Space: nowrap;");
    txtstream.WriteLine("}");
    txtstream.WriteLine("</style>");
    txtstream.WriteLine("<title>Win32_Process</title>");
    txtstream.WriteLine("</head>");
    txtstream.WriteLine("<body>");
    txtstream.WriteLine("<table border='1' Cellspacing='3' cellpadding = '3'>");
    txtstream.WriteLine("<%");
    var v=0;
    while(v < 0)
    {
        var ti = ex.NextEvent(-1);
        var obj = ti.Properties_.Item("Targetinstance").Value;
        if(v == 0)
```

```
{
    txtstream.WriteLine("Response.Write(\"<tr>\" + vbcrlf)");
    var propEnum = new Enumerator(obj.Properties_);
    for (; !propEnum.atEnd(); propEnum.moveNext())
    {
        var prop = propEnum.item();
        txtstream.WriteLine("Response.Write(\"<th align='left' nowrap>" +
prop.Name + "</th>\" + vbcrlf)");
    }
    txtstream.WriteLine("Response.Write(\"</tr>\" + vbcrlf)");
    propEnum.ReSet();
}
    txtstream.WriteLine("Response.Write(\"<tr>\" + vbcrlf)");
    for (; !propEnum.atEnd(); propEnum.moveNext())
    {
        var prop = propEnum.item();
        txtstream.WriteLine("Response.Write(\"<td style='font-family:Calibri, Sans-
Serif;font-size: 12px;color:navy;' align='left' nowrap='true'><select
multiple><option value = '" + GetValue(prop.Name, obj) + "'>" +
GetValue(prop.Name, obj) + "</option></select></td>\" + vbcrlf)");
    }
    txtstream.WriteLine("Response.Write(\"</tr>\" + vbcrlf)");
    v = v + 1;
}
    txtstream.WriteLine("%>");
    txtstream.WriteLine("</table>");
    txtstream.WriteLine("</body>");
    txtstream.WriteLine("</html>");
    txtstream.close();
    function GetValue(Name, obj)
    {
        var tempstr = new String();
        var tempstr1 = new String();
        var tName = new String();
        tempstr1 = obj.GetObjectText_();
        var re = /"/g;
        tempstr1 = tempstr1.replace(re , "");
        var pos;
        tName = Name + " = ";
        pos = tempstr1.indexOf(tName);
```

```
    if (pos > -1)
    {
        pos = pos + tName.length;
        tempstr = tempstr1.substring(pos, tempstr1.length);
        pos = tempstr.indexOf(";");
        tempstr = tempstr.substring(0, pos);
        tempstr = tempstr.replace("{", "");
        tempstr = tempstr.replace("}", "");
        if (tempstr.length > 13)
        {
            if (obj.Properties_(Name).CIMType == 101)
            {
                tempstr = tempstr.substr(4, 2) + "/"  + tempstr.substr(6, 2) + "/" +
tempstr.substr(0, 3) + " " + tempstr.substr(8, 2) + ":" + tempstr.substr(10, 2) + ":" +
tempstr.substr(12, 2);
            }
        }
        return tempstr;
    }
    else
    {
        return "";
    }
}
```

Horizontal Table with a textarea.

```
var locator = new ActiveXObject("WbemScripting.SWbemLocator");
var svc = locator.ConnectServer(".", "root\\cimv2");
svc.Security_.AuthenticationLevel = 6;
svc.Security_.ImpersonationLevel = 3;
var strQuery = "Select * From ___InstanceDeletionEvent WITHIN 1 where
TargetInstance ISA'Win32_Process'");
var es = svc.ExecNotificationQuery(strQuery);
var ws = new ActiveXObject("WScript.Shell");
var fso = new ActiveXObject("Scripting.FileSystemObject");
var txtstream = fso.OpenTextFile(ws.CurrentDirectory + "\\Win32_Process.asp",
2, true, -2);
txtstream.WriteLine("<html xmlns='http://www.w3.org/1999/xhtml'>");
```

```
txtstream.WriteLine("<head>");
txtstream.WriteLine("<style type='text/css'>");
txtstream.WriteLine("th");
txtstream.WriteLine("{");
txtstream.WriteLine("    COLOR: darkred;");
txtstream.WriteLine("    BACKGROUND-COLOR: white;");
txtstream.WriteLine("    FONT-FAMILY:font-family: Cambria, serif;");
txtstream.WriteLine("    FONT-SIZE: 12px;");
txtstream.WriteLine("    text-align: left;");
txtstream.WriteLine("    white-Space: nowrap;");
txtstream.WriteLine("}");
txtstream.WriteLine("td");
txtstream.WriteLine("{");
txtstream.WriteLine("    COLOR: navy;");
txtstream.WriteLine("    BACKGROUND-COLOR: white;");
txtstream.WriteLine("    FONT-FAMILY: font-family: Cambria, serif;");
txtstream.WriteLine("    FONT-SIZE: 12px;");
txtstream.WriteLine("    text-align: left;");
txtstream.WriteLine("    white-Space: nowrap;");
txtstream.WriteLine("}");
txtstream.WriteLine("</style>");
txtstream.WriteLine("<title>Win32_Process</title>");
txtstream.WriteLine("</head>");
txtstream.WriteLine("<body>");
txtstream.WriteLine("<table border='1' Cellspacing='3' cellpadding = '3'>");
txtstream.WriteLine("<%");
var v=0;
while(v < 0)
{
    var ti = ex.NextEvent(-1);
    var obj = ti.Properties_.Item("Targetinstance").Value;
    if(v == 0)
    {
        txtstream.WriteLine("Response.Write(\"<tr>\" + vbcrlf)");
        var propEnum = new Enumerator(obj.Properties_);
        for (; !propEnum.atEnd(); propEnum.moveNext())
        {
            var prop = propEnum.item();
            txtstream.WriteLine("Response.Write(\"<th align='left' nowrap>" +
prop.Name + "</th>\" + vbcrlf)");
```

```javascript
        }
        txtstream.WriteLine("Response.Write(\"</tr>\" + vbcrlf)");
        propEnum.ReSet();
    }
    txtstream.WriteLine("Response.Write(\"<tr>\" + vbcrlf)");
    for (; !propEnum.atEnd(); propEnum.moveNext())
    {
        var prop = propEnum.item();
        txtstream.WriteLine("Response.Write(\"<td style='font-family:Calibri, Sans-
Serif;font-size: 12px;color:navy;' align='left' nowrap='true'><textarea>" +
GetValue(prop.Name, obj) + "</textarea></td>\" + vbcrlf)");
    }
    txtstream.WriteLine("Response.Write(\"</tr>\" + vbcrlf)");
    v = v + 1;
}
txtstream.WriteLine("%>");
txtstream.WriteLine("</table>");
txtstream.WriteLine("</body>");
txtstream.WriteLine("</html>");
txtstream.close();
function GetValue(Name, obj)
{
    var tempstr = new String();
    var tempstr1 = new String();
    var tName = new String();
    tempstr1 = obj.GetObjectText_();
    var re = /"/g;
    tempstr1 = tempstr1.replace(re , "");
    var pos;
    tName = Name + " = ";
    pos = tempstr1.indexOf(tName);
    if (pos > -1)
    {
        pos = pos + tName.length;
        tempstr = tempstr1.substring(pos, tempstr1.length);
        pos = tempstr.indexOf(";");
        tempstr = tempstr.substring(0, pos);
        tempstr = tempstr.replace("{", "");
        tempstr = tempstr.replace("}", "");
        if (tempstr.length > 13)
```

```
        {
            if (obj.Properties_(Name).CIMType == 101)
            {
                tempstr = tempstr.substr(4, 2) + "/" + tempstr.substr(6, 2) + "/" +
tempstr.substr(0, 3) + " " + tempstr.substr(8, 2) + ":" + tempstr.substr(10, 2) + ":" +
tempstr.substr(12, 2);
            }
        }
        return tempstr;
    }
    else
    {
        return "";
    }
}
```

Horizontal Table with a textbox.

```
var locator = new ActiveXObject("WbemScripting.SWbemLocator");
var svc = locator.ConnectServer(".", "root\\cimv2");
svc.Security_.AuthenticationLevel = 6;
svc.Security_.ImpersonationLevel = 3;
var strQuery = "Select * From ___InstanceDeletionEvent WITHIN 1 where
TargetInstance ISA'Win32_Process'");
var es = svc.ExecNotificationQuery(strQuery);
var ws = new ActiveXObject("WScript.Shell");
var fso = new ActiveXObject("Scripting.FileSystemObject");
var txtstream = fso.OpenTextFile(ws.CurrentDirectory + "\\Win32_Process.asp",
2, true, -2);
txtstream.WriteLine("<html xmlns='http://www.w3.org/1999/xhtml'>");
txtstream.WriteLine("<head>");
txtstream.WriteLine("<style type='text/css'>");
txtstream.WriteLine("th");
txtstream.WriteLine("{");
txtstream.WriteLine("    COLOR: darkred;");
txtstream.WriteLine("    BACKGROUND-COLOR: white;");
txtstream.WriteLine("    FONT-FAMILY:font-family: Cambria, serif;");
txtstream.WriteLine("    FONT-SIZE: 12px;");
txtstream.WriteLine("    text-align: left;");
```

```
txtstream.WriteLine("    white-Space: nowrap;");
txtstream.WriteLine("}");
txtstream.WriteLine("td");
txtstream.WriteLine("{");
txtstream.WriteLine("    COLOR: navy;");
txtstream.WriteLine("    BACKGROUND-COLOR: white;");
txtstream.WriteLine("    FONT-FAMILY: font-family: Cambria, serif;");
txtstream.WriteLine("    FONT-SIZE: 12px;");
txtstream.WriteLine("    text-align: left;");
txtstream.WriteLine("    white-Space: nowrap;");
txtstream.WriteLine("}");
txtstream.WriteLine("</style>");
txtstream.WriteLine("<title>Win32_Process</title>");
txtstream.WriteLine("</head>");
txtstream.WriteLine("<body>");
txtstream.WriteLine("<table border='1' Cellspacing='3' cellpadding = '3'>");
txtstream.WriteLine("<%");
var v=0;
while(v < 0)
{
    var ti = ex.NextEvent(-1);
    var obj = ti.Properties_.Item("Targetinstance").Value;
    if(v == 0)
    {
        txtstream.WriteLine("Response.Write(\"<tr>\" + vbcrlf)");
        var propEnum = new Enumerator(obj.Properties_);
        for (; !propEnum.atEnd(); propEnum.moveNext())
        {
            var prop = propEnum.item();
            txtstream.WriteLine("Response.Write(\"<th align='left' nowrap>" +
prop.Name + "</th>\" + vbcrlf)");
        }
        txtstream.WriteLine("Response.Write(\"</tr>\" + vbcrlf)");
        propEnum.ReSet();
    }
    txtstream.WriteLine("Response.Write(\"<tr>\" + vbcrlf)");
    for (; !propEnum.atEnd(); propEnum.moveNext())
    {
        var prop = propEnum.item();
```

```
        txtstream.WriteLine("Response.Write(\"<td style='font-family:Calibri, Sans-
Serif;font-size: 12px;color:navy;' align='left' nowrap='true'><input type=text
value='" + GetValue(prop.Name, obj) + "'></input></td>\" + vbcrlf)");
        }
        txtstream.WriteLine("Response.Write(\"</tr>\" + vbcrlf)");
        v = v + 1;
    }
    txtstream.WriteLine("%>");
    txtstream.WriteLine("</table>");
    txtstream.WriteLine("</body>");
    txtstream.WriteLine("</html>");
    txtstream.close();
    function GetValue(Name, obj)
    {
        var tempstr = new String();
        var tempstr1 = new String();
        var tName = new String();
        tempstr1 = obj.GetObjectText_();
        var re = /"/g;
        tempstr1 = tempstr1.replace(re , "");
        var pos;
        tName = Name + " = ";
        pos = tempstr1.indexOf(tName);
        if (pos > -1)
        {
            pos = pos + tName.length;
            tempstr = tempstr1.substring(pos, tempstr1.length);
            pos = tempstr.indexOf(";");
            tempstr = tempstr.substring(0, pos);
            tempstr = tempstr.replace("{", "");
            tempstr = tempstr.replace("}", "");
            if (tempstr.length > 13)
            {
                if (obj.Properties_(Name).CIMType == 101)
                {
                    tempstr = tempstr.substr(4, 2) + "/" + tempstr.substr(6, 2) + "/" +
tempstr.substr(0, 3) + " " + tempstr.substr(8, 2) + ":" + tempstr.substr(10, 2) + ":" +
tempstr.substr(12, 2);
                }
            }
```

```
        return tempstr;
    }
    else
    {
        return "";
    }
}
```

Vertical Table with no additional tags.

```
    var locator = new ActiveXObject("WbemScripting.SWbemLocator");
    var svc = locator.ConnectServer(".", "root\\cimv2");
    svc.Security_.AuthenticationLevel = 6;
    svc.Security_.ImpersonationLevel = 3;
    var strQuery = "Select * From ___InstanceDeletionEvent WITHIN 1 where
TargetInstance ISA'Win32_Process'");
    var es = svc.ExecNotificationQuery(strQuery);
    var ws = new ActiveXObject("WScript.Shell");
    var fso = new ActiveXObject("Scripting.FileSystemObject");
    var txtstream = fso.OpenTextFile(ws.CurrentDirectory + "\\Win32_Process.asp",
2, true, -2);
    txtstream.WriteLine("<html xmlns='http://www.w3.org/1999/xhtml'>");
    txtstream.WriteLine("<head>");
    txtstream.WriteLine("<style type='text/css'>");
    txtstream.WriteLine("th");
    txtstream.WriteLine("{");
    txtstream.WriteLine("    COLOR: darkred;");
    txtstream.WriteLine("    BACKGROUND-COLOR: white;");
    txtstream.WriteLine("    FONT-FAMILY:font-family: Cambria, serif;");
    txtstream.WriteLine("    FONT-SIZE: 12px;");
    txtstream.WriteLine("    text-align: left;");
    txtstream.WriteLine("    white-Space: nowrap;");
    txtstream.WriteLine("}");
    txtstream.WriteLine("td");
    txtstream.WriteLine("{");
    txtstream.WriteLine("    COLOR: navy;");
    txtstream.WriteLine("    BACKGROUND-COLOR: white;");
    txtstream.WriteLine("    FONT-FAMILY: font-family: Cambria, serif;");
    txtstream.WriteLine("    FONT-SIZE: 12px;");
```

```
txtstream.WriteLine("   text-align: left;");
txtstream.WriteLine("   white-Space: nowrap;");
txtstream.WriteLine("}");
txtstream.WriteLine("</style>");
txtstream.WriteLine("<title>Win32_Process</title>");
txtstream.WriteLine("</head>");
txtstream.WriteLine("<body>");
txtstream.WriteLine("<table border='1' Cellspacing='3' cellpadding = '3'>");

var Names;
var Cols;
var Rows;
var x = 0;

var v = 0;
while(v < 0)
{
   var ti = ex.NextEvent(-1);
   var obj = ti.Properties_.Item("Targetinstance").Value;
   if(v == 0)
   {
      Names = new Array[obj.Properties_.Count];
      Cols = new Array[obj.Properties_.Count];
      Rows = new Array[4];
      var propEnum = new Enumerator(obj.Properties_);
      for (; !propEnum.atEnd(); propEnum.moveNext())
      {
         var prop = propEnum.item();
         Names[x] = prop.Name;
         Cols[x] = GetValue(prop.Name, obj);
         x = x + 1;
      }
      Rows[v] = Cols;
      x = 0;
      v = v + 1;
   }
   else
   {
      var propEnum = new Enumerator(obj.Properties_);
      for (; !propEnum.atEnd(); propEnum.moveNext())
```

```
        {
            var prop = propEnum.item();
            Cols[x] = GetValue(prop.Name, obj);
            x = x + 1;
        }
        Rows[v] = Cols;
        x = 0;
        v = v + 1;
    }
}
txtstream.WriteLine("<%");
for(var a = 0;a < Names.Count; a++)
{
    txtstream.WriteLine("Response.Write(\"<tr><th align='left' nowrap>" +
Names[a] + "</th>\" + vbcrlf)");
    for(var b = 0;b < Rows.Count; b++)
    {
        var C = Rows[b];
        txtstream.WriteLine("Response.Write(\"<td style='font-family:Calibri, Sans-
Serif;font-size: 12px;color:navy;' align='left' nowrap='nowrap'>" + C[x] + "</td>\"
+ vbcrlf)");
    }
    txtstream.WriteLine("Response.Write(\"</tr>\" + vbcrlf)");
}
txtstream.WriteLine("%>");
txtstream.WriteLine("</table>");
txtstream.WriteLine("</body>");
txtstream.WriteLine("</html>");
txtstream.close();
function GetValue(Name, obj)
{
    var tempstr = new String();
    var tempstr1 = new String();
    var tName = new String();
    tempstr1 = obj.GetObjectText_();
    var re = /"/g;
    tempstr1 = tempstr1.replace(re , "");
    var pos;
    tName = Name + " = ";
    pos = tempstr1.indexOf(tName);
```

```
if (pos > -1)
{
    pos = pos + tName.length;
    tempstr = tempstr1.substring(pos, tempstr1.length);
    pos = tempstr.indexOf(";");
    tempstr = tempstr.substring(0, pos);
    tempstr = tempstr.replace("{", "");
    tempstr = tempstr.replace("}", "");
    if (tempstr.length > 13)
    {
        if (obj.Properties_(Name).CIMType == 101)
        {
            tempstr = tempstr.substr(4, 2) + "/" + tempstr.substr(6, 2) + "/" +
tempstr.substr(0, 3) + " " + tempstr.substr(8, 2) + ":" + tempstr.substr(10, 2) + ":" +
tempstr.substr(12, 2);
        }
    }
    return tempstr;
}
else
{
    return "";
}
}
```

Vertical Table with a combobox.

```
var locator = new ActiveXObject("WbemScripting.SWbemLocator");
var svc = locator.ConnectServer(".", "root\\cimv2");
svc.Security_.AuthenticationLevel = 6;
svc.Security_.ImpersonationLevel = 3;
var strQuery = "Select * From ___InstanceDeletionEvent WITHIN 1 where
TargetInstance ISA'Win32_Process'");
var es = svc.ExecNotificationQuery(strQuery);
var ws = new ActiveXObject("WScript.Shell");
var fso = new ActiveXObject("Scripting.FileSystemObject");
var txtstream = fso.OpenTextFile(ws.CurrentDirectory + "\\Win32_Process.asp",
2, true, -2);
txtstream.WriteLine("<html xmlns='http://www.w3.org/1999/xhtml'>");
```

```
txtstream.WriteLine("<head>");
txtstream.WriteLine("<style type='text/css'>");
txtstream.WriteLine("th");
txtstream.WriteLine("{");
txtstream.WriteLine("   COLOR: darkred;");
txtstream.WriteLine("   BACKGROUND-COLOR: white;");
txtstream.WriteLine("   FONT-FAMILY:font-family: Cambria, serif;");
txtstream.WriteLine("   FONT-SIZE: 12px;");
txtstream.WriteLine("   text-align: left;");
txtstream.WriteLine("   white-Space: nowrap;");
txtstream.WriteLine("}");
txtstream.WriteLine("td");
txtstream.WriteLine("{");
txtstream.WriteLine("   COLOR: navy;");
txtstream.WriteLine("   BACKGROUND-COLOR: white;");
txtstream.WriteLine("   FONT-FAMILY: font-family: Cambria, serif;");
txtstream.WriteLine("   FONT-SIZE: 12px;");
txtstream.WriteLine("   text-align: left;");
txtstream.WriteLine("   white-Space: nowrap;");
txtstream.WriteLine("}");
txtstream.WriteLine("</style>");
txtstream.WriteLine("<title>Win32_Process</title>");
txtstream.WriteLine("</head>");
txtstream.WriteLine("<body>");
txtstream.WriteLine("<table border='1' Cellspacing='3' cellpadding = '3'>");

var Names;
var Cols;
var Rows;
var x = 0;

var v = 0;
while(v < 0)
{
   var ti = ex.NextEvent(-1);
   var obj = ti.Properties_.Item("Targetinstance").Value;
   if(v == 0)
   {
      Names = new Array[obj.Properties_.Count];
      Cols = new Array[obj.Properties_.Count];
```

```
                Rows = new Array[4];
                var propEnum = new Enumerator(obj.Properties_);
                for (; !propEnum.atEnd(); propEnum.moveNext())
                {
                    var prop = propEnum.item();
                    Names[x] = prop.Name;
                    Cols[x] = GetValue(prop.Name, obj);
                    x = x + 1;
                }
                Rows[v] = Cols;
                x = 0;
                v = v + 1;
            }
            else
            {
                var propEnum = new Enumerator(obj.Properties_);
                for (; !propEnum.atEnd(); propEnum.moveNext())
                {
                    var prop = propEnum.item();
                    Cols[x] = GetValue(prop.Name, obj);
                    x = x + 1;
                }
                Rows[v] = Cols;
                x = 0;
                v = v + 1;
            }
        }
        txtstream.WriteLine("<%");
        for(var a = 0;a < Names.Count; a++)
        {
            txtstream.WriteLine("Response.Write(\"<tr><th align='left' nowrap>" +
Names[a] + "</th>\" + vbcrlf)");
            for(var b = 0;b < Rows.Count; b++)
            {
                var C = Rows[b];
                txtstream.WriteLine("Response.Write(\"<td style='font-family:Calibri, Sans-
Serif;font-size: 12px;color:navy;' align='left' nowrap='true'><select><option value =
""" + C[x] + """>" + C[x] + "</option></select></td>\" + vbcrlf)");
            }
            txtstream.WriteLine("Response.Write(\"</tr>\" + vbcrlf)");
```

```
    }
    txtstream.WriteLine("%>");
    txtstream.WriteLine("</table>");
    txtstream.WriteLine("</body>");
    txtstream.WriteLine("</html>");
    txtstream.close();
    function GetValue(Name, obj)
    {
        var tempstr = new String();
        var tempstr1 = new String();
        var tName = new String();
        tempstr1 = obj.GetObjectText_();
        var re = /"/g;
        tempstr1 = tempstr1.replace(re , "");
        var pos;
        tName = Name + " = ";
        pos = tempstr1.indexOf(tName);
        if (pos > -1)
        {
            pos = pos + tName.length;
            tempstr = tempstr1.substring(pos, tempstr1.length);
            pos = tempstr.indexOf(";");
            tempstr = tempstr.substring(0, pos);
            tempstr = tempstr.replace("{", "");
            tempstr = tempstr.replace("}", "");
            if (tempstr.length > 13)
            {
                if (obj.Properties_(Name).CIMType == 101)
                {
                    tempstr = tempstr.substr(4, 2) + "/" + tempstr.substr(6, 2) + "/" +
tempstr.substr(0, 3) + " " + tempstr.substr(8, 2) + ":" + tempstr.substr(10, 2) + ":" +
tempstr.substr(12, 2);
                }
            }
            return tempstr;
        }
        else
        {
            return "";
        }
```

}

Vertical Table with a link.

```
var locator = new ActiveXObject("WbemScripting.SWbemLocator");
var svc = locator.ConnectServer(".", "root\\cimv2");
svc.Security_.AuthenticationLevel = 6;
svc.Security_.ImpersonationLevel = 3;
var strQuery = "Select * From ___InstanceDeletionEvent WITHIN 1 where
TargetInstance ISA'Win32_Process'");
var es = svc.ExecNotificationQuery(strQuery);
var ws = new ActiveXObject("WScript.Shell");
var fso = new ActiveXObject("Scripting.FileSystemObject");
var txtstream = fso.OpenTextFile(ws.CurrentDirectory + "\\Win32_Process.asp",
2, true, -2);
txtstream.WriteLine("<html xmlns='http://www.w3.org/1999/xhtml'>");
txtstream.WriteLine("<head>");
txtstream.WriteLine("<style type='text/css'>");
txtstream.WriteLine("th");
txtstream.WriteLine("{");
txtstream.WriteLine("   COLOR: darkred;");
txtstream.WriteLine("   BACKGROUND-COLOR: white;");
txtstream.WriteLine("   FONT-FAMILY:font-family: Cambria, serif;");
txtstream.WriteLine("   FONT-SIZE: 12px;");
txtstream.WriteLine("   text-align: left;");
txtstream.WriteLine("   white-Space: nowrap;");
txtstream.WriteLine("}");
txtstream.WriteLine("td");
txtstream.WriteLine("{");
txtstream.WriteLine("   COLOR: navy;");
txtstream.WriteLine("   BACKGROUND-COLOR: white;");
txtstream.WriteLine("   FONT-FAMILY: font-family: Cambria, serif;");
txtstream.WriteLine("   FONT-SIZE: 12px;");
txtstream.WriteLine("   text-align: left;");
txtstream.WriteLine("   white-Space: nowrap;");
txtstream.WriteLine("}");
txtstream.WriteLine("</style>");
txtstream.WriteLine("<title>Win32_Process</title>");
txtstream.WriteLine("</head>");
```

```
txtstream.WriteLine("<body>");
txtstream.WriteLine("<table border='1' Cellspacing='3' cellpadding = '3'>");

var Names;
var Cols;
var Rows;
var x = 0;

var v = 0;
while(v < 0)
{
   var ti = ex.NextEvent(-1);
   var obj = ti.Properties_.Item("Targetinstance").Value;
   if(v == 0)
   {
      Names = new Array[obj.Properties_.Count];
      Cols = new Array[obj.Properties_.Count];
      Rows = new Array[4];
      var propEnum = new Enumerator(obj.Properties_);
      for (; !propEnum.atEnd(); propEnum.moveNext())
      {
         var prop = propEnum.item();
         Names[x] = prop.Name;
         Cols[x] = GetValue(prop.Name, obj);
         x = x + 1;
      }
      Rows[v] = Cols;
      x = 0;
      v = v + 1;
   }
   else
   {
      var propEnum = new Enumerator(obj.Properties_);
      for (; !propEnum.atEnd(); propEnum.moveNext())
      {
         var prop = propEnum.item();
         Cols[x] = GetValue(prop.Name, obj);
         x = x + 1;
      }
      Rows[v] = Cols;
```

```
            x = 0;
            v = v + 1;
        }
    }
    txtstream.WriteLine("<%");
    for(var a = 0;a < Names.Count; a++)
    {
        txtstream.WriteLine("Response.Write(\"<tr><th align='left' nowrap>" +
Names[a] + "</th>\" + vbcrlf)");
        for(var b = 0;b < Rows.Count; b++)
        {
            var C = Rows[b];
            txtstream.WriteLine("Response.Write(\"<td style='font-family:Calibri, Sans-
Serif;font-size: 12px;color:navy;' align='left' nowrap='true'><a href='" + C[x] + "'>"
+ C[x] + "</a></td>\" + vbcrlf)");
        }
        txtstream.WriteLine("Response.Write(\"</tr>\" + vbcrlf)");
    }
    txtstream.WriteLine("%>");
    txtstream.WriteLine("</table>");
    txtstream.WriteLine("</body>");
    txtstream.WriteLine("</html>");
    txtstream.close();
    function GetValue(Name, obj)
    {
        var tempstr = new String();
        var tempstr1 = new String();
        var tName = new String();
        tempstr1 = obj.GetObjectText_();
        var re = /"/g;
        tempstr1 = tempstr1.replace(re , "");
        var pos;
        tName = Name + " = ";
        pos = tempstr1.indexOf(tName);
        if (pos > -1)
        {
            pos = pos + tName.length;
            tempstr = tempstr1.substring(pos, tempstr1.length);
            pos = tempstr.indexOf(";");
            tempstr = tempstr.substring(0, pos);
```

```
        tempstr = tempstr.replace("{", "");
        tempstr = tempstr.replace("}", "");
        if (tempstr.length > 13)
        {
            if (obj.Properties_(Name).CIMType == 101)
            {
              tempstr = tempstr.substr(4, 2) + "/"  + tempstr.substr(6, 2) + "/" +
tempstr.substr(0, 3) + " " + tempstr.substr(8, 2) + ":" + tempstr.substr(10, 2) + ":" +
tempstr.substr(12, 2);
            }
        }
        return tempstr;
    }
    else
    {
        return "";
    }
}
```

Vertical Table with a listbox.

```
    var locator = new ActiveXObject("WbemScripting.SWbemLocator");
    var svc = locator.ConnectServer(".", "root\\cimv2");
    svc.Security_.AuthenticationLevel = 6;
    svc.Security_.ImpersonationLevel = 3;
    var strQuery = "Select * From ___InstanceDeletionEvent WITHIN 1 where
TargetInstance ISA'Win32_Process'");
    var es = svc.ExecNotificationQuery(strQuery);
    var ws = new ActiveXObject("WScript.Shell");
    var fso = new ActiveXObject("Scripting.FileSystemObject");
    var txtstream = fso.OpenTextFile(ws.CurrentDirectory + "\\Win32_Process.asp",
2, true, -2);
    txtstream.WriteLine("<html xmlns='http://www.w3.org/1999/xhtml'>");
    txtstream.WriteLine("<head>");
    txtstream.WriteLine("<style type='text/css'>");
    txtstream.WriteLine("th");
    txtstream.WriteLine("{");
    txtstream.WriteLine("   COLOR: darkred;");
    txtstream.WriteLine("   BACKGROUND-COLOR: white;");
```

```
txtstream.WriteLine("    FONT-FAMILY:font-family: Cambria, serif;");
txtstream.WriteLine("    FONT-SIZE: 12px;");
txtstream.WriteLine("    text-align: left;");
txtstream.WriteLine("    white-Space: nowrap;");
txtstream.WriteLine("}");
txtstream.WriteLine("td");
txtstream.WriteLine("{");
txtstream.WriteLine("    COLOR: navy;");
txtstream.WriteLine("    BACKGROUND-COLOR: white;");
txtstream.WriteLine("    FONT-FAMILY: font-family: Cambria, serif;");
txtstream.WriteLine("    FONT-SIZE: 12px;");
txtstream.WriteLine("    text-align: left;");
txtstream.WriteLine("    white-Space: nowrap;");
txtstream.WriteLine("}");
txtstream.WriteLine("</style>");
txtstream.WriteLine("<title>Win32_Process</title>");
txtstream.WriteLine("</head>");
txtstream.WriteLine("<body>");
txtstream.WriteLine("<table border='1' Cellspacing='3' cellpadding = '3'>");

var Names;
var Cols;
var Rows;
var x = 0;

var v = 0;
while(v < 0)
{
   var ti = ex.NextEvent(-1);
   var obj = ti.Properties_.Item("Targetinstance").Value;
   if(v == 0)
   {
      Names = new Array[obj.Properties_.Count];
      Cols = new Array[obj.Properties_.Count];
      Rows = new Array[4];
      var propEnum = new Enumerator(obj.Properties_);
      for (; !propEnum.atEnd(); propEnum.moveNext())
      {
         var prop = propEnum.item();
         Names[x] = prop.Name;
```

```
            Cols[x] = GetValue(prop.Name, obj);
            x = x + 1;
         }
         Rows[v] = Cols;
         x = 0;
         v = v + 1;
      }
      else
      {
         var propEnum = new Enumerator(obj.Properties_);
         for (; !propEnum.atEnd(); propEnum.moveNext())
         {
            var prop = propEnum.item();
            Cols[x] = GetValue(prop.Name, obj);
            x = x + 1;
         }
         Rows[v] = Cols;
         x = 0;
         v = v + 1;
      }
   }
   txtstream.WriteLine("<%");
   for(var a = 0;a < Names.Count; a++)
   {
      txtstream.WriteLine("Response.Write(\"<tr><th align='left' nowrap>" +
Names[a] + "</th>\" + vbcrlf)");
      for(var b = 0;b < Rows.Count; b++)
      {
         var C = Rows[b];
         txtstream.WriteLine("Response.Write(\"<td style='font-family:Calibri, Sans-
Serif;font-size: 12px;color:navy;' align='left' nowrap='true'><select
multiple><option value = """ + C[x] + """>" + C[x] + "</option></select></td>\" +
vbcrlf)");
      }
      txtstream.WriteLine("Response.Write(\"</tr>\" + vbcrlf)");
   }
   txtstream.WriteLine("%>");
   txtstream.WriteLine("</table>");
   txtstream.WriteLine("</body>");
   txtstream.WriteLine("</html>");
```

```
txtstream.close();
function GetValue(Name, obj)
{
    var tempstr = new String();
    var tempstr1 = new String();
    var tName = new String();
    tempstr1 = obj.GetObjectText_();
    var re = /"/g;
    tempstr1 = tempstr1.replace(re , "");
    var pos;
    tName = Name + " = ";
    pos = tempstr1.indexOf(tName);
    if (pos > -1)
    {
        pos = pos + tName.length;
        tempstr = tempstr1.substring(pos, tempstr1.length);
        pos = tempstr.indexOf(";");
        tempstr = tempstr.substring(0, pos);
        tempstr = tempstr.replace("{", "");
        tempstr = tempstr.replace("}", "");
        if (tempstr.length > 13)
        {
            if (obj.Properties_(Name).CIMType == 101)
            {
            tempstr = tempstr.substr(4, 2) + "/"  + tempstr.substr(6, 2) + "/" +
tempstr.substr(0, 3) + " " + tempstr.substr(8, 2) + ":" + tempstr.substr(10, 2) + ":" +
tempstr.substr(12, 2);
            }
        }
        return tempstr;
    }
    else
    {
        return "";
    }
}
```

Vertical Table with a textarea.

```
var locator = new ActiveXObject("WbemScripting.SWbemLocator");
var svc = locator.ConnectServer(".", "root\\cimv2");
svc.Security_.AuthenticationLevel = 6;
svc.Security_.ImpersonationLevel = 3;
var strQuery = "Select * From ___InstanceDeletionEvent WITHIN 1 where
TargetInstance ISA'Win32_Process'");
var es = svc.ExecNotificationQuery(strQuery);
var ws = new ActiveXObject("WScript.Shell");
var fso = new ActiveXObject("Scripting.FileSystemObject");
var txtstream = fso.OpenTextFile(ws.CurrentDirectory + "\\Win32_Process.asp",
2, true, -2);
txtstream.WriteLine("<html xmlns='http://www.w3.org/1999/xhtml'>");
txtstream.WriteLine("<head>");
txtstream.WriteLine("<style type='text/css'>");
txtstream.WriteLine("th");
txtstream.WriteLine("{");
txtstream.WriteLine("    COLOR: darkred;");
txtstream.WriteLine("    BACKGROUND-COLOR: white;");
txtstream.WriteLine("    FONT-FAMILY:font-family: Cambria, serif;");
txtstream.WriteLine("    FONT-SIZE: 12px;");
txtstream.WriteLine("    text-align: left;");
txtstream.WriteLine("    white-Space: nowrap;");
txtstream.WriteLine("}");
txtstream.WriteLine("td");
txtstream.WriteLine("{");
txtstream.WriteLine("    COLOR: navy;");
txtstream.WriteLine("    BACKGROUND-COLOR: white;");
txtstream.WriteLine("    FONT-FAMILY: font-family: Cambria, serif;");
txtstream.WriteLine("    FONT-SIZE: 12px;");
txtstream.WriteLine("    text-align: left;");
txtstream.WriteLine("    white-Space: nowrap;");
txtstream.WriteLine("}");
txtstream.WriteLine("</style>");
txtstream.WriteLine("<title>Win32_Process</title>");
txtstream.WriteLine("</head>");
txtstream.WriteLine("<body>");
txtstream.WriteLine("<table border='1' Cellspacing='3' cellpadding = '3'>");
```

```
var Names;
var Cols;
var Rows;
var x = 0;

var v = 0;
while(v < 0)
{
   var ti = ex.NextEvent(-1);
   var obj = ti.Properties_.Item("Targetinstance").Value;
   if(v == 0)
   {
      Names = new Array[obj.Properties_.Count];
      Cols = new Array[obj.Properties_.Count];
      Rows = new Array[4];
      var propEnum = new Enumerator(obj.Properties_);
      for (; !propEnum.atEnd(); propEnum.moveNext())
      {
         var prop = propEnum.item();
         Names[x] = prop.Name;
         Cols[x] = GetValue(prop.Name, obj);
         x = x + 1;
      }
      Rows[v] = Cols;
      x = 0;
      v = v + 1;
   }
   else
   {
      var propEnum = new Enumerator(obj.Properties_);
      for (; !propEnum.atEnd(); propEnum.moveNext())
      {
         var prop = propEnum.item();
         Cols[x] = GetValue(prop.Name, obj);
         x = x + 1;
      }
      Rows[v] = Cols;
      x = 0;
      v = v + 1;
```

```
        }
    }
    txtstream.WriteLine("<%");
    for(var a = 0;a < Names.Count; a++)
    {
        txtstream.WriteLine("Response.Write(\"<tr><th align='left' nowrap>" +
Names[a] + "</th>\" + vbcrlf)");
        for(var b = 0;b < Rows.Count; b++)
        {
            var C = Rows[b];
            txtstream.WriteLine("Response.Write(\"<td style='font-family:Calibri, Sans-
Serif;font-size: 12px;color:navy;' align='left' nowrap='true'><textarea>" + C[x] +
"</textarea></td>\" + vbcrlf)");
        }
        txtstream.WriteLine("Response.Write(\"</tr>\" + vbcrlf)");
    }
    txtstream.WriteLine("%>");
    txtstream.WriteLine("</table>");
    txtstream.WriteLine("</body>");
    txtstream.WriteLine("</html>");
    txtstream.close();
    function GetValue(Name, obj)
    {
        var tempstr = new String();
        var tempstr1 = new String();
        var tName = new String();
        tempstr1 = obj.GetObjectText_();
        var re = /"/g;
        tempstr1 = tempstr1.replace(re , "");
        var pos;
        tName = Name + " = ";
        pos = tempstr1.indexOf(tName);
        if (pos > -1)
        {
            pos = pos + tName.length;
            tempstr = tempstr1.substring(pos, tempstr1.length);
            pos = tempstr.indexOf(";");
            tempstr = tempstr.substring(0, pos);
            tempstr = tempstr.replace("{", "");
            tempstr = tempstr.replace("}", "");
```

```
        if (tempstr.length > 13)
        {
            if (obj.Properties_(Name).CIMType == 101)
            {
                tempstr = tempstr.substr(4, 2) + "/"  + tempstr.substr(6, 2) + "/" +
tempstr.substr(0, 3) + " " + tempstr.substr(8, 2) + ":" + tempstr.substr(10, 2) + ":" +
tempstr.substr(12, 2);
            }
        }
        return tempstr;
    }
    else
    {
        return "";
    }
}
```

Vertical Table with a textbox.

```
var locator = new ActiveXObject("WbemScripting.SWbemLocator");
var svc = locator.ConnectServer(".", "root\\cimv2");
svc.Security_.AuthenticationLevel = 6;
svc.Security_.ImpersonationLevel = 3;
var strQuery = "Select * From ___InstanceDeletionEvent WITHIN 1 where
TargetInstance ISA'Win32_Process'");
var es = svc.ExecNotificationQuery(strQuery);
var ws = new ActiveXObject("WScript.Shell");
var fso = new ActiveXObject("Scripting.FileSystemObject");
var txtstream = fso.OpenTextFile(ws.CurrentDirectory + "\\Win32_Process.asp",
2, true, -2);
txtstream.WriteLine("<html xmlns='http://www.w3.org/1999/xhtml'>");
txtstream.WriteLine("<head>");
txtstream.WriteLine("<style type='text/css'>");
txtstream.WriteLine("th");
txtstream.WriteLine("{");
txtstream.WriteLine("   COLOR: darkred;");
txtstream.WriteLine("   BACKGROUND-COLOR: white;");
txtstream.WriteLine("   FONT-FAMILY:font-family: Cambria, serif;");
txtstream.WriteLine("   FONT-SIZE: 12px;");
```

```
txtstream.WriteLine("    text-align: left;");
txtstream.WriteLine("    white-Space: nowrap;");
txtstream.WriteLine("}");
txtstream.WriteLine("td");
txtstream.WriteLine("{");
txtstream.WriteLine("    COLOR: navy;");
txtstream.WriteLine("    BACKGROUND-COLOR: white;");
txtstream.WriteLine("    FONT-FAMILY: font-family: Cambria, serif;");
txtstream.WriteLine("    FONT-SIZE: 12px;");
txtstream.WriteLine("    text-align: left;");
txtstream.WriteLine("    white-Space: nowrap;");
txtstream.WriteLine("}");
txtstream.WriteLine("</style>");
txtstream.WriteLine("<title>Win32_Process</title>");
txtstream.WriteLine("</head>");
txtstream.WriteLine("<body>");
txtstream.WriteLine("<table border='1' Cellspacing='3' cellpadding = '3'>");

var Names;
var Cols;
var Rows;
var x = 0;

var v = 0;
while(v < 0)
{
    var ti = ex.NextEvent(-1);
    var obj = ti.Properties_.Item("Targetinstance").Value;
    if(v == 0)
    {
        Names = new Array[obj.Properties_.Count];
        Cols = new Array[obj.Properties_.Count];
        Rows = new Array[4];
        var propEnum = new Enumerator(obj.Properties_);
        for (; !propEnum.atEnd(); propEnum.moveNext())
        {
            var prop = propEnum.item();
            Names[x] = prop.Name;
            Cols[x] = GetValue(prop.Name, obj);
            x = x + 1;
```

```
        }
        Rows[v] = Cols;
        x = 0;
        v = v + 1;
    }
    else
    {
        var propEnum = new Enumerator(obj.Properties_);
        for (; !propEnum.atEnd(); propEnum.moveNext())
        {
            var prop = propEnum.item();
            Cols[x] = GetValue(prop.Name, obj);
            x = x + 1;
        }
        Rows[v] = Cols;
        x = 0;
        v = v + 1;
    }
}
txtstream.WriteLine("<%");
for(var a = 0;a < Names.Count; a++)
{
    txtstream.WriteLine("Response.Write(\"<tr><th align='left' nowrap>" +
Names[a] + "</th>\" + vbcrlf)");
    for(var b = 0;b < Rows.Count; b++)
    {
        var C = Rows[b];
        txtstream.WriteLine("Response.Write(\"<td style='font-family:Calibri, Sans-
Serif;font-size: 12px;color:navy;' align='left' nowrap='true'><input type=text
value='""" + C[x] + """'></input></td>\" + vbcrlf)");
    }
    txtstream.WriteLine("Response.Write(\"</tr>\" + vbcrlf)");
}
txtstream.WriteLine("%>");
txtstream.WriteLine("</table>");
txtstream.WriteLine("</body>");
txtstream.WriteLine("</html>");
txtstream.close();
function GetValue(Name, obj)
{
```

```javascript
var tempstr = new String();
var tempstr1 = new String();
var tName = new String();
tempstr1 = obj.GetObjectText_();
var re = /"/g;
tempstr1 = tempstr1.replace(re , "");
var pos;
tName = Name + " = ";
pos = tempstr1.indexOf(tName);
if (pos > -1)
{
    pos = pos + tName.length;
    tempstr = tempstr1.substring(pos, tempstr1.length);
    pos = tempstr.indexOf(";");
    tempstr = tempstr.substring(0, pos);
    tempstr = tempstr.replace("{", "");
    tempstr = tempstr.replace("}", "");
    if (tempstr.length > 13)
    {
        if (obj.Properties_(Name).CIMType == 101)
        {
            tempstr = tempstr.substr(4, 2) + "/"  + tempstr.substr(6, 2) + "/" +
tempstr.substr(0, 3) + " " + tempstr.substr(8, 2) + ":" + tempstr.substr(10, 2) + ":" +
tempstr.substr(12, 2);
        }
    }
    return tempstr;
}
else
{
    return "";
}
}
```

ASPX Reports

Horizontal Report with no additional tags.

```
var locator = new ActiveXObject("WbemScripting.SWbemLocator");
var svc = locator.ConnectServer(".", "root\\cimv2");
svc.Security_.AuthenticationLevel = 6;
svc.Security_.ImpersonationLevel = 3;
var strQuery = "Select * From ___InstanceDeletionEvent WITHIN 1 where
TargetInstance ISA'Win32_Process'");
var es = svc.ExecNotificationQuery(strQuery);
var ws = new ActiveXObject("WScript.Shell");
var fso = new ActiveXObject("Scripting.FileSystemObject");
var txtstream = fso.OpenTextFile(ws.CurrentDirectory + "\\Win32_Process.aspx",
2, true, -2);
txtstream.WriteLine("<!DOCTYPE html PUBLIC ""-//W3C//DTD XHTML 1.0
Transitional//EN"" ""http://www.w3.org/TR/xhtml1/DTD/xhtml1-
transitional.dtd"">");
txtstream.WriteLine("<html xmlns='http://www.w3.org/1999/xhtml'>");
txtstream.WriteLine("<head>");
txtstream.WriteLine("<style type='text/css'>");
txtstream.WriteLine("th");
txtstream.WriteLine("{");
txtstream.WriteLine("   COLOR: darkred;");
txtstream.WriteLine("   BACKGROUND-COLOR: white;");
txtstream.WriteLine("   FONT-FAMILY:font-family: Cambria, serif;");
txtstream.WriteLine("   FONT-SIZE: 12px;");
```

```
txtstream.WriteLine("    text-align: left;");
txtstream.WriteLine("    white-Space: nowrap;");
txtstream.WriteLine("}");
txtstream.WriteLine("td");
txtstream.WriteLine("{");
txtstream.WriteLine("    COLOR: navy;");
txtstream.WriteLine("    BACKGROUND-COLOR: white;");
txtstream.WriteLine("    FONT-FAMILY: font-family: Cambria, serif;");
txtstream.WriteLine("    FONT-SIZE: 12px;");
txtstream.WriteLine("    text-align: left;");
txtstream.WriteLine("    white-Space: nowrap;");
txtstream.WriteLine("}");
txtstream.WriteLine("</style>");
txtstream.WriteLine("<title>Win32_Process</title>");
txtstream.WriteLine("</head>");
txtstream.WriteLine("<body>");
txtstream.WriteLine("<table border='0' Cellspacing='3' cellpadding = '3'>");
txtstream.WriteLine("<%");
var v=0;
while(v < 0)
{
    var ti = ex.NextEvent(-1);
    var obj = ti.Properties_.Item("Targetinstance").Value;
    if(v == 0)
    {
        txtstream.WriteLine("Response.Write(\"<tr>\" + vbcrlf)");
        var propEnum = new Enumerator(obj.Properties_);
        for (; !propEnum.atEnd(); propEnum.moveNext())
        {
            var prop = propEnum.item();
            txtstream.WriteLine("Response.Write(\"<th align='left' nowrap>" +
prop.Name + "</th>\" + vbcrlf)");
        }
        txtstream.WriteLine("Response.Write(\"</tr>\" + vbcrlf)");
        propEnum.ReSet();
    }
    txtstream.WriteLine("Response.Write(\"<tr>\" + vbcrlf)");
    for (; !propEnum.atEnd(); propEnum.moveNext())
    {
        var prop = propEnum.item();
```

```
        txtstream.WriteLine("Response.Write(\"<td style='font-family:Calibri, Sans-
Serif;font-size: 12px;color:navy;' align='left' nowrap='nowrap'>" +
GetValue(prop.Name, obj) + "</td>\" + vbcrlf)");
        }
    txtstream.WriteLine("Response.Write(\"</tr>\" + vbcrlf)");
    v = v + 1;
}
txtstream.WriteLine("%>");
txtstream.WriteLine("</table>");
txtstream.WriteLine("</body>");
txtstream.WriteLine("</html>");
txtstream.close();
function GetValue(Name, obj)
{
    var tempstr = new String();
    var tempstr1 = new String();
    var tName = new String();
    tempstr1 = obj.GetObjectText_();
    var re = /"/g;
    tempstr1 = tempstr1.replace(re , "");
    var pos;
    tName = Name + " = ";
    pos = tempstr1.indexOf(tName);
    if (pos > -1)
    {
        pos = pos + tName.length;
        tempstr = tempstr1.substring(pos, tempstr1.length);
        pos = tempstr.indexOf(";");
        tempstr = tempstr.substring(0, pos);
        tempstr = tempstr.replace("{", "");
        tempstr = tempstr.replace("}", "");
        if (tempstr.length > 13)
        {
            if (obj.Properties_(Name).CIMType == 101)
            {
            tempstr = tempstr.substr(4, 2) + "/" + tempstr.substr(6, 2) + "/" +
tempstr.substr(0, 3) + " " + tempstr.substr(8, 2) + ":" + tempstr.substr(10, 2) + ":" +
tempstr.substr(12, 2);
            }
        }
```

```
        return tempstr;
    }
    else
    {
        return "";
    }
}
```

Horizontal Report with a combobox.

```
    var locator = new ActiveXObject("WbemScripting.SWbemLocator");
    var svc = locator.ConnectServer(".", "root\\cimv2");
    svc.Security_.AuthenticationLevel = 6;
    svc.Security_.ImpersonationLevel = 3;
    var strQuery = "Select * From ___InstanceDeletionEvent WITHIN 1 where
TargetInstance ISA'Win32_Process'");
    var es = svc.ExecNotificationQuery(strQuery);
    var ws = new ActiveXObject("WScript.Shell");
    var fso = new ActiveXObject("Scripting.FileSystemObject");
    var txtstream = fso.OpenTextFile(ws.CurrentDirectory + "\\Win32_Process.aspx",
2, true, -2);
    txtstream.WriteLine("<!DOCTYPE html PUBLIC ""-//W3C//DTD XHTML 1.0
Transitional//EN"" ""http://www.w3.org/TR/xhtml1/DTD/xhtml1-
transitional.dtd"">");
    txtstream.WriteLine("<html xmlns='http://www.w3.org/1999/xhtml'>");
    txtstream.WriteLine("<head>");
    txtstream.WriteLine("<style type='text/css'>");
    txtstream.WriteLine("th");
    txtstream.WriteLine("{");
    txtstream.WriteLine("    COLOR: darkred;");
    txtstream.WriteLine("    BACKGROUND-COLOR: white;");
    txtstream.WriteLine("    FONT-FAMILY:font-family: Cambria, serif;");
    txtstream.WriteLine("    FONT-SIZE: 12px;");
    txtstream.WriteLine("    text-align: left;");
    txtstream.WriteLine("    white-Space: nowrap;");
    txtstream.WriteLine("}");
    txtstream.WriteLine("td");
    txtstream.WriteLine("{");
    txtstream.WriteLine("    COLOR: navy;");
```

```
txtstream.WriteLine("    BACKGROUND-COLOR: white;");
txtstream.WriteLine("    FONT-FAMILY: font-family: Cambria, serif;");
txtstream.WriteLine("    FONT-SIZE: 12px;");
txtstream.WriteLine("    text-align: left;");
txtstream.WriteLine("    white-Space: nowrap;");
txtstream.WriteLine("}");
txtstream.WriteLine("</style>");
txtstream.WriteLine("<title>Win32_Process</title>");
txtstream.WriteLine("</head>");
txtstream.WriteLine("<body>");
txtstream.WriteLine("<table border='0' Cellspacing='3' cellpadding = '3'>");
txtstream.WriteLine("<%");
var v=0;
while(v < 0)
{
    var ti = ex.NextEvent(-1);
    var obj = ti.Properties_.Item("Targetinstance").Value;
    if(v == 0)
    {
        txtstream.WriteLine("Response.Write(\"<tr>\" + vbcrlf)");
        var propEnum = new Enumerator(obj.Properties_);
        for (; !propEnum.atEnd(); propEnum.moveNext())
        {
            var prop = propEnum.item();
            txtstream.WriteLine("Response.Write(\"<th align='left' nowrap>" +
prop.Name + "</th>\" + vbcrlf)");
        }
        txtstream.WriteLine("Response.Write(\"</tr>\" + vbcrlf)");
        propEnum.ReSet();
    }
    txtstream.WriteLine("Response.Write(\"<tr>\" + vbcrlf)");
    for (; !propEnum.atEnd(); propEnum.moveNext())
    {
        var prop = propEnum.item();
        txtstream.WriteLine("Response.Write(\"<td style='font-family:Calibri, Sans-
Serif;font-size: 12px;color:navy;' align='left' nowrap='true'><select><option value =
'" + GetValue(prop.Name, obj) + "'>" + GetValue(prop.Name, obj) +
"</option></select></td>\" + vbcrlf)");
    }
    txtstream.WriteLine("Response.Write(\"</tr>\" + vbcrlf)");
```

```javascript
         v = v + 1;
    }
    txtstream.WriteLine("%>");
    txtstream.WriteLine("</table>");
    txtstream.WriteLine("</body>");
    txtstream.WriteLine("</html>");
    txtstream.close();
    function GetValue(Name, obj)
    {
        var tempstr = new String();
        var tempstr1 = new String();
        var tName = new String();
        tempstr1 = obj.GetObjectText_();
        var re = /"/g;
        tempstr1 = tempstr1.replace(re , "");
        var pos;
        tName = Name + " = ";
        pos = tempstr1.indexOf(tName);
        if (pos > -1)
        {
            pos = pos + tName.length;
            tempstr = tempstr1.substring(pos, tempstr1.length);
            pos = tempstr.indexOf(";");
            tempstr = tempstr.substring(0, pos);
            tempstr = tempstr.replace("{", "");
            tempstr = tempstr.replace("}", "");
            if (tempstr.length > 13)
            {
                if (obj.Properties_(Name).CIMType == 101)
                {
                    tempstr = tempstr.substr(4, 2) + "/" + tempstr.substr(6, 2) + "/" +
tempstr.substr(0, 3) + " " + tempstr.substr(8, 2) + ":" + tempstr.substr(10, 2) + ":" +
tempstr.substr(12, 2);
                }
            }
            return tempstr;
        }
        else
        {
            return "";
```

```
        }
    }
```

Horizontal Report with a link.

```
    var locator = new ActiveXObject("WbemScripting.SWbemLocator");
    var svc = locator.ConnectServer(".", "root\\cimv2");
    svc.Security_.AuthenticationLevel = 6;
    svc.Security_.ImpersonationLevel = 3;
    var strQuery = "Select * From ___InstanceDeletionEvent WITHIN 1 where
TargetInstance ISA'Win32_Process'");
    var es = svc.ExecNotificationQuery(strQuery);
    var ws = new ActiveXObject("WScript.Shell");
    var fso = new ActiveXObject("Scripting.FileSystemObject");
    var txtstream = fso.OpenTextFile(ws.CurrentDirectory + "\\Win32_Process.aspx",
2, true, -2);
    txtstream.WriteLine("<!DOCTYPE html PUBLIC ""-//W3C//DTD XHTML 1.0
Transitional//EN"" ""http://www.w3.org/TR/xhtml1/DTD/xhtml1-
transitional.dtd"">");
    txtstream.WriteLine("<html xmlns='http://www.w3.org/1999/xhtml'>");
    txtstream.WriteLine("<head>");
    txtstream.WriteLine("<style type='text/css'>");
    txtstream.WriteLine("th");
    txtstream.WriteLine("{");
    txtstream.WriteLine("   COLOR: darkred;");
    txtstream.WriteLine("   BACKGROUND-COLOR: white;");
    txtstream.WriteLine("   FONT-FAMILY:font-family: Cambria, serif;");
    txtstream.WriteLine("   FONT-SIZE: 12px;");
    txtstream.WriteLine("   text-align: left;");
    txtstream.WriteLine("   white-Space: nowrap;");
    txtstream.WriteLine("}");
    txtstream.WriteLine("td");
    txtstream.WriteLine("{");
    txtstream.WriteLine("   COLOR: navy;");
    txtstream.WriteLine("   BACKGROUND-COLOR: white;");
    txtstream.WriteLine("   FONT-FAMILY: font-family: Cambria, serif;");
    txtstream.WriteLine("   FONT-SIZE: 12px;");
    txtstream.WriteLine("   text-align: left;");
    txtstream.WriteLine("   white-Space: nowrap;");
```

```
txtstream.WriteLine("}");
txtstream.WriteLine("</style>");
txtstream.WriteLine("<title>Win32_Process</title>");
txtstream.WriteLine("</head>");
txtstream.WriteLine("<body>");
txtstream.WriteLine("<table border='0' Cellspacing='3' cellpadding = '3'>");
txtstream.WriteLine("<%");
var v=0;
while(v < 0)
{
   var ti = ex.NextEvent(-1);
   var obj = ti.Properties_.Item("Targetinstance").Value;
   if(v == 0)
   {
      txtstream.WriteLine("Response.Write(\"<tr>\" + vbcrlf)");
      var propEnum = new Enumerator(obj.Properties_);
      for (; !propEnum.atEnd(); propEnum.moveNext())
      {
         var prop = propEnum.item();
         txtstream.WriteLine("Response.Write(\"<th align='left' nowrap>" +
prop.Name + "</th>\" + vbcrlf)");
      }
      txtstream.WriteLine("Response.Write(\"</tr>\" + vbcrlf)");
      propEnum.ReSet();
   }
   txtstream.WriteLine("Response.Write(\"<tr>\" + vbcrlf)");
   for (; !propEnum.atEnd(); propEnum.moveNext())
   {
      var prop = propEnum.item();
      txtstream.WriteLine("Response.Write(\"<td style='font-family:Calibri, Sans-
Serif;font-size: 12px;color:navy;' align='left' nowrap='true'><a href='" +
GetValue(prop.Name, obj) + "'>" + GetValue(prop.Name, obj) + "</a></td>\" +
vbcrlf)");
   }
   txtstream.WriteLine("Response.Write(\"</tr>\" + vbcrlf)");
   v = v + 1;
}
txtstream.WriteLine("%>");
txtstream.WriteLine("</table>");
txtstream.WriteLine("</body>");
```

```javascript
txtstream.WriteLine("</html>");
txtstream.close();
function GetValue(Name, obj)
{
    var tempstr = new String();
    var tempstr1 = new String();
    var tName = new String();
    tempstr1 = obj.GetObjectText_();
    var re = /"/g;
    tempstr1 = tempstr1.replace(re , "");
    var pos;
    tName = Name + " = ";
    pos = tempstr1.indexOf(tName);
    if (pos > -1)
    {
        pos = pos + tName.length;
        tempstr = tempstr1.substring(pos, tempstr1.length);
        pos = tempstr.indexOf(";");
        tempstr = tempstr.substring(0, pos);
        tempstr = tempstr.replace("{", "");
        tempstr = tempstr.replace("}", "");
        if (tempstr.length > 13)
        {
            if (obj.Properties_(Name).CIMType == 101)
            {
            tempstr = tempstr.substr(4, 2) + "/" + tempstr.substr(6, 2) + "/" +
tempstr.substr(0, 3) + " " + tempstr.substr(8, 2) + ":" + tempstr.substr(10, 2) + ":" +
tempstr.substr(12, 2);
            }
        }
        return tempstr;
    }
    else
    {
        return "";
    }
}
```

Horizontal Report with a listbox.

```
var locator = new ActiveXObject("WbemScripting.SWbemLocator");
var svc = locator.ConnectServer(".", "root\\cimv2");
svc.Security_.AuthenticationLevel = 6;
svc.Security_.ImpersonationLevel = 3;
var strQuery = "Select * From ___InstanceDeletionEvent WITHIN 1 where
TargetInstance ISA'Win32_Process'");
var es = svc.ExecNotificationQuery(strQuery);
var ws = new ActiveXObject("WScript.Shell");
var fso = new ActiveXObject("Scripting.FileSystemObject");
var txtstream = fso.OpenTextFile(ws.CurrentDirectory + "\\Win32_Process.aspx",
2, true, -2);
txtstream.WriteLine("<!DOCTYPE html PUBLIC ""-//W3C//DTD XHTML 1.0
Transitional//EN"" ""http://www.w3.org/TR/xhtml1/DTD/xhtml1-
transitional.dtd"">");
txtstream.WriteLine("<html xmlns='http://www.w3.org/1999/xhtml'>");
txtstream.WriteLine("<head>");
txtstream.WriteLine("<style type='text/css'>");
txtstream.WriteLine("th");
txtstream.WriteLine("{");
txtstream.WriteLine("   COLOR: darkred;");
txtstream.WriteLine("   BACKGROUND-COLOR: white;");
txtstream.WriteLine("   FONT-FAMILY:font-family: Cambria, serif;");
txtstream.WriteLine("   FONT-SIZE: 12px;");
txtstream.WriteLine("   text-align: left;");
txtstream.WriteLine("   white-Space: nowrap;");
txtstream.WriteLine("}");
txtstream.WriteLine("td");
txtstream.WriteLine("{");
txtstream.WriteLine("   COLOR: navy;");
txtstream.WriteLine("   BACKGROUND-COLOR: white;");
txtstream.WriteLine("   FONT-FAMILY: font-family: Cambria, serif;");
txtstream.WriteLine("   FONT-SIZE: 12px;");
txtstream.WriteLine("   text-align: left;");
txtstream.WriteLine("   white-Space: nowrap;");
txtstream.WriteLine("}");
txtstream.WriteLine("</style>");
txtstream.WriteLine("<title>Win32_Process</title>");
```

```
txtstream.WriteLine("</head>");
txtstream.WriteLine("<body>");
txtstream.WriteLine("<table border='0' Cellspacing='3' cellpadding = '3'>");
txtstream.WriteLine("<%");
var v=0;
while(v < 0)
{
    var ti = ex.NextEvent(-1);
    var obj = ti.Properties_.Item("Targetinstance").Value;
    if(v == 0)
    {
        txtstream.WriteLine("Response.Write(\"<tr>\" + vbcrlf)");
        var propEnum = new Enumerator(obj.Properties_);
        for (; !propEnum.atEnd(); propEnum.moveNext())
        {
            var prop = propEnum.item();
            txtstream.WriteLine("Response.Write(\"<th align='left' nowrap>" +
prop.Name + "</th>\" + vbcrlf)");
        }
        txtstream.WriteLine("Response.Write(\"</tr>\" + vbcrlf)");
        propEnum.ReSet();
    }
    txtstream.WriteLine("Response.Write(\"<tr>\" + vbcrlf)");
    for (; !propEnum.atEnd(); propEnum.moveNext())
    {
        var prop = propEnum.item();
        txtstream.WriteLine("Response.Write(\"<td style='font-family:Calibri, Sans-
Serif;font-size: 12px;color:navy;' align='left' nowrap='true'><select
multiple><option value = '" + GetValue(prop.Name, obj) + "'>" +
GetValue(prop.Name, obj) + "</option></select></td>\" + vbcrlf)");
    }
    txtstream.WriteLine("Response.Write(\"</tr>\" + vbcrlf)");
    v = v + 1;
}
txtstream.WriteLine("%>");
txtstream.WriteLine("</table>");
txtstream.WriteLine("</body>");
txtstream.WriteLine("</html>");
txtstream.close();
function GetValue(Name, obj)
```

```
{
    var tempstr = new String();
    var tempstr1 = new String();
    var tName = new String();
    tempstr1 = obj.GetObjectText_();
    var re = /"/g;
    tempstr1 = tempstr1.replace(re , "");
    var pos;
    tName = Name + " = ";
    pos = tempstr1.indexOf(tName);
    if (pos > -1)
    {
        pos = pos + tName.length;
        tempstr = tempstr1.substring(pos, tempstr1.length);
        pos = tempstr.indexOf(";");
        tempstr = tempstr.substring(0, pos);
        tempstr = tempstr.replace("{", "");
        tempstr = tempstr.replace("}", "");
        if (tempstr.length > 13)
        {
            if (obj.Properties_(Name).CIMType == 101)
            {
              tempstr = tempstr.substr(4, 2) + "/"  + tempstr.substr(6, 2) + "/" +
tempstr.substr(0, 3) + " " + tempstr.substr(8, 2) + ":" + tempstr.substr(10, 2) + ":" +
tempstr.substr(12, 2);
            }
        }
        return tempstr;
    }
    else
    {
        return "";
    }
}
```

Horizontal Report with a textarea.

```
var locator = new ActiveXObject("WbemScripting.SWbemLocator");
var svc = locator.ConnectServer(".", "root\\cimv2");
```

```
svc.Security_.AuthenticationLevel = 6;
svc.Security_.ImpersonationLevel = 3;
var strQuery = "Select * From ___InstanceDeletionEvent WITHIN 1 where
TargetInstance ISA'Win32_Process'");
var es = svc.ExecNotificationQuery(strQuery);
var ws = new ActiveXObject("WScript.Shell");
var fso = new ActiveXObject("Scripting.FileSystemObject");
var txtstream = fso.OpenTextFile(ws.CurrentDirectory + "\\Win32_Process.aspx",
2, true, -2);
txtstream.WriteLine("<!DOCTYPE html PUBLIC ""-//W3C//DTD XHTML 1.0
Transitional//EN"" ""http://www.w3.org/TR/xhtml1/DTD/xhtml1-
transitional.dtd"">");
txtstream.WriteLine("<html xmlns='http://www.w3.org/1999/xhtml'>");
txtstream.WriteLine("<head>");
txtstream.WriteLine("<style type='text/css'>");
txtstream.WriteLine("th");
txtstream.WriteLine("{");
txtstream.WriteLine("   COLOR: darkred;");
txtstream.WriteLine("   BACKGROUND-COLOR: white;");
txtstream.WriteLine("   FONT-FAMILY:font-family: Cambria, serif;");
txtstream.WriteLine("   FONT-SIZE: 12px;");
txtstream.WriteLine("   text-align: left;");
txtstream.WriteLine("   white-Space: nowrap;");
txtstream.WriteLine("}");
txtstream.WriteLine("td");
txtstream.WriteLine("{");
txtstream.WriteLine("   COLOR: navy;");
txtstream.WriteLine("   BACKGROUND-COLOR: white;");
txtstream.WriteLine("   FONT-FAMILY: font-family: Cambria, serif;");
txtstream.WriteLine("   FONT-SIZE: 12px;");
txtstream.WriteLine("   text-align: left;");
txtstream.WriteLine("   white-Space: nowrap;");
txtstream.WriteLine("}");
txtstream.WriteLine("</style>");
txtstream.WriteLine("<title>Win32_Process</title>");
txtstream.WriteLine("</head>");
txtstream.WriteLine("<body>");
txtstream.WriteLine("<table border='0' Cellspacing='3' cellpadding = '3'>");
txtstream.WriteLine("<%");
var v=0;
```

```
while(v < 0)
{
    var ti = ex.NextEvent(-1);
    var obj = ti.Properties_.Item("Targetinstance").Value;
    if(v == 0)
    {
        txtstream.WriteLine("Response.Write(\"<tr>\" + vbcrlf)");
        var propEnum = new Enumerator(obj.Properties_);
        for (; !propEnum.atEnd(); propEnum.moveNext())
        {
            var prop = propEnum.item();
            txtstream.WriteLine("Response.Write(\"<th align='left' nowrap>" +
prop.Name + "</th>\" + vbcrlf)");
        }
        txtstream.WriteLine("Response.Write(\"</tr>\" + vbcrlf)");
        propEnum.ReSet();
    }
    txtstream.WriteLine("Response.Write(\"<tr>\" + vbcrlf)");
    for (; !propEnum.atEnd(); propEnum.moveNext())
    {
        var prop = propEnum.item();
        txtstream.WriteLine("Response.Write(\"<td style='font-family:Calibri, Sans-
Serif;font-size: 12px;color:navy;' align='left' nowrap='true'><textarea>" +
GetValue(prop.Name, obj) + "</textarea></td>\" + vbcrlf)");
    }
    txtstream.WriteLine("Response.Write(\"</tr>\" + vbcrlf)");
    v = v + 1;
}
txtstream.WriteLine("%>");
txtstream.WriteLine("</table>");
txtstream.WriteLine("</body>");
txtstream.WriteLine("</html>");
txtstream.close();
function GetValue(Name, obj)
{
    var tempstr = new String();
    var tempstr1 = new String();
    var tName = new String();
    tempstr1 = obj.GetObjectText_();
    var re = /"/g;
```

```
tempstr1 = tempstr1.replace(re , "");
var pos;
tName = Name + " = ";
pos = tempstr1.indexOf(tName);
if (pos > -1)
{
    pos = pos + tName.length;
    tempstr = tempstr1.substring(pos, tempstr1.length);
    pos = tempstr.indexOf(";");
    tempstr = tempstr.substring(0, pos);
    tempstr = tempstr.replace("{", "");
    tempstr = tempstr.replace("}", "");
    if (tempstr.length > 13)
    {
        if (obj.Properties_(Name).CIMType == 101)
        {
        tempstr = tempstr.substr(4, 2) + "/"  + tempstr.substr(6, 2) + "/" +
tempstr.substr(0, 3) + " " + tempstr.substr(8, 2) + ":" + tempstr.substr(10, 2) + ":" +
tempstr.substr(12, 2);
        }
    }
    return tempstr;
}
else
{
    return "";
}
}
```

Horizontal Report with a textbox.

```
var locator = new ActiveXObject("WbemScripting.SWbemLocator");
var svc = locator.ConnectServer(".", "root\\cimv2");
svc.Security_.AuthenticationLevel = 6;
svc.Security_.ImpersonationLevel = 3;
var strQuery = "Select * From ___InstanceDeletionEvent WITHIN 1 where
TargetInstance ISA'Win32_Process'");
var es = svc.ExecNotificationQuery(strQuery);
var ws = new ActiveXObject("WScript.Shell");
```

```
var fso = new ActiveXObject("Scripting.FileSystemObject");
var txtstream = fso.OpenTextFile(ws.CurrentDirectory + "\\Win32_Process.aspx",
2, true, -2);
txtstream.WriteLine("<!DOCTYPE html PUBLIC ""-//W3C//DTD XHTML 1.0
Transitional//EN"" ""http://www.w3.org/TR/xhtml1/DTD/xhtml1-
transitional.dtd"">");
txtstream.WriteLine("<html xmlns='http://www.w3.org/1999/xhtml'>");
txtstream.WriteLine("<head>");
txtstream.WriteLine("<style type='text/css'>");
txtstream.WriteLine("th");
txtstream.WriteLine("{");
txtstream.WriteLine("   COLOR: darkred;");
txtstream.WriteLine("   BACKGROUND-COLOR: white;");
txtstream.WriteLine("   FONT-FAMILY:font-family: Cambria, serif;");
txtstream.WriteLine("   FONT-SIZE: 12px;");
txtstream.WriteLine("   text-align: left;");
txtstream.WriteLine("   white-Space: nowrap;");
txtstream.WriteLine("}");
txtstream.WriteLine("td");
txtstream.WriteLine("{");
txtstream.WriteLine("   COLOR: navy;");
txtstream.WriteLine("   BACKGROUND-COLOR: white;");
txtstream.WriteLine("   FONT-FAMILY: font-family: Cambria, serif;");
txtstream.WriteLine("   FONT-SIZE: 12px;");
txtstream.WriteLine("   text-align: left;");
txtstream.WriteLine("   white-Space: nowrap;");
txtstream.WriteLine("}");
txtstream.WriteLine("</style>");
txtstream.WriteLine("<title>Win32_Process</title>");
txtstream.WriteLine("</head>");
txtstream.WriteLine("<body>");
txtstream.WriteLine("<table border='0' Cellspacing='3' cellpadding = '3'>");
txtstream.WriteLine("<%");
var v=0;
while(v < 0)
{
    var ti = ex.NextEvent(-1);
    var obj = ti.Properties_.Item("Targetinstance").Value;
    if(v == 0)
    {
```

```
txtstream.WriteLine("Response.Write(\"<tr>\" + vbcrlf)");
var propEnum = new Enumerator(obj.Properties_);
for (; !propEnum.atEnd(); propEnum.moveNext())
{
    var prop = propEnum.item();
    txtstream.WriteLine("Response.Write(\"<th align='left' nowrap>" +
prop.Name + "</th>\" + vbcrlf)");
}
txtstream.WriteLine("Response.Write(\"</tr>\" + vbcrlf)");
propEnum.ReSet();
}
txtstream.WriteLine("Response.Write(\"<tr>\" + vbcrlf)");
for (; !propEnum.atEnd(); propEnum.moveNext())
{
    var prop = propEnum.item();
    txtstream.WriteLine("Response.Write(\"<td style='font-family:Calibri, Sans-
Serif;font-size: 12px;color:navy;' align='left' nowrap='true'><input type=text
value='" + GetValue(prop.Name, obj) + "'></input></td>\" + vbcrlf)");
}
txtstream.WriteLine("Response.Write(\"</tr>\" + vbcrlf)");
v = v + 1;
}
txtstream.WriteLine("%>");
txtstream.WriteLine("</table>");
txtstream.WriteLine("</body>");
txtstream.WriteLine("</html>");
txtstream.close();
function GetValue(Name, obj)
{
    var tempstr = new String();
    var tempstr1 = new String();
    var tName = new String();
    tempstr1 = obj.GetObjectText_();
    var re = /"/g;
    tempstr1 = tempstr1.replace(re , "");
    var pos;
    tName = Name + " = ";
    pos = tempstr1.indexOf(tName);
    if (pos > -1)
    {
```

```
      pos = pos + tName.length;
      tempstr = tempstr1.substring(pos, tempstr1.length);
      pos = tempstr.indexOf(";");
      tempstr = tempstr.substring(0, pos);
      tempstr = tempstr.replace("{", "");
      tempstr = tempstr.replace("}", "");
      if (tempstr.length > 13)
      {
         if (obj.Properties_(Name).CIMType == 101)
         {
           tempstr = tempstr.substr(4, 2) + "/"  + tempstr.substr(6, 2) + "/" +
tempstr.substr(0, 3) + " " + tempstr.substr(8, 2) + ":" + tempstr.substr(10, 2) + ":" +
tempstr.substr(12, 2);
         }
      }
      return tempstr;
   }
   else
   {
      return "";
   }
}
```

Vertical Report with no additional tags.

```
   var locator = new ActiveXObject("WbemScripting.SWbemLocator");
   var svc = locator.ConnectServer(".", "root\\cimv2");
   svc.Security_.AuthenticationLevel = 6;
   svc.Security_.ImpersonationLevel = 3;
   var strQuery = "Select * From ___InstanceDeletionEvent WITHIN 1 where
TargetInstance ISA'Win32_Process'");
   var es = svc.ExecNotificationQuery(strQuery);
   var ws = new ActiveXObject("WScript.Shell");
   var fso = new ActiveXObject("Scripting.FileSystemObject");
   var txtstream = fso.OpenTextFile(ws.CurrentDirectory + "\\Win32_Process.aspx",
2, true, -2);
   txtstream.WriteLine("<!DOCTYPE html PUBLIC ""-//W3C//DTD XHTML 1.0
Transitional//EN"" ""http://www.w3.org/TR/xhtml1/DTD/xhtml1-
transitional.dtd"">");
```

```
txtstream.WriteLine("<html xmlns='http://www.w3.org/1999/xhtml'>");
txtstream.WriteLine("<head>");
txtstream.WriteLine("<style type='text/css'>");
txtstream.WriteLine("th");
txtstream.WriteLine("{");
txtstream.WriteLine("   COLOR: darkred;");
txtstream.WriteLine("   BACKGROUND-COLOR: white;");
txtstream.WriteLine("   FONT-FAMILY:font-family: Cambria, serif;");
txtstream.WriteLine("   FONT-SIZE: 12px;");
txtstream.WriteLine("   text-align: left;");
txtstream.WriteLine("   white-Space: nowrap;");
txtstream.WriteLine("}");
txtstream.WriteLine("td");
txtstream.WriteLine("{");
txtstream.WriteLine("   COLOR: navy;");
txtstream.WriteLine("   BACKGROUND-COLOR: white;");
txtstream.WriteLine("   FONT-FAMILY: font-family: Cambria, serif;");
txtstream.WriteLine("   FONT-SIZE: 12px;");
txtstream.WriteLine("   text-align: left;");
txtstream.WriteLine("   white-Space: nowrap;");
txtstream.WriteLine("}");
txtstream.WriteLine("</style>");
txtstream.WriteLine("<title>Win32_Process</title>");
txtstream.WriteLine("</head>");
txtstream.WriteLine("<body>");
txtstream.WriteLine("<table border='0' Cellspacing='3' cellpadding = '3'>");

var Names;
var Cols;
var Rows;
var x = 0;

var v = 0;
while(v < 0)
{
   var ti = ex.NextEvent(-1);
   var obj = ti.Properties_.Item("Targetinstance").Value;
   if(v == 0)
   {
      Names = new Array[obj.Properties_.Count];
```

```
            Cols = new Array[obj.Properties_.Count];
            Rows = new Array[4];
            var propEnum = new Enumerator(obj.Properties_);
            for (; !propEnum.atEnd(); propEnum.moveNext())
            {
                var prop = propEnum.item();
                Names[x] = prop.Name;
                Cols[x] = GetValue(prop.Name, obj);
                x = x + 1;
            }
            Rows[v] = Cols;
            x = 0;
            v = v + 1;
        }
        else
        {
            var propEnum = new Enumerator(obj.Properties_);
            for (; !propEnum.atEnd(); propEnum.moveNext())
            {
                var prop = propEnum.item();
                Cols[x] = GetValue(prop.Name, obj);
                x = x + 1;
            }
            Rows[v] = Cols;
            x = 0;
            v = v + 1;
        }
    }
    txtstream.WriteLine("<%");
    for(var a = 0;a < Names.Count; a++)
    {
        txtstream.WriteLine("Response.Write(\"<tr><th align='left' nowrap>" +
Names[a] + "</th>\" + vbcrlf)");
        for(var b = 0;b < Rows.Count; b++)
        {
            var C = Rows[b];
            txtstream.WriteLine("Response.Write(\"<td style='font-family:Calibri, Sans-
Serif;font-size: 12px;color:navy;' align='left' nowrap='nowrap'>" + C[x] + "</td>\"
+ vbcrlf)");
        }
```

```
            txtstream.WriteLine("Response.Write(\"</tr>\" + vbcrlf)");
        }
        txtstream.WriteLine("%>");
        txtstream.WriteLine("</table>");
        txtstream.WriteLine("</body>");
        txtstream.WriteLine("</html>");
        txtstream.close();
        function GetValue(Name, obj)
        {
            var tempstr = new String();
            var tempstr1 = new String();
            var tName = new String();
            tempstr1 = obj.GetObjectText_();
            var re = /"/g;
            tempstr1 = tempstr1.replace(re , "");
            var pos;
            tName = Name + " = ";
            pos = tempstr1.indexOf(tName);
            if (pos > -1)
            {
                pos = pos + tName.length;
                tempstr = tempstr1.substring(pos, tempstr1.length);
                pos = tempstr.indexOf(";");
                tempstr = tempstr.substring(0, pos);
                tempstr = tempstr.replace("{", "");
                tempstr = tempstr.replace("}", "");
                if (tempstr.length > 13)
                {
                    if (obj.Properties_(Name).CIMType == 101)
                    {
                        tempstr = tempstr.substr(4, 2) + "/"  + tempstr.substr(6, 2) + "/" +
tempstr.substr(0, 3) + " " + tempstr.substr(8, 2) + ":" + tempstr.substr(10, 2) + ":" +
tempstr.substr(12, 2);
                    }
                }
                return tempstr;
            }
            else
            {
                return "";
```

```
        }
    }
```

Vertical Report with a combobox.

```
var locator = new ActiveXObject("WbemScripting.SWbemLocator");
var svc = locator.ConnectServer(".", "root\\cimv2");
svc.Security_.AuthenticationLevel = 6;
svc.Security_.ImpersonationLevel = 3;
var strQuery = "Select * From __InstanceDeletionEvent WITHIN 1 where
TargetInstance ISA'Win32_Process'");
var es = svc.ExecNotificationQuery(strQuery);
var ws = new ActiveXObject("WScript.Shell");
var fso = new ActiveXObject("Scripting.FileSystemObject");
var txtstream = fso.OpenTextFile(ws.CurrentDirectory + "\\Win32_Process.aspx",
2, true, -2);
txtstream.WriteLine("<!DOCTYPE html PUBLIC ""-//W3C//DTD XHTML 1.0
Transitional//EN"" ""http://www.w3.org/TR/xhtml1/DTD/xhtml1-
transitional.dtd"">");
txtstream.WriteLine("<html xmlns='http://www.w3.org/1999/xhtml'>");
txtstream.WriteLine("<head>");
txtstream.WriteLine("<style type='text/css'>");
txtstream.WriteLine("th");
txtstream.WriteLine("{");
txtstream.WriteLine("    COLOR: darkred;");
txtstream.WriteLine("    BACKGROUND-COLOR: white;");
txtstream.WriteLine("    FONT-FAMILY:font-family: Cambria, serif;");
txtstream.WriteLine("    FONT-SIZE: 12px;");
txtstream.WriteLine("    text-align: left;");
txtstream.WriteLine("    white-Space: nowrap;");
txtstream.WriteLine("}");
txtstream.WriteLine("td");
txtstream.WriteLine("{");
txtstream.WriteLine("    COLOR: navy;");
txtstream.WriteLine("    BACKGROUND-COLOR: white;");
txtstream.WriteLine("    FONT-FAMILY: font-family: Cambria, serif;");
txtstream.WriteLine("    FONT-SIZE: 12px;");
txtstream.WriteLine("    text-align: left;");
txtstream.WriteLine("    white-Space: nowrap;");
```

```
txtstream.WriteLine("}");
txtstream.WriteLine("</style>");
txtstream.WriteLine("<title>Win32_Process</title>");
txtstream.WriteLine("</head>");
txtstream.WriteLine("<body>");
txtstream.WriteLine("<table border='0' Cellspacing='3' cellpadding = '3'>");

var Names;
var Cols;
var Rows;
var x = 0;

var v = 0;
while(v < 0)
{
    var ti = ex.NextEvent(-1);
    var obj = ti.Properties_.Item("Targetinstance").Value;
    if(v == 0)
    {
        Names = new Array[obj.Properties_.Count];
        Cols = new Array[obj.Properties_.Count];
        Rows = new Array[4];
        var propEnum = new Enumerator(obj.Properties_);
        for (; !propEnum.atEnd(); propEnum.moveNext())
        {
            var prop = propEnum.item();
            Names[x] = prop.Name;
            Cols[x] = GetValue(prop.Name, obj);
            x = x + 1;
        }
        Rows[v] = Cols;
        x = 0;
        v = v + 1;
    }
    else
    {
        var propEnum = new Enumerator(obj.Properties_);
        for (; !propEnum.atEnd(); propEnum.moveNext())
        {
            var prop = propEnum.item();
```

```javascript
        Cols[x] = GetValue(prop.Name, obj);
        x = x + 1;
      }
      Rows[v] = Cols;
      x = 0;
      v = v + 1;
    }
  }
  txtstream.WriteLine("<%");
  for(var a = 0;a < Names.Count; a++)
  {
    txtstream.WriteLine("Response.Write(\"<tr><th align='left' nowrap>" +
Names[a] + "</th>\" + vbcrlf)");
    for(var b = 0;b < Rows.Count; b++)
    {
      var C = Rows[b];
      txtstream.WriteLine("Response.Write(\"<td style='font-family:Calibri, Sans-
Serif;font-size: 12px;color:navy;' align='left' nowrap='true'><select><option value =
"'" + C[x] + "'">" + C[x] + "</option></select></td>\" + vbcrlf)");
    }
    txtstream.WriteLine("Response.Write(\"</tr>\" + vbcrlf)");
  }
  txtstream.WriteLine("%>");
  txtstream.WriteLine("</table>");
  txtstream.WriteLine("</body>");
  txtstream.WriteLine("</html>");
  txtstream.close();
  function GetValue(Name, obj)
  {
    var tempstr = new String();
    var tempstr1 = new String();
    var tName = new String();
    tempstr1 = obj.GetObjectText_();
    var re = /"/g;
    tempstr1 = tempstr1.replace(re , "");
    var pos;
    tName = Name + " = ";
    pos = tempstr1.indexOf(tName);
    if (pos > -1)
    {
```

```
            pos = pos + tName.length;
            tempstr = tempstr1.substring(pos, tempstr1.length);
            pos = tempstr.indexOf(";");
            tempstr = tempstr.substring(0, pos);
            tempstr = tempstr.replace("{", "");
            tempstr = tempstr.replace("}", "");
            if (tempstr.length > 13)
            {
                if (obj.Properties_(Name).CIMType == 101)
                {
                  tempstr = tempstr.substr(4, 2) + "/" + tempstr.substr(6, 2) + "/" +
tempstr.substr(0, 3) + " " + tempstr.substr(8, 2) + ":" + tempstr.substr(10, 2) + ":" +
tempstr.substr(12, 2);
                }
            }
            return tempstr;
        }
        else
        {
            return "";
        }
    }
```

Vertical Report with a link.

```
        var locator = new ActiveXObject("WbemScripting.SWbemLocator");
        var svc = locator.ConnectServer(".", "root\\cimv2");
        svc.Security_.AuthenticationLevel = 6;
        svc.Security_.ImpersonationLevel = 3;
        var strQuery = "Select * From ___InstanceDeletionEvent WITHIN 1 where
TargetInstance ISA'Win32_Process'");
        var es = svc.ExecNotificationQuery(strQuery);
        var ws = new ActiveXObject("WScript.Shell");
        var fso = new ActiveXObject("Scripting.FileSystemObject");
        var txtstream = fso.OpenTextFile(ws.CurrentDirectory + "\\Win32_Process.aspx",
2, true, -2);
        txtstream.WriteLine("<!DOCTYPE html PUBLIC ""-//W3C//DTD XHTML 1.0
Transitional//EN"" ""http://www.w3.org/TR/xhtml1/DTD/xhtml1-
transitional.dtd"">");
```

```
txtstream.WriteLine("<html xmlns='http://www.w3.org/1999/xhtml'>");
txtstream.WriteLine("<head>");
txtstream.WriteLine("<style type='text/css'>");
txtstream.WriteLine("th");
txtstream.WriteLine("{");
txtstream.WriteLine("    COLOR: darkred;");
txtstream.WriteLine("    BACKGROUND-COLOR: white;");
txtstream.WriteLine("    FONT-FAMILY:font-family: Cambria, serif;");
txtstream.WriteLine("    FONT-SIZE: 12px;");
txtstream.WriteLine("    text-align: left;");
txtstream.WriteLine("    white-Space: nowrap;");
txtstream.WriteLine("}");
txtstream.WriteLine("td");
txtstream.WriteLine("{");
txtstream.WriteLine("    COLOR: navy;");
txtstream.WriteLine("    BACKGROUND-COLOR: white;");
txtstream.WriteLine("    FONT-FAMILY: font-family: Cambria, serif;");
txtstream.WriteLine("    FONT-SIZE: 12px;");
txtstream.WriteLine("    text-align: left;");
txtstream.WriteLine("    white-Space: nowrap;");
txtstream.WriteLine("}");
txtstream.WriteLine("</style>");
txtstream.WriteLine("<title>Win32_Process</title>");
txtstream.WriteLine("</head>");
txtstream.WriteLine("<body>");
txtstream.WriteLine("<table border='0' Cellspacing='3' cellpadding = '3'>");

var Names;
var Cols;
var Rows;
var x = 0;

var v = 0;
while(v < 0)
{
    var ti = ex.NextEvent(-1);
    var obj = ti.Properties_.Item("Targetinstance").Value;
    if(v == 0)
    {
        Names = new Array[obj.Properties_.Count];
```

```
        Cols = new Array[obj.Properties_.Count];
        Rows = new Array[4];
        var propEnum = new Enumerator(obj.Properties_);
        for (; !propEnum.atEnd(); propEnum.moveNext())
        {
            var prop = propEnum.item();
            Names[x] = prop.Name;
            Cols[x] = GetValue(prop.Name, obj);
            x = x + 1;
        }
        Rows[v] = Cols;
        x = 0;
        v = v + 1;
    }
    else
    {
        var propEnum = new Enumerator(obj.Properties_);
        for (; !propEnum.atEnd(); propEnum.moveNext())
        {
            var prop = propEnum.item();
            Cols[x] = GetValue(prop.Name, obj);
            x = x + 1;
        }
        Rows[v] = Cols;
        x = 0;
        v = v + 1;
    }
}
txtstream.WriteLine("<%");
for(var a = 0;a < Names.Count; a++)
{
    txtstream.WriteLine("Response.Write(\"<tr><th align='left' nowrap>" +
Names[a] + "</th>\" + vbcrlf)");
    for(var b = 0;b < Rows.Count; b++)
    {
        var C = Rows[b];
        txtstream.WriteLine("Response.Write(\"<td style='font-family:Calibri, Sans-
Serif;font-size: 12px;color:navy;' align='left' nowrap='true'><a href='" + C[x] + "'>"
+ C[x] + "</a></td>\" + vbcrlf)");
    }
```

```javascript
        txtstream.WriteLine("Response.Write(\"</tr>\" + vbcrlf)");
    }
    txtstream.WriteLine("%>");
    txtstream.WriteLine("</table>");
    txtstream.WriteLine("</body>");
    txtstream.WriteLine("</html>");
    txtstream.close();
    function GetValue(Name, obj)
    {
        var tempstr = new String();
        var tempstr1 = new String();
        var tName = new String();
        tempstr1 = obj.GetObjectText_();
        var re = /"/g;
        tempstr1 = tempstr1.replace(re , "");
        var pos;
        tName = Name + " = ";
        pos = tempstr1.indexOf(tName);
        if (pos > -1)
        {
            pos = pos + tName.length;
            tempstr = tempstr1.substring(pos, tempstr1.length);
            pos = tempstr.indexOf(";");
            tempstr = tempstr.substring(0, pos);
            tempstr = tempstr.replace("{", "");
            tempstr = tempstr.replace("}", "");
            if (tempstr.length > 13)
            {
                if (obj.Properties_(Name).CIMType == 101)
                {
                    tempstr = tempstr.substr(4, 2) + "/" + tempstr.substr(6, 2) + "/" +
tempstr.substr(0, 3) + " " + tempstr.substr(8, 2) + ":" + tempstr.substr(10, 2) + ":" +
tempstr.substr(12, 2);
                }
            }
            return tempstr;
        }
        else
        {
            return "";
```

```
        }
    }
```

Vertical Report with a listbox.

```
    var locator = new ActiveXObject("WbemScripting.SWbemLocator");
    var svc = locator.ConnectServer(".", "root\\cimv2");
    svc.Security_.AuthenticationLevel = 6;
    svc.Security_.ImpersonationLevel = 3;
    var strQuery = "Select * From __InstanceDeletionEvent WITHIN 1 where
TargetInstance ISA'Win32_Process'");
    var es = svc.ExecNotificationQuery(strQuery);
    var ws = new ActiveXObject("WScript.Shell");
    var fso = new ActiveXObject("Scripting.FileSystemObject");
    var txtstream = fso.OpenTextFile(ws.CurrentDirectory + "\\Win32_Process.aspx",
2, true, -2);
    txtstream.WriteLine("<!DOCTYPE html PUBLIC ""-//W3C//DTD XHTML 1.0
Transitional//EN""" ""http://www.w3.org/TR/xhtml1/DTD/xhtml1-
transitional.dtd"">");
    txtstream.WriteLine("<html xmlns='http://www.w3.org/1999/xhtml'>");
    txtstream.WriteLine("<head>");
    txtstream.WriteLine("<style type='text/css'>");
    txtstream.WriteLine("th");
    txtstream.WriteLine("{");
    txtstream.WriteLine("    COLOR: darkred;");
    txtstream.WriteLine("    BACKGROUND-COLOR: white;");
    txtstream.WriteLine("    FONT-FAMILY:font-family: Cambria, serif;");
    txtstream.WriteLine("    FONT-SIZE: 12px;");
    txtstream.WriteLine("    text-align: left;");
    txtstream.WriteLine("    white-Space: nowrap;");
    txtstream.WriteLine("}");
    txtstream.WriteLine("td");
    txtstream.WriteLine("{");
    txtstream.WriteLine("    COLOR: navy;");
    txtstream.WriteLine("    BACKGROUND-COLOR: white;");
    txtstream.WriteLine("    FONT-FAMILY: font-family: Cambria, serif;");
    txtstream.WriteLine("    FONT-SIZE: 12px;");
    txtstream.WriteLine("    text-align: left;");
    txtstream.WriteLine("    white-Space: nowrap;");
```

```
txtstream.WriteLine("}");
txtstream.WriteLine("</style>");
txtstream.WriteLine("<title>Win32_Process</title>");
txtstream.WriteLine("</head>");
txtstream.WriteLine("<body>");
txtstream.WriteLine("<table border='0' Cellspacing='3' cellpadding = '3'>");

var Names;
var Cols;
var Rows;
var x = 0;

var v = 0;
while(v < 0)
{
    var ti = ex.NextEvent(-1);
    var obj = ti.Properties_.Item("Targetinstance").Value;
    if(v == 0)
    {
        Names = new Array[obj.Properties_.Count];
        Cols = new Array[obj.Properties_.Count];
        Rows = new Array[4];
        var propEnum = new Enumerator(obj.Properties_);
        for (; !propEnum.atEnd(); propEnum.moveNext())
        {
            var prop = propEnum.item();
            Names[x] = prop.Name;
            Cols[x] = GetValue(prop.Name, obj);
            x = x + 1;
        }
        Rows[v] = Cols;
        x = 0;
        v = v + 1;
    }
    else
    {
        var propEnum = new Enumerator(obj.Properties_);
        for (; !propEnum.atEnd(); propEnum.moveNext())
        {
            var prop = propEnum.item();
```

```
                Cols[x] = GetValue(prop.Name, obj);
                x = x + 1;
            }
            Rows[v] = Cols;
            x = 0;
            v = v + 1;
        }
    }
    txtstream.WriteLine("<%");
    for(var a = 0;a < Names.Count; a++)
    {
        txtstream.WriteLine("Response.Write(\"<tr><th align='left' nowrap>" +
Names[a] + "</th>\" + vbcrlf)");
        for(var b = 0;b < Rows.Count; b++)
        {
            var C = Rows[b];
            txtstream.WriteLine("Response.Write(\"<td style='font-family:Calibri, Sans-
Serif;font-size: 12px;color:navy;' align='left' nowrap='true'><select
multiple><option value = """ + C[x] + """>" + C[x] + "</option></select></td>\" +
vbcrlf)");
        }
        txtstream.WriteLine("Response.Write(\"</tr>\" + vbcrlf)");
    }
    txtstream.WriteLine("%>");
    txtstream.WriteLine("</table>");
    txtstream.WriteLine("</body>");
    txtstream.WriteLine("</html>");
    txtstream.close();
    function GetValue(Name, obj)
    {
        var tempstr = new String();
        var tempstr1 = new String();
        var tName = new String();
        tempstr1 = obj.GetObjectText_();
        var re = /"/g;
        tempstr1 = tempstr1.replace(re , "");
        var pos;
        tName = Name + " = ";
        pos = tempstr1.indexOf(tName);
        if (pos > -1)
```

```
        {
            pos = pos + tName.length;
            tempstr = tempstr1.substring(pos, tempstr1.length);
            pos = tempstr.indexOf(";");
            tempstr = tempstr.substring(0, pos);
            tempstr = tempstr.replace("{", "");
            tempstr = tempstr.replace("}", "");
            if (tempstr.length > 13)
            {
                if (obj.Properties_(Name).CIMType == 101)
                {
                    tempstr = tempstr.substr(4, 2) + "/"  + tempstr.substr(6, 2) + "/" +
tempstr.substr(0, 3) + " " + tempstr.substr(8, 2) + ":" + tempstr.substr(10, 2) + ":" +
tempstr.substr(12, 2);
                }
            }
            return tempstr;
        }
        else
        {
            return "";
        }
    }
```

Vertical Report with a textarea.

```
    var locator = new ActiveXObject("WbemScripting.SWbemLocator");
    var svc = locator.ConnectServer(".", "root\\cimv2");
    svc.Security_.AuthenticationLevel = 6;
    svc.Security_.ImpersonationLevel = 3;
    var strQuery = "Select * From ___InstanceDeletionEvent WITHIN 1 where
TargetInstance ISA'Win32_Process'");
    var es = svc.ExecNotificationQuery(strQuery);
    var ws = new ActiveXObject("WScript.Shell");
    var fso = new ActiveXObject("Scripting.FileSystemObject");
    var txtstream = fso.OpenTextFile(ws.CurrentDirectory + "\\Win32_Process.aspx",
2, true, -2);
```

```
txtstream.WriteLine("<!DOCTYPE html PUBLIC ""-//W3C//DTD XHTML 1.0
Transitional//EN"" ""http://www.w3.org/TR/xhtml1/DTD/xhtml1-
transitional.dtd"">");
txtstream.WriteLine("<html xmlns='http://www.w3.org/1999/xhtml'>");
txtstream.WriteLine("<head>");
txtstream.WriteLine("<style type='text/css'>");
txtstream.WriteLine("th");
txtstream.WriteLine("{");
txtstream.WriteLine("   COLOR: darkred;");
txtstream.WriteLine("   BACKGROUND-COLOR: white;");
txtstream.WriteLine("   FONT-FAMILY:font-family: Cambria, serif;");
txtstream.WriteLine("   FONT-SIZE: 12px;");
txtstream.WriteLine("   text-align: left;");
txtstream.WriteLine("   white-Space: nowrap;");
txtstream.WriteLine("}");
txtstream.WriteLine("td");
txtstream.WriteLine("{");
txtstream.WriteLine("   COLOR: navy;");
txtstream.WriteLine("   BACKGROUND-COLOR: white;");
txtstream.WriteLine("   FONT-FAMILY: font-family: Cambria, serif;");
txtstream.WriteLine("   FONT-SIZE: 12px;");
txtstream.WriteLine("   text-align: left;");
txtstream.WriteLine("   white-Space: nowrap;");
txtstream.WriteLine("}");
txtstream.WriteLine("</style>");
txtstream.WriteLine("<title>Win32_Process</title>");
txtstream.WriteLine("</head>");
txtstream.WriteLine("<body>");
txtstream.WriteLine("<table border='0' Cellspacing='3' cellpadding = '3'>");

var Names;
var Cols;
var Rows;
var x = 0;

var v = 0;
while(v < 0)
{
    var ti = ex.NextEvent(-1);
    var obj = ti.Properties_.Item("Targetinstance").Value;
```

```
      if(v == 0)
      {
         Names = new Array[obj.Properties_.Count];
         Cols = new Array[obj.Properties_.Count];
         Rows = new Array[4];
         var propEnum = new Enumerator(obj.Properties_);
         for (; !propEnum.atEnd(); propEnum.moveNext())
         {
            var prop = propEnum.item();
            Names[x] = prop.Name;
            Cols[x] = GetValue(prop.Name, obj);
            x = x + 1;
         }
         Rows[v] = Cols;
         x = 0;
         v = v + 1;
      }
      else
      {
         var propEnum = new Enumerator(obj.Properties_);
         for (; !propEnum.atEnd(); propEnum.moveNext())
         {
            var prop = propEnum.item();
            Cols[x] = GetValue(prop.Name, obj);
            x = x + 1;
         }
         Rows[v] = Cols;
         x = 0;
         v = v + 1;
      }
   }
   txtstream.WriteLine("<%");
   for(var a = 0;a < Names.Count; a++)
   {
      txtstream.WriteLine("Response.Write(\"<tr><th align='left' nowrap>" +
Names[a] + "</th>\" + vbcrlf)");
      for(var b = 0;b < Rows.Count; b++)
      {
         var C = Rows[b];
```

```
            txtstream.WriteLine("Response.Write(\"<td style='font-family:Calibri, Sans-
Serif;font-size: 12px;color:navy;' align='left' nowrap='true'><textarea>" + C[x] +
"</textarea></td>\" + vbcrlf)");
        }
        txtstream.WriteLine("Response.Write(\"</tr>\" + vbcrlf)");
    }
    txtstream.WriteLine("%>");
    txtstream.WriteLine("</table>");
    txtstream.WriteLine("</body>");
    txtstream.WriteLine("</html>");
    txtstream.close();
    function GetValue(Name, obj)
    {
        var tempstr = new String();
        var tempstr1 = new String();
        var tName = new String();
        tempstr1 = obj.GetObjectText_();
        var re = /"/g;
        tempstr1 = tempstr1.replace(re , "");
        var pos;
        tName = Name + " = ";
        pos = tempstr1.indexOf(tName);
        if (pos > -1)
        {
            pos = pos + tName.length;
            tempstr = tempstr1.substring(pos, tempstr1.length);
            pos = tempstr.indexOf(";");
            tempstr = tempstr.substring(0, pos);
            tempstr = tempstr.replace("{", "");
            tempstr = tempstr.replace("}", "");
            if (tempstr.length > 13)
            {
                if (obj.Properties_(Name).CIMType == 101)
                {
                    tempstr = tempstr.substr(4, 2) + "/" + tempstr.substr(6, 2) + "/" +
tempstr.substr(0, 3) + " " + tempstr.substr(8, 2) + ":" + tempstr.substr(10, 2) + ":" +
tempstr.substr(12, 2);
                }
            }
            return tempstr;
```

```
      }
      else
      {
         return "";
      }
   }
```

Vertical Report with a textbox.

```
   var locator = new ActiveXObject("WbemScripting.SWbemLocator");
   var svc = locator.ConnectServer(".", "root\\cimv2");
   svc.Security_.AuthenticationLevel = 6;
   svc.Security_.ImpersonationLevel = 3;
   var strQuery = "Select * From ___InstanceDeletionEvent WITHIN 1 where
TargetInstance ISA'Win32_Process'");
   var es = svc.ExecNotificationQuery(strQuery);
   var ws = new ActiveXObject("WScript.Shell");
   var fso = new ActiveXObject("Scripting.FileSystemObject");
   var txtstream = fso.OpenTextFile(ws.CurrentDirectory + "\\Win32_Process.aspx",
2, true, -2);
   txtstream.WriteLine("<!DOCTYPE html PUBLIC ""-//W3C//DTD XHTML 1.0
Transitional//EN"" ""http://www.w3.org/TR/xhtml1/DTD/xhtml1-
transitional.dtd"">");
   txtstream.WriteLine("<html xmlns='http://www.w3.org/1999/xhtml'>");
   txtstream.WriteLine("<head>");
   txtstream.WriteLine("<style type='text/css'>");
   txtstream.WriteLine("th");
   txtstream.WriteLine("{");
   txtstream.WriteLine("    COLOR: darkred;");
   txtstream.WriteLine("    BACKGROUND-COLOR: white;");
   txtstream.WriteLine("    FONT-FAMILY:font-family: Cambria, serif;");
   txtstream.WriteLine("    FONT-SIZE: 12px;");
   txtstream.WriteLine("    text-align: left;");
   txtstream.WriteLine("    white-Space: nowrap;");
   txtstream.WriteLine("}");
   txtstream.WriteLine("td");
   txtstream.WriteLine("{");
   txtstream.WriteLine("    COLOR: navy;");
   txtstream.WriteLine("    BACKGROUND-COLOR: white;");
```

```
txtstream.WriteLine("   FONT-FAMILY: font-family: Cambria, serif;");
txtstream.WriteLine("   FONT-SIZE: 12px;");
txtstream.WriteLine("   text-align: left;");
txtstream.WriteLine("   white-Space: nowrap;");
txtstream.WriteLine("}");
txtstream.WriteLine("</style>");
txtstream.WriteLine("<title>Win32_Process</title>");
txtstream.WriteLine("</head>");
txtstream.WriteLine("<body>");
txtstream.WriteLine("<table border='0' Cellspacing='3' cellpadding = '3'>");

var Names;
var Cols;
var Rows;
var x = 0;

var v = 0;
while(v < 0)
{
    var ti = ex.NextEvent(-1);
    var obj = ti.Properties_.Item("Targetinstance").Value;
    if(v == 0)
    {
        Names = new Array[obj.Properties_.Count];
        Cols = new Array[obj.Properties_.Count];
        Rows = new Array[4];
        var propEnum = new Enumerator(obj.Properties_);
        for (; !propEnum.atEnd(); propEnum.moveNext())
        {
            var prop = propEnum.item();
            Names[x] = prop.Name;
            Cols[x] = GetValue(prop.Name, obj);
            x = x + 1;
        }
        Rows[v] = Cols;
        x = 0;
        v = v + 1;
    }
    else
    {
```

```javascript
        var propEnum = new Enumerator(obj.Properties_);
        for (; !propEnum.atEnd(); propEnum.moveNext())
        {
            var prop = propEnum.item();
            Cols[x] = GetValue(prop.Name, obj);
            x = x + 1;
        }
        Rows[v] = Cols;
        x = 0;
        v = v + 1;
    }
}
txtstream.WriteLine("<%");
for(var a = 0;a < Names.Count; a++)
{
    txtstream.WriteLine("Response.Write(\"<tr><th align='left' nowrap>" +
Names[a] + "</th>\" + vbcrlf)");
    for(var b = 0;b < Rows.Count; b++)
    {
        var C = Rows[b];
        txtstream.WriteLine("Response.Write(\"<td style='font-family:Calibri, Sans-
Serif;font-size: 12px;color:navy;' align='left' nowrap='true'><input type=text
value=\"\"" + C[x] + "\"\"></input></td>\" + vbcrlf)");
    }
    txtstream.WriteLine("Response.Write(\"</tr>\" + vbcrlf)");
}
txtstream.WriteLine("%>");
txtstream.WriteLine("</table>");
txtstream.WriteLine("</body>");
txtstream.WriteLine("</html>");
txtstream.close();
function GetValue(Name, obj)
{
    var tempstr = new String();
    var tempstr1 = new String();
    var tName = new String();
    tempstr1 = obj.GetObjectText_();
    var re = /"/g;
    tempstr1 = tempstr1.replace(re , "");
    var pos;
```

```
tName = Name + " = ";
pos = tempstr1.indexOf(tName);
if (pos > -1)
{
    pos = pos + tName.length;
    tempstr = tempstr1.substring(pos, tempstr1.length);
    pos = tempstr.indexOf(";");
    tempstr = tempstr.substring(0, pos);
    tempstr = tempstr.replace("{", "");
    tempstr = tempstr.replace("}", "");
    if (tempstr.length > 13)
    {
        if (obj.Properties_(Name).CIMType == 101)
        {
            tempstr = tempstr.substr(4, 2) + "/"  + tempstr.substr(6, 2) + "/" +
tempstr.substr(0, 3) + " " + tempstr.substr(8, 2) + ":" + tempstr.substr(10, 2) + ":" +
tempstr.substr(12, 2);
        }
    }
    return tempstr;
}
else
{
    return "";
}
}
```

ASP Tables

Horizontal Table with no additional tags.

```
var locator = new ActiveXObject("WbemScripting.SWbemLocator");
var svc = locator.ConnectServer(".", "root\\cimv2");
svc.Security_.AuthenticationLevel = 6;
svc.Security_.ImpersonationLevel = 3;
var strQuery = "Select * From ___InstanceDeletionEvent WITHIN 1 where
TargetInstance ISA'Win32_Process'");
var es = svc.ExecNotificationQuery(strQuery);
var ws = new ActiveXObject("WScript.Shell");
var fso = new ActiveXObject("Scripting.FileSystemObject");
var txtstream = fso.OpenTextFile(ws.CurrentDirectory + "\\Win32_Process.aspx",
2, true, -2);
txtstream.WriteLine("<!DOCTYPE html PUBLIC ""-//W3C//DTD XHTML 1.0
Transitional//EN"" ""http://www.w3.org/TR/xhtml1/DTD/xhtml1-
transitional.dtd"">");
txtstream.WriteLine("<html xmlns='http://www.w3.org/1999/xhtml'>");
txtstream.WriteLine("<head>");
txtstream.WriteLine("<style type='text/css'>");
txtstream.WriteLine("th");
txtstream.WriteLine("{");
txtstream.WriteLine("    COLOR: darkred;");
txtstream.WriteLine("    BACKGROUND-COLOR: white;");
```

```
txtstream.WriteLine("   FONT-FAMILY:font-family: Cambria, serif;");
txtstream.WriteLine("   FONT-SIZE: 12px;");
txtstream.WriteLine("   text-align: left;");
txtstream.WriteLine("   white-Space: nowrap;");
txtstream.WriteLine("}");
txtstream.WriteLine("td");
txtstream.WriteLine("{");
txtstream.WriteLine("   COLOR: navy;");
txtstream.WriteLine("   BACKGROUND-COLOR: white;");
txtstream.WriteLine("   FONT-FAMILY: font-family: Cambria, serif;");
txtstream.WriteLine("   FONT-SIZE: 12px;");
txtstream.WriteLine("   text-align: left;");
txtstream.WriteLine("   white-Space: nowrap;");
txtstream.WriteLine("}");
txtstream.WriteLine("</style>");
txtstream.WriteLine("<title>Win32_Process</title>");
txtstream.WriteLine("</head>");
txtstream.WriteLine("<body>");
txtstream.WriteLine("<table border='1' Cellspacing='3' cellpadding = '3'>");
txtstream.WriteLine("<%");
var v=0;
while(v < 0)
{
    var ti = ex.NextEvent(-1);
    var obj = ti.Properties_.Item("Targetinstance").Value;
    if(v == 0)
    {
        txtstream.WriteLine("Response.Write(\"<tr>\" + vbcrlf)");
        var propEnum = new Enumerator(obj.Properties_);
        for (; !propEnum.atEnd(); propEnum.moveNext())
        {
            var prop = propEnum.item();
            txtstream.WriteLine("Response.Write(\"<th align='left' nowrap>" +
prop.Name + "</th>\" + vbcrlf)");
        }
        txtstream.WriteLine("Response.Write(\"</tr>\" + vbcrlf)");
        propEnum.ReSet();
    }
    txtstream.WriteLine("Response.Write(\"<tr>\" + vbcrlf)");
    for (; !propEnum.atEnd(); propEnum.moveNext())
```

```
        {
            var prop = propEnum.item();
            txtstream.WriteLine("Response.Write(\"<td style='font-family:Calibri, Sans-
Serif;font-size: 12px;color:navy;' align='left' nowrap='nowrap'>" +
GetValue(prop.Name, obj) + "</td>\" + vbcrlf)");
        }
        txtstream.WriteLine("Response.Write(\"</tr>\" + vbcrlf)");
        v = v + 1;
    }
    txtstream.WriteLine("%>");
    txtstream.WriteLine("</table>");
    txtstream.WriteLine("</body>");
    txtstream.WriteLine("</html>");
    txtstream.close();
    function GetValue(Name, obj)
    {
        var tempstr = new String();
        var tempstr1 = new String();
        var tName = new String();
        tempstr1 = obj.GetObjectText_();
        var re = /"/g;
        tempstr1 = tempstr1.replace(re , "");
        var pos;
        tName = Name + " = ";
        pos = tempstr1.indexOf(tName);
        if (pos > -1)
        {
            pos = pos + tName.length;
            tempstr = tempstr1.substring(pos, tempstr1.length);
            pos = tempstr.indexOf(";");
            tempstr = tempstr.substring(0, pos);
            tempstr = tempstr.replace("{", "");
            tempstr = tempstr.replace("}", "");
            if (tempstr.length > 13)
            {
                if (obj.Properties_(Name).CIMType == 101)
                {
                    tempstr = tempstr.substr(4, 2) + "/" + tempstr.substr(6, 2) + "/" +
tempstr.substr(0, 3) + " " + tempstr.substr(8, 2) + ":" + tempstr.substr(10, 2) + ":" +
tempstr.substr(12, 2);
```

```
        }
      }
      return tempstr;
    }
    else
    {
      return "";
    }
}
```

Horizontal Table with a combobox.

```
    var locator = new ActiveXObject("WbemScripting.SWbemLocator");
    var svc = locator.ConnectServer(".", "root\\cimv2");
    svc.Security_.AuthenticationLevel = 6;
    svc.Security_.ImpersonationLevel = 3;
    var strQuery = "Select * From ___InstanceDeletionEvent WITHIN 1 where
TargetInstance ISA'Win32_Process'");
    var es = svc.ExecNotificationQuery(strQuery);
    var ws = new ActiveXObject("WScript.Shell");
    var fso = new ActiveXObject("Scripting.FileSystemObject");
    var txtstream = fso.OpenTextFile(ws.CurrentDirectory + "\\Win32_Process.aspx",
2, true, -2);
    txtstream.WriteLine("<!DOCTYPE html PUBLIC ""-//W3C//DTD XHTML 1.0
Transitional//EN"" ""http://www.w3.org/TR/xhtml1/DTD/xhtml1-
transitional.dtd"">");
    txtstream.WriteLine("<html xmlns='http://www.w3.org/1999/xhtml'>");
    txtstream.WriteLine("<head>");
    txtstream.WriteLine("<style type='text/css'>");
    txtstream.WriteLine("th");
    txtstream.WriteLine("{");
    txtstream.WriteLine("   COLOR: darkred;");
    txtstream.WriteLine("   BACKGROUND-COLOR: white;");
    txtstream.WriteLine("   FONT-FAMILY:font-family: Cambria, serif;");
    txtstream.WriteLine("   FONT-SIZE: 12px;");
    txtstream.WriteLine("   text-align: left;");
    txtstream.WriteLine("   white-Space: nowrap;");
    txtstream.WriteLine("}");
    txtstream.WriteLine("td");
```

```
txtstream.WriteLine("{");
txtstream.WriteLine("    COLOR: navy;");
txtstream.WriteLine("    BACKGROUND-COLOR: white;");
txtstream.WriteLine("    FONT-FAMILY: font-family: Cambria, serif;");
txtstream.WriteLine("    FONT-SIZE: 12px;");
txtstream.WriteLine("    text-align: left;");
txtstream.WriteLine("    white-Space: nowrap;");
txtstream.WriteLine("}");
txtstream.WriteLine("</style>");
txtstream.WriteLine("<title>Win32_Process</title>");
txtstream.WriteLine("</head>");
txtstream.WriteLine("<body>");
txtstream.WriteLine("<table border='1' Cellspacing='3' cellpadding = '3'>");
txtstream.WriteLine("<%");
var v=0;
while(v < 0)
{
   var ti = ex.NextEvent(-1);
   var obj = ti.Properties_.Item("Targetinstance").Value;
   if(v == 0)
   {
      txtstream.WriteLine("Response.Write(\"<tr>\" + vbcrlf)");
      var propEnum = new Enumerator(obj.Properties_);
      for (; !propEnum.atEnd(); propEnum.moveNext())
      {
         var prop = propEnum.item();
         txtstream.WriteLine("Response.Write(\"<th align='left' nowrap>" +
prop.Name + "</th>\" + vbcrlf)");
      }
      txtstream.WriteLine("Response.Write(\"</tr>\" + vbcrlf)");
      propEnum.ReSet();
   }
   txtstream.WriteLine("Response.Write(\"<tr>\" + vbcrlf)");
   for (; !propEnum.atEnd(); propEnum.moveNext())
   {
      var prop = propEnum.item();
      txtstream.WriteLine("Response.Write(\"<td style='font-family:Calibri, Sans-
Serif;font-size: 12px;color:navy;' align='left' nowrap='true'><select><option value =
'" + GetValue(prop.Name, obj) + "'>" + GetValue(prop.Name, obj) +
"</option></select></td>\" + vbcrlf)");
```

```
        }
        txtstream.WriteLine("Response.Write(\"</tr>\" + vbcrlf)");
        v = v + 1;
    }
    txtstream.WriteLine("%>");
    txtstream.WriteLine("</table>");
    txtstream.WriteLine("</body>");
    txtstream.WriteLine("</html>");
    txtstream.close();
    function GetValue(Name, obj)
    {
        var tempstr = new String();
        var tempstr1 = new String();
        var tName = new String();
        tempstr1 = obj.GetObjectText_();
        var re = /"/g;
        tempstr1 = tempstr1.replace(re , "");
        var pos;
        tName = Name + " = ";
        pos = tempstr1.indexOf(tName);
        if (pos > -1)
        {
            pos = pos + tName.length;
            tempstr = tempstr1.substring(pos, tempstr1.length);
            pos = tempstr.indexOf(";");
            tempstr = tempstr.substring(0, pos);
            tempstr = tempstr.replace("{", "");
            tempstr = tempstr.replace("}", "");
            if (tempstr.length > 13)
            {
                if (obj.Properties_(Name).CIMType == 101)
                {
                 tempstr = tempstr.substr(4, 2) + "/"  + tempstr.substr(6, 2) + "/" +
tempstr.substr(0, 3) + " " + tempstr.substr(8, 2) + ":" + tempstr.substr(10, 2) + ":" +
tempstr.substr(12, 2);
                }
            }
            return tempstr;
        }
        else
```

```
    {
      return "";
    }
  }
```

Horizontal Table with a link.

```
  var locator = new ActiveXObject("WbemScripting.SWbemLocator");
  var svc = locator.ConnectServer(".", "root\\cimv2");
  svc.Security_.AuthenticationLevel = 6;
  svc.Security_.ImpersonationLevel = 3;
  var strQuery = "Select * From ___InstanceDeletionEvent WITHIN 1 where
TargetInstance ISA'Win32_Process'");
  var es = svc.ExecNotificationQuery(strQuery);
  var ws = new ActiveXObject("WScript.Shell");
  var fso = new ActiveXObject("Scripting.FileSystemObject");
  var txtstream = fso.OpenTextFile(ws.CurrentDirectory + "\\Win32_Process.aspx",
2, true, -2);
  txtstream.WriteLine("<!DOCTYPE html PUBLIC ""-//W3C//DTD XHTML 1.0
Transitional//EN"" ""http://www.w3.org/TR/xhtml1/DTD/xhtml1-
transitional.dtd"">");
  txtstream.WriteLine("<html xmlns='http://www.w3.org/1999/xhtml'>");
  txtstream.WriteLine("<head>");
  txtstream.WriteLine("<style type='text/css'>");
  txtstream.WriteLine("th");
  txtstream.WriteLine("{");
  txtstream.WriteLine("   COLOR: darkred;");
  txtstream.WriteLine("   BACKGROUND-COLOR: white;");
  txtstream.WriteLine("   FONT-FAMILY:font-family: Cambria, serif;");
  txtstream.WriteLine("   FONT-SIZE: 12px;");
  txtstream.WriteLine("   text-align: left;");
  txtstream.WriteLine("   white-Space: nowrap;");
  txtstream.WriteLine("}");
  txtstream.WriteLine("td");
  txtstream.WriteLine("{");
  txtstream.WriteLine("   COLOR: navy;");
  txtstream.WriteLine("   BACKGROUND-COLOR: white;");
  txtstream.WriteLine("   FONT-FAMILY: font-family: Cambria, serif;");
  txtstream.WriteLine("   FONT-SIZE: 12px;");
```

```
txtstream.WriteLine("    text-align: left;");
txtstream.WriteLine("    white-Space: nowrap;");
txtstream.WriteLine("}");
txtstream.WriteLine("</style>");
txtstream.WriteLine("<title>Win32_Process</title>");
txtstream.WriteLine("</head>");
txtstream.WriteLine("<body>");
txtstream.WriteLine("<table border='1' Cellspacing='3' cellpadding = '3'>");
txtstream.WriteLine("<%");
var v=0;
while(v < 0)
{
    var ti = ex.NextEvent(-1);
    var obj = ti.Properties_.Item("Targetinstance").Value;
    if(v == 0)
    {
        txtstream.WriteLine("Response.Write(\"<tr>\" + vbcrlf)");
        var propEnum = new Enumerator(obj.Properties_);
        for (; !propEnum.atEnd(); propEnum.moveNext())
        {
            var prop = propEnum.item();
            txtstream.WriteLine("Response.Write(\"<th align='left' nowrap>" +
prop.Name + "</th>\" + vbcrlf)");
        }
        txtstream.WriteLine("Response.Write(\"</tr>\" + vbcrlf)");
        propEnum.ReSet();
    }
    txtstream.WriteLine("Response.Write(\"<tr>\" + vbcrlf)");
    for (; !propEnum.atEnd(); propEnum.moveNext())
    {
        var prop = propEnum.item();
        txtstream.WriteLine("Response.Write(\"<td style='font-family:Calibri, Sans-
Serif;font-size: 12px;color:navy;' align='left' nowrap='true'><a href='" +
GetValue(prop.Name, obj) + "'>" + GetValue(prop.Name, obj) + "</a></td>\" +
vbcrlf)");
    }
    txtstream.WriteLine("Response.Write(\"</tr>\" + vbcrlf)");
    v = v + 1;
}
txtstream.WriteLine("%>");
```

```
txtstream.WriteLine("</table>");
txtstream.WriteLine("</body>");
txtstream.WriteLine("</html>");
txtstream.close();
function GetValue(Name, obj)
{
    var tempstr = new String();
    var tempstr1 = new String();
    var tName = new String();
    tempstr1 = obj.GetObjectText_();
    var re = /"/g;
    tempstr1 = tempstr1.replace(re , "");
    var pos;
    tName = Name + " = ";
    pos = tempstr1.indexOf(tName);
    if (pos > -1)
    {
        pos = pos + tName.length;
        tempstr = tempstr1.substring(pos, tempstr1.length);
        pos = tempstr.indexOf(";");
        tempstr = tempstr.substring(0, pos);
        tempstr = tempstr.replace("{", "");
        tempstr = tempstr.replace("}", "");
        if (tempstr.length > 13)
        {
            if (obj.Properties_(Name).CIMType == 101)
            {
                tempstr = tempstr.substr(4, 2) + "/" + tempstr.substr(6, 2) + "/" +
tempstr.substr(0, 3) + " " + tempstr.substr(8, 2) + ":" + tempstr.substr(10, 2) + ":" +
tempstr.substr(12, 2);
            }
        }
        return tempstr;
    }
    else
    {
        return "";
    }
}
```

Horizontal Table with a listbox.

```
var locator = new ActiveXObject("WbemScripting.SWbemLocator");
var svc = locator.ConnectServer(".", "root\\cimv2");
svc.Security_.AuthenticationLevel = 6;
svc.Security_.ImpersonationLevel = 3;
var strQuery = "Select * From __InstanceDeletionEvent WITHIN 1 where
TargetInstance ISA'Win32_Process'");
var es = svc.ExecNotificationQuery(strQuery);
var ws = new ActiveXObject("WScript.Shell");
var fso = new ActiveXObject("Scripting.FileSystemObject");
var txtstream = fso.OpenTextFile(ws.CurrentDirectory + "\\Win32_Process.aspx",
2, true, -2);
txtstream.WriteLine("<!DOCTYPE html PUBLIC ""-//W3C//DTD XHTML 1.0
Transitional//EN"" ""http://www.w3.org/TR/xhtml1/DTD/xhtml1-
transitional.dtd"">");
txtstream.WriteLine("<html xmlns='http://www.w3.org/1999/xhtml'>");
txtstream.WriteLine("<head>");
txtstream.WriteLine("<style type='text/css'>");
txtstream.WriteLine("th");
txtstream.WriteLine("{");
txtstream.WriteLine("    COLOR: darkred;");
txtstream.WriteLine("    BACKGROUND-COLOR: white;");
txtstream.WriteLine("    FONT-FAMILY:font-family: Cambria, serif;");
txtstream.WriteLine("    FONT-SIZE: 12px;");
txtstream.WriteLine("    text-align: left;");
txtstream.WriteLine("    white-Space: nowrap;");
txtstream.WriteLine("}");
txtstream.WriteLine("td");
txtstream.WriteLine("{");
txtstream.WriteLine("    COLOR: navy;");
txtstream.WriteLine("    BACKGROUND-COLOR: white;");
txtstream.WriteLine("    FONT-FAMILY: font-family: Cambria, serif;");
txtstream.WriteLine("    FONT-SIZE: 12px;");
txtstream.WriteLine("    text-align: left;");
txtstream.WriteLine("    white-Space: nowrap;");
txtstream.WriteLine("}");
txtstream.WriteLine("</style>");
txtstream.WriteLine("<title>Win32_Process</title>");
```

```
txtstream.WriteLine("</head>");
txtstream.WriteLine("<body>");
txtstream.WriteLine("<table border='1' Cellspacing='3' cellpadding = '3'>");
txtstream.WriteLine("<%");
var v=0;
while(v < 0)
{
    var ti = ex.NextEvent(-1);
    var obj = ti.Properties_.Item("Targetinstance").Value;
    if(v == 0)
    {
        txtstream.WriteLine("Response.Write(\"<tr>\" + vbcrlf)");
        var propEnum = new Enumerator(obj.Properties_);
        for (; !propEnum.atEnd(); propEnum.moveNext())
        {
            var prop = propEnum.item();
            txtstream.WriteLine("Response.Write(\"<th align='left' nowrap>" +
prop.Name + "</th>\" + vbcrlf)");
        }
        txtstream.WriteLine("Response.Write(\"</tr>\" + vbcrlf)");
        propEnum.ReSet();
    }
    txtstream.WriteLine("Response.Write(\"<tr>\" + vbcrlf)");
    for (; !propEnum.atEnd(); propEnum.moveNext())
    {
        var prop = propEnum.item();
        txtstream.WriteLine("Response.Write(\"<td style='font-family:Calibri, Sans-
Serif;font-size: 12px;color:navy;' align='left' nowrap='true'><select
multiple><option value = '" + GetValue(prop.Name, obj) + "'>" +
GetValue(prop.Name, obj) + "</option></select></td>\" + vbcrlf)");
    }
    txtstream.WriteLine("Response.Write(\"</tr>\" + vbcrlf)");
    v = v + 1;
}
txtstream.WriteLine("%>");
txtstream.WriteLine("</table>");
txtstream.WriteLine("</body>");
txtstream.WriteLine("</html>");
txtstream.close();
function GetValue(Name, obj)
```

```javascript
{
    var tempstr = new String();
    var tempstr1 = new String();
    var tName = new String();
    tempstr1 = obj.GetObjectText_();
    var re = /"/g;
    tempstr1 = tempstr1.replace(re , "");
    var pos;
    tName = Name + " = ";
    pos = tempstr1.indexOf(tName);
    if (pos > -1)
    {
        pos = pos + tName.length;
        tempstr = tempstr1.substring(pos, tempstr1.length);
        pos = tempstr.indexOf(";");
        tempstr = tempstr.substring(0, pos);
        tempstr = tempstr.replace("{", "");
        tempstr = tempstr.replace("}", "");
        if (tempstr.length > 13)
        {
            if (obj.Properties_(Name).CIMType == 101)
            {
                tempstr = tempstr.substr(4, 2) + "/" + tempstr.substr(6, 2) + "/" +
tempstr.substr(0, 3) + " " + tempstr.substr(8, 2) + ":" + tempstr.substr(10, 2) + ":" +
tempstr.substr(12, 2);
            }
        }
        return tempstr;
    }
    else
    {
        return "";
    }
}
```

Horizontal Table with a textarea.

```
var locator = new ActiveXObject("WbemScripting.SWbemLocator");
var svc = locator.ConnectServer(".", "root\\cimv2");
svc.Security_.AuthenticationLevel = 6;
svc.Security_.ImpersonationLevel = 3;
var strQuery = "Select * From ___InstanceDeletionEvent WITHIN 1 where
TargetInstance ISA'Win32_Process'");
var es = svc.ExecNotificationQuery(strQuery);
var ws = new ActiveXObject("WScript.Shell");
var fso = new ActiveXObject("Scripting.FileSystemObject");
var txtstream = fso.OpenTextFile(ws.CurrentDirectory + "\\Win32_Process.aspx",
2, true, -2);
txtstream.WriteLine("<!DOCTYPE html PUBLIC ""-//W3C//DTD XHTML 1.0
Transitional//EN"" ""http://www.w3.org/TR/xhtml1/DTD/xhtml1-
transitional.dtd"">");
txtstream.WriteLine("<html xmlns='http://www.w3.org/1999/xhtml'>");
txtstream.WriteLine("<head>");
txtstream.WriteLine("<style type='text/css'>");
txtstream.WriteLine("th");
txtstream.WriteLine("{");
txtstream.WriteLine("    COLOR: darkred;");
txtstream.WriteLine("    BACKGROUND-COLOR: white;");
txtstream.WriteLine("    FONT-FAMILY:font-family: Cambria, serif;");
txtstream.WriteLine("    FONT-SIZE: 12px;");
txtstream.WriteLine("    text-align: left;");
txtstream.WriteLine("    white-Space: nowrap;");
txtstream.WriteLine("}");
txtstream.WriteLine("td");
txtstream.WriteLine("{");
txtstream.WriteLine("    COLOR: navy;");
txtstream.WriteLine("    BACKGROUND-COLOR: white;");
txtstream.WriteLine("    FONT-FAMILY: font-family: Cambria, serif;");
txtstream.WriteLine("    FONT-SIZE: 12px;");
txtstream.WriteLine("    text-align: left;");
txtstream.WriteLine("    white-Space: nowrap;");
txtstream.WriteLine("}");
txtstream.WriteLine("</style>");
txtstream.WriteLine("<title>Win32_Process</title>");
```

```
txtstream.WriteLine("</head>");
txtstream.WriteLine("<body>");
txtstream.WriteLine("<table border='1' Cellspacing='3' cellpadding = '3'>");
txtstream.WriteLine("<%");
var v=0;
while(v < 0)
{
    var ti = ex.NextEvent(-1);
    var obj = ti.Properties_.Item("Targetinstance").Value;
    if(v == 0)
    {
        txtstream.WriteLine("Response.Write(\"<tr>\" + vbcrlf)");
        var propEnum = new Enumerator(obj.Properties_);
        for (; !propEnum.atEnd(); propEnum.moveNext())
        {
            var prop = propEnum.item();
            txtstream.WriteLine("Response.Write(\"<th align='left' nowrap>" +
prop.Name + "</th>\" + vbcrlf)");
        }
        txtstream.WriteLine("Response.Write(\"</tr>\" + vbcrlf)");
        propEnum.ReSet();
    }
    txtstream.WriteLine("Response.Write(\"<tr>\" + vbcrlf)");
    for (; !propEnum.atEnd(); propEnum.moveNext())
    {
        var prop = propEnum.item();
        txtstream.WriteLine("Response.Write(\"<td style='font-family:Calibri, Sans-
Serif;font-size: 12px;color:navy;' align='left' nowrap='true'><textarea>" +
GetValue(prop.Name, obj) + "</textarea></td>\" + vbcrlf)");
    }
    txtstream.WriteLine("Response.Write(\"</tr>\" + vbcrlf)");
    v = v + 1;
}
txtstream.WriteLine("%>");
txtstream.WriteLine("</table>");
txtstream.WriteLine("</body>");
txtstream.WriteLine("</html>");
txtstream.close();
function GetValue(Name, obj)
{
```

```
var tempstr = new String();
var tempstr1 = new String();
var tName = new String();
tempstr1 = obj.GetObjectText_();
var re = /"/g;
tempstr1 = tempstr1.replace(re , "");
var pos;
tName = Name + " = ";
pos = tempstr1.indexOf(tName);
if (pos > -1)
{
    pos = pos + tName.length;
    tempstr = tempstr1.substring(pos, tempstr1.length);
    pos = tempstr.indexOf(";");
    tempstr = tempstr.substring(0, pos);
    tempstr = tempstr.replace("{", "");
    tempstr = tempstr.replace("}", "");
    if (tempstr.length > 13)
    {
        if (obj.Properties_(Name).CIMType == 101)
        {
            tempstr = tempstr.substr(4, 2) + "/"  + tempstr.substr(6, 2) + "/" +
tempstr.substr(0, 3) + " " + tempstr.substr(8, 2) + ":" + tempstr.substr(10, 2) + ":" +
tempstr.substr(12, 2);
        }
    }
    return tempstr;
}
else
{
    return "";
}
}
```

Horizontal Table with a textbox.

```
var locator = new ActiveXObject("WbemScripting.SWbemLocator");
var svc = locator.ConnectServer(".", "root\\cimv2");
svc.Security_.AuthenticationLevel = 6;
svc.Security_.ImpersonationLevel = 3;
var strQuery = "Select * From ___InstanceDeletionEvent WITHIN 1 where
TargetInstance ISA'Win32_Process'");
var es = svc.ExecNotificationQuery(strQuery);
var ws = new ActiveXObject("WScript.Shell");
var fso = new ActiveXObject("Scripting.FileSystemObject");
var txtstream = fso.OpenTextFile(ws.CurrentDirectory + "\\Win32_Process.aspx",
2, true, -2);
txtstream.WriteLine("<!DOCTYPE html PUBLIC ""-//W3C//DTD XHTML 1.0
Transitional//EN"" ""http://www.w3.org/TR/xhtml1/DTD/xhtml1-
transitional.dtd"">");
txtstream.WriteLine("<html xmlns='http://www.w3.org/1999/xhtml'>");
txtstream.WriteLine("<head>");
txtstream.WriteLine("<style type='text/css'>");
txtstream.WriteLine("th");
txtstream.WriteLine("{");
txtstream.WriteLine("    COLOR: darkred;");
txtstream.WriteLine("    BACKGROUND-COLOR: white;");
txtstream.WriteLine("    FONT-FAMILY:font-family: Cambria, serif;");
txtstream.WriteLine("    FONT-SIZE: 12px;");
txtstream.WriteLine("    text-align: left;");
txtstream.WriteLine("    white-Space: nowrap;");
txtstream.WriteLine("}");
txtstream.WriteLine("td");
txtstream.WriteLine("{");
txtstream.WriteLine("    COLOR: navy;");
txtstream.WriteLine("    BACKGROUND-COLOR: white;");
txtstream.WriteLine("    FONT-FAMILY: font-family: Cambria, serif;");
txtstream.WriteLine("    FONT-SIZE: 12px;");
txtstream.WriteLine("    text-align: left;");
txtstream.WriteLine("    white-Space: nowrap;");
txtstream.WriteLine("}");
txtstream.WriteLine("</style>");
txtstream.WriteLine("<title>Win32_Process</title>");
```

```
txtstream.WriteLine("</head>");
txtstream.WriteLine("<body>");
txtstream.WriteLine("<table border='1' Cellspacing='3' cellpadding = '3'>");
txtstream.WriteLine("<%");
var v=0;
while(v < 0)
{
    var ti = ex.NextEvent(-1);
    var obj = ti.Properties_.Item("Targetinstance").Value;
    if(v == 0)
    {
        txtstream.WriteLine("Response.Write(\"<tr>\" + vbcrlf)");
        var propEnum = new Enumerator(obj.Properties_);
        for (; !propEnum.atEnd(); propEnum.moveNext())
        {
            var prop = propEnum.item();
            txtstream.WriteLine("Response.Write(\"<th align='left' nowrap>" +
prop.Name + "</th>\" + vbcrlf)");
        }
        txtstream.WriteLine("Response.Write(\"</tr>\" + vbcrlf)");
        propEnum.ReSet();
    }
    txtstream.WriteLine("Response.Write(\"<tr>\" + vbcrlf)");
    for (; !propEnum.atEnd(); propEnum.moveNext())
    {
        var prop = propEnum.item();
        txtstream.WriteLine("Response.Write(\"<td style='font-family:Calibri, Sans-
Serif;font-size: 12px;color:navy;' align='left' nowrap='true'><input type=text
value='" + GetValue(prop.Name, obj) + "'></input></td>\" + vbcrlf)");
    }
    txtstream.WriteLine("Response.Write(\"</tr>\" + vbcrlf)");
    v = v + 1;
}
txtstream.WriteLine("%>");
txtstream.WriteLine("</table>");
txtstream.WriteLine("</body>");
txtstream.WriteLine("</html>");
txtstream.close();
function GetValue(Name, obj)
{
```

```
var tempstr = new String();
var tempstr1 = new String();
var tName = new String();
tempstr1 = obj.GetObjectText_();
var re = /"/g;
tempstr1 = tempstr1.replace(re , "");
var pos;
tName = Name + " = ";
pos = tempstr1.indexOf(tName);
if (pos > -1)
{
    pos = pos + tName.length;
    tempstr = tempstr1.substring(pos, tempstr1.length);
    pos = tempstr.indexOf(";");
    tempstr = tempstr.substring(0, pos);
    tempstr = tempstr.replace("{", "");
    tempstr = tempstr.replace("}", "");
    if (tempstr.length > 13)
    {
        if (obj.Properties_(Name).CIMType == 101)
        {
        tempstr = tempstr.substr(4, 2) + "/"  + tempstr.substr(6, 2) + "/" +
tempstr.substr(0, 3) + " " + tempstr.substr(8, 2) + ":" + tempstr.substr(10, 2) + ":" +
tempstr.substr(12, 2);
        }
    }
    return tempstr;
}
else
{
    return "";
}
}
```

Vertical Table with no additional tags.

```
var locator = new ActiveXObject("WbemScripting.SWbemLocator");
var svc = locator.ConnectServer(".", "root\\cimv2");
svc.Security_.AuthenticationLevel = 6;
svc.Security_.ImpersonationLevel = 3;
var strQuery = "Select * From __InstanceDeletionEvent WITHIN 1 where
TargetInstance ISA'Win32_Process'");
var es = svc.ExecNotificationQuery(strQuery);
var ws = new ActiveXObject("WScript.Shell");
var fso = new ActiveXObject("Scripting.FileSystemObject");
var txtstream = fso.OpenTextFile(ws.CurrentDirectory + "\\Win32_Process.aspx",
2, true, -2);
txtstream.WriteLine("<!DOCTYPE html PUBLIC ""-//W3C//DTD XHTML 1.0
Transitional//EN"" ""http://www.w3.org/TR/xhtml1/DTD/xhtml1-
transitional.dtd"">");
txtstream.WriteLine("<html xmlns='http://www.w3.org/1999/xhtml'>");
txtstream.WriteLine("<head>");
txtstream.WriteLine("<style type='text/css'>");
txtstream.WriteLine("th");
txtstream.WriteLine("{");
txtstream.WriteLine("    COLOR: darkred;");
txtstream.WriteLine("    BACKGROUND-COLOR: white;");
txtstream.WriteLine("    FONT-FAMILY:font-family: Cambria, serif;");
txtstream.WriteLine("    FONT-SIZE: 12px;");
txtstream.WriteLine("    text-align: left;");
txtstream.WriteLine("    white-Space: nowrap;");
txtstream.WriteLine("}");
txtstream.WriteLine("td");
txtstream.WriteLine("{");
txtstream.WriteLine("    COLOR: navy;");
txtstream.WriteLine("    BACKGROUND-COLOR: white;");
txtstream.WriteLine("    FONT-FAMILY: font-family: Cambria, serif;");
txtstream.WriteLine("    FONT-SIZE: 12px;");
txtstream.WriteLine("    text-align: left;");
txtstream.WriteLine("    white-Space: nowrap;");
txtstream.WriteLine("}");
txtstream.WriteLine("</style>");
txtstream.WriteLine("<title>Win32_Process</title>");
```

```
txtstream.WriteLine("</head>");
txtstream.WriteLine("<body>");
txtstream.WriteLine("<table border='1' Cellspacing='3' cellpadding = '3'>");

var Names;
var Cols;
var Rows;
var x = 0;

var v = 0;
while(v < 0)
{
   var ti = ex.NextEvent(-1);
   var obj = ti.Properties_.Item("Targetinstance").Value;
   if(v == 0)
   {
     Names = new Array[obj.Properties_.Count];
     Cols = new Array[obj.Properties_.Count];
     Rows = new Array[4];
     var propEnum = new Enumerator(obj.Properties_);
     for (; !propEnum.atEnd(); propEnum.moveNext())
     {
        var prop = propEnum.item();
        Names[x] = prop.Name;
        Cols[x] = GetValue(prop.Name, obj);
        x = x + 1;
     }
     Rows[v] = Cols;
     x = 0;
     v = v + 1;
   }
   else
   {
     var propEnum = new Enumerator(obj.Properties_);
     for (; !propEnum.atEnd(); propEnum.moveNext())
     {
        var prop = propEnum.item();
        Cols[x] = GetValue(prop.Name, obj);
        x = x + 1;
     }
```

```
        Rows[v] = Cols;
        x = 0;
        v = v + 1;
    }
}
txtstream.WriteLine("<%");
for(var a = 0;a < Names.Count; a++)
{
    txtstream.WriteLine("Response.Write(\"<tr><th align='left' nowrap>" +
Names[a] + "</th>\" + vbcrlf)");
    for(var b = 0;b < Rows.Count; b++)
    {
        var C = Rows[b];
        txtstream.WriteLine("Response.Write(\"<td style='font-family:Calibri, Sans-
Serif;font-size: 12px;color:navy;' align='left' nowrap='nowrap'>" + C[x] + "</td>\"
+ vbcrlf)");
    }
    txtstream.WriteLine("Response.Write(\"</tr>\" + vbcrlf)");
}
txtstream.WriteLine("%>");
txtstream.WriteLine("</table>");
txtstream.WriteLine("</body>");
txtstream.WriteLine("</html>");
txtstream.close();
function GetValue(Name, obj)
{
    var tempstr = new String();
    var tempstr1 = new String();
    var tName = new String();
    tempstr1 = obj.GetObjectText_();
    var re = /"/g;
    tempstr1 = tempstr1.replace(re , "");
    var pos;
    tName = Name + " = ";
    pos = tempstr1.indexOf(tName);
    if (pos > -1)
    {
        pos = pos + tName.length;
        tempstr = tempstr1.substring(pos, tempstr1.length);
        pos = tempstr.indexOf(";");
```

```
    tempstr = tempstr.substring(0, pos);
    tempstr = tempstr.replace("{", "");
    tempstr = tempstr.replace("}", "");
    if (tempstr.length > 13)
    {
        if (obj.Properties_(Name).CIMType == 101)
        {
        tempstr = tempstr.substr(4, 2) + "/" + tempstr.substr(6, 2) + "/" +
tempstr.substr(0, 3) + " " + tempstr.substr(8, 2) + ":" + tempstr.substr(10, 2) + ":" +
tempstr.substr(12, 2);
        }
    }
    return tempstr;
    }
    else
    {
        return "";
    }
}
```

Vertical Table with a combobox.

```
var locator = new ActiveXObject("WbemScripting.SWbemLocator");
var svc = locator.ConnectServer(".", "root\\cimv2");
svc.Security_.AuthenticationLevel = 6;
svc.Security_.ImpersonationLevel = 3;
var strQuery = "Select * From ___InstanceDeletionEvent WITHIN 1 where
TargetInstance ISA'Win32_Process'");
var es = svc.ExecNotificationQuery(strQuery);
var ws = new ActiveXObject("WScript.Shell");
var fso = new ActiveXObject("Scripting.FileSystemObject");
var txtstream = fso.OpenTextFile(ws.CurrentDirectory + "\\Win32_Process.aspx",
2, true, -2);
txtstream.WriteLine("<!DOCTYPE html PUBLIC ""-//W3C//DTD XHTML 1.0
Transitional//EN"" ""http://www.w3.org/TR/xhtml1/DTD/xhtml1-
transitional.dtd"">");
txtstream.WriteLine("<html xmlns='http://www.w3.org/1999/xhtml'>");
txtstream.WriteLine("<head>");
txtstream.WriteLine("<style type='text/css'>");
```

```
txtstream.WriteLine("th");
txtstream.WriteLine("{");
txtstream.WriteLine("   COLOR: darkred;");
txtstream.WriteLine("   BACKGROUND-COLOR: white;");
txtstream.WriteLine("   FONT-FAMILY:font-family: Cambria, serif;");
txtstream.WriteLine("   FONT-SIZE: 12px;");
txtstream.WriteLine("   text-align: left;");
txtstream.WriteLine("   white-Space: nowrap;");
txtstream.WriteLine("}");
txtstream.WriteLine("td");
txtstream.WriteLine("{");
txtstream.WriteLine("   COLOR: navy;");
txtstream.WriteLine("   BACKGROUND-COLOR: white;");
txtstream.WriteLine("   FONT-FAMILY: font-family: Cambria, serif;");
txtstream.WriteLine("   FONT-SIZE: 12px;");
txtstream.WriteLine("   text-align: left;");
txtstream.WriteLine("   white-Space: nowrap;");
txtstream.WriteLine("}");
txtstream.WriteLine("</style>");
txtstream.WriteLine("<title>Win32_Process</title>");
txtstream.WriteLine("</head>");
txtstream.WriteLine("<body>");
txtstream.WriteLine("<table border='1' Cellspacing='3' cellpadding = '3'>");

var Names;
var Cols;
var Rows;
var x = 0;

var v = 0;
while(v < 0)
{
   var ti = ex.NextEvent(-1);
   var obj = ti.Properties_.Item("Targetinstance").Value;
   if(v == 0)
   {
      Names = new Array[obj.Properties_.Count];
      Cols = new Array[obj.Properties_.Count];
      Rows = new Array[4];
      var propEnum = new Enumerator(obj.Properties_);
```

```
      for (; !propEnum.atEnd(); propEnum.moveNext())
      {
         var prop = propEnum.item();
         Names[x] = prop.Name;
         Cols[x] = GetValue(prop.Name, obj);
         x = x + 1;
      }
      Rows[v] = Cols;
      x = 0;
      v = v + 1;
   }
   else
   {
      var propEnum = new Enumerator(obj.Properties_);
      for (; !propEnum.atEnd(); propEnum.moveNext())
      {
         var prop = propEnum.item();
         Cols[x] = GetValue(prop.Name, obj);
         x = x + 1;
      }
      Rows[v] = Cols;
      x = 0;
      v = v + 1;
   }
}
txtstream.WriteLine("<%");
for(var a = 0;a < Names.Count; a++)
{
   txtstream.WriteLine("Response.Write(\"<tr><th align='left' nowrap>" +
Names[a] + "</th>\" + vbcrlf)");
   for(var b = 0;b < Rows.Count; b++)
   {
      var C = Rows[b];
      txtstream.WriteLine("Response.Write(\"<td style='font-family:Calibri, Sans-
Serif;font-size: 12px;color:navy;' align='left' nowrap='true'><select><option value =
"""" + C[x] + """">" + C[x] + "</option></select></td>\" + vbcrlf)");
   }
   txtstream.WriteLine("Response.Write(\"</tr>\" + vbcrlf)");
}
txtstream.WriteLine("%>");
```

```javascript
txtstream.WriteLine("</table>");
txtstream.WriteLine("</body>");
txtstream.WriteLine("</html>");
txtstream.close();
function GetValue(Name, obj)
{
    var tempstr = new String();
    var tempstr1 = new String();
    var tName = new String();
    tempstr1 = obj.GetObjectText_();
    var re = /"/g;
    tempstr1 = tempstr1.replace(re , "");
    var pos;
    tName = Name + " = ";
    pos = tempstr1.indexOf(tName);
    if (pos > -1)
    {
        pos = pos + tName.length;
        tempstr = tempstr1.substring(pos, tempstr1.length);
        pos = tempstr.indexOf(";");
        tempstr = tempstr.substring(0, pos);
        tempstr = tempstr.replace("{", "");
        tempstr = tempstr.replace("}", "");
        if (tempstr.length > 13)
        {
            if (obj.Properties_(Name).CIMType == 101)
            {
              tempstr = tempstr.substr(4, 2) + "/" + tempstr.substr(6, 2) + "/" +
tempstr.substr(0, 3) + " " + tempstr.substr(8, 2) + ":" + tempstr.substr(10, 2) + ":" +
tempstr.substr(12, 2);
            }
        }
        return tempstr;
    }
    else
    {
        return "";
    }
}
```

Vertical Table with a link.

```
var locator = new ActiveXObject("WbemScripting.SWbemLocator");
var svc = locator.ConnectServer(".", "root\\cimv2");
svc.Security_.AuthenticationLevel = 6;
svc.Security_.ImpersonationLevel = 3;
var strQuery = "Select * From ___InstanceDeletionEvent WITHIN 1 where
TargetInstance ISA'Win32_Process'");
var es = svc.ExecNotificationQuery(strQuery);
var ws = new ActiveXObject("WScript.Shell");
var fso = new ActiveXObject("Scripting.FileSystemObject");
var txtstream = fso.OpenTextFile(ws.CurrentDirectory + "\\Win32_Process.aspx",
2, true, -2);
txtstream.WriteLine("<!DOCTYPE html PUBLIC ""-//W3C//DTD XHTML 1.0
Transitional//EN"" ""http://www.w3.org/TR/xhtml1/DTD/xhtml1-
transitional.dtd"">");
txtstream.WriteLine("<html xmlns='http://www.w3.org/1999/xhtml'>");
txtstream.WriteLine("<head>");
txtstream.WriteLine("<style type='text/css'>");
txtstream.WriteLine("th");
txtstream.WriteLine("{");
txtstream.WriteLine("    COLOR: darkred;");
txtstream.WriteLine("    BACKGROUND-COLOR: white;");
txtstream.WriteLine("    FONT-FAMILY:font-family: Cambria, serif;");
txtstream.WriteLine("    FONT-SIZE: 12px;");
txtstream.WriteLine("    text-align: left;");
txtstream.WriteLine("    white-Space: nowrap;");
txtstream.WriteLine("}");
txtstream.WriteLine("td");
txtstream.WriteLine("{");
txtstream.WriteLine("    COLOR: navy;");
txtstream.WriteLine("    BACKGROUND-COLOR: white;");
txtstream.WriteLine("    FONT-FAMILY: font-family: Cambria, serif;");
txtstream.WriteLine("    FONT-SIZE: 12px;");
txtstream.WriteLine("    text-align: left;");
txtstream.WriteLine("    white-Space: nowrap;");
txtstream.WriteLine("}");
txtstream.WriteLine("</style>");
txtstream.WriteLine("<title>Win32_Process</title>");
```

```
txtstream.WriteLine("</head>");
txtstream.WriteLine("<body>");
txtstream.WriteLine("<table border='1' Cellspacing='3' cellpadding = '3'>");

var Names;
var Cols;
var Rows;
var x = 0;

var v = 0;
while(v < 0)
{
    var ti = ex.NextEvent(-1);
    var obj = ti.Properties_.Item("Targetinstance").Value;
    if(v == 0)
    {
        Names = new Array[obj.Properties_.Count];
        Cols = new Array[obj.Properties_.Count];
        Rows = new Array[4];
        var propEnum = new Enumerator(obj.Properties_);
        for (; !propEnum.atEnd(); propEnum.moveNext())
        {
            var prop = propEnum.item();
            Names[x] = prop.Name;
            Cols[x] = GetValue(prop.Name, obj);
            x = x + 1;
        }
        Rows[v] = Cols;
        x = 0;
        v = v + 1;
    }
    else
    {
        var propEnum = new Enumerator(obj.Properties_);
        for (; !propEnum.atEnd(); propEnum.moveNext())
        {
            var prop = propEnum.item();
            Cols[x] = GetValue(prop.Name, obj);
            x = x + 1;
        }
```

```
        Rows[v] = Cols;
        x = 0;
        v = v + 1;
    }
}
txtstream.WriteLine("<%");
for(var a = 0;a < Names.Count; a++)
{
    txtstream.WriteLine("Response.Write(\"<tr><th align='left' nowrap>" +
Names[a] + "</th>\" + vbcrlf)");
    for(var b = 0;b < Rows.Count; b++)
    {
        var C = Rows[b];
        txtstream.WriteLine("Response.Write(\"<td style='font-family:Calibri, Sans-
Serif;font-size: 12px;color:navy;' align='left' nowrap='true'><a href='" + C[x] + "'>"
+ C[x] + "</a></td>\" + vbcrlf)");
    }
    txtstream.WriteLine("Response.Write(\"</tr>\" + vbcrlf)");
}
txtstream.WriteLine("%>");
txtstream.WriteLine("</table>");
txtstream.WriteLine("</body>");
txtstream.WriteLine("</html>");
txtstream.close();
function GetValue(Name, obj)
{
    var tempstr = new String();
    var tempstr1 = new String();
    var tName = new String();
    tempstr1 = obj.GetObjectText_();
    var re = /"/g;
    tempstr1 = tempstr1.replace(re , "");
    var pos;
    tName = Name + " = ";
    pos = tempstr1.indexOf(tName);
    if (pos > -1)
    {
        pos = pos + tName.length;
        tempstr = tempstr1.substring(pos, tempstr1.length);
        pos = tempstr.indexOf(";");
```

```
        tempstr = tempstr.substring(0, pos);
        tempstr = tempstr.replace("{", "");
        tempstr = tempstr.replace("}", "");
        if (tempstr.length > 13)
        {
            if (obj.Properties_(Name).CIMType == 101)
            {
                tempstr = tempstr.substr(4, 2) + "/" + tempstr.substr(6, 2) + "/" +
tempstr.substr(0, 3) + " " + tempstr.substr(8, 2) + ":" + tempstr.substr(10, 2) + ":" +
tempstr.substr(12, 2);
            }
        }
        return tempstr;
    }
    else
    {
        return "";
    }
}
```

Vertical Table with a listbox.

```
var locator = new ActiveXObject("WbemScripting.SWbemLocator");
var svc = locator.ConnectServer(".", "root\\cimv2");
svc.Security_.AuthenticationLevel = 6;
svc.Security_.ImpersonationLevel = 3;
var strQuery = "Select * From ___InstanceDeletionEvent WITHIN 1 where
TargetInstance ISA'Win32_Process'");
var es = svc.ExecNotificationQuery(strQuery);
var ws = new ActiveXObject("WScript.Shell");
var fso = new ActiveXObject("Scripting.FileSystemObject");
var txtstream = fso.OpenTextFile(ws.CurrentDirectory + "\\Win32_Process.aspx",
2, true, -2);
txtstream.WriteLine("<!DOCTYPE html PUBLIC ""-//W3C//DTD XHTML 1.0
Transitional//EN"" ""http://www.w3.org/TR/xhtml1/DTD/xhtml1-
transitional.dtd"">");
txtstream.WriteLine("<html xmlns='http://www.w3.org/1999/xhtml'>");
txtstream.WriteLine("<head>");
txtstream.WriteLine("<style type='text/css'>");
```

```
txtstream.WriteLine("th");
txtstream.WriteLine("{");
txtstream.WriteLine("   COLOR: darkred;");
txtstream.WriteLine("   BACKGROUND-COLOR: white;");
txtstream.WriteLine("   FONT-FAMILY:font-family: Cambria, serif;");
txtstream.WriteLine("   FONT-SIZE: 12px;");
txtstream.WriteLine("   text-align: left;");
txtstream.WriteLine("   white-Space: nowrap;");
txtstream.WriteLine("}");
txtstream.WriteLine("td");
txtstream.WriteLine("{");
txtstream.WriteLine("   COLOR: navy;");
txtstream.WriteLine("   BACKGROUND-COLOR: white;");
txtstream.WriteLine("   FONT-FAMILY: font-family: Cambria, serif;");
txtstream.WriteLine("   FONT-SIZE: 12px;");
txtstream.WriteLine("   text-align: left;");
txtstream.WriteLine("   white-Space: nowrap;");
txtstream.WriteLine("}");
txtstream.WriteLine("</style>");
txtstream.WriteLine("<title>Win32_Process</title>");
txtstream.WriteLine("</head>");
txtstream.WriteLine("<body>");
txtstream.WriteLine("<table border='1' Cellspacing='3' cellpadding = '3'>");

var Names;
var Cols;
var Rows;
var x = 0;

var v = 0;
while(v < 0)
{
   var ti = ex.NextEvent(-1);
   var obj = ti.Properties_.Item("Targetinstance").Value;
   if(v == 0)
   {
      Names = new Array[obj.Properties_.Count];
      Cols = new Array[obj.Properties_.Count];
      Rows = new Array[4];
      var propEnum = new Enumerator(obj.Properties_);
```

```
    for (; !propEnum.atEnd(); propEnum.moveNext())
    {
      var prop = propEnum.item();
      Names[x] = prop.Name;
      Cols[x] = GetValue(prop.Name, obj);
      x = x + 1;
    }
    Rows[v] = Cols;
    x = 0;
    v = v + 1;
  }
  else
  {
    var propEnum = new Enumerator(obj.Properties_);
    for (; !propEnum.atEnd(); propEnum.moveNext())
    {
      var prop = propEnum.item();
      Cols[x] = GetValue(prop.Name, obj);
      x = x + 1;
    }
    Rows[v] = Cols;
    x = 0;
    v = v + 1;
  }
}
txtstream.WriteLine("<%");
for(var a = 0;a < Names.Count; a++)
{
    txtstream.WriteLine("Response.Write(\"<tr><th align='left' nowrap>" +
Names[a] + "</th>\" + vbcrlf)");
    for(var b = 0;b < Rows.Count; b++)
    {
        var C = Rows[b];
        txtstream.WriteLine("Response.Write(\"<td style='font-family:Calibri, Sans-
Serif;font-size: 12px;color:navy;' align='left' nowrap='true'><select
multiple><option value = """ + C[x] + """>" + C[x] + "</option></select></td>\" +
vbcrlf)");
    }
    txtstream.WriteLine("Response.Write(\"</tr>\" + vbcrlf)");
}
```

```
txtstream.WriteLine("%>");
txtstream.WriteLine("</table>");
txtstream.WriteLine("</body>");
txtstream.WriteLine("</html>");
txtstream.close();
function GetValue(Name, obj)
{
    var tempstr = new String();
    var tempstr1 = new String();
    var tName = new String();
    tempstr1 = obj.GetObjectText_();
    var re = /"/g;
    tempstr1 = tempstr1.replace(re , "");
    var pos;
    tName = Name + " = ";
    pos = tempstr1.indexOf(tName);
    if (pos > -1)
    {
        pos = pos + tName.length;
        tempstr = tempstr1.substring(pos, tempstr1.length);
        pos = tempstr.indexOf(";");
        tempstr = tempstr.substring(0, pos);
        tempstr = tempstr.replace("{", "");
        tempstr = tempstr.replace("}", "");
        if (tempstr.length > 13)
        {
            if (obj.Properties_(Name).CIMType == 101)
            {
            tempstr = tempstr.substr(4, 2) + "/" + tempstr.substr(6, 2) + "/" +
tempstr.substr(0, 3) + " " + tempstr.substr(8, 2) + ":" + tempstr.substr(10, 2) + ":" +
tempstr.substr(12, 2);
            }
        }
        return tempstr;
    }
    else
    {
        return "";
    }
}
```

Vertical Table with a textarea.

```
var locator = new ActiveXObject("WbemScripting.SWbemLocator");
var svc = locator.ConnectServer(".", "root\\cimv2");
svc.Security_.AuthenticationLevel = 6;
svc.Security_.ImpersonationLevel = 3;
var strQuery = "Select * From ___InstanceDeletionEvent WITHIN 1 where
TargetInstance ISA'Win32_Process'");
var es = svc.ExecNotificationQuery(strQuery);
var ws = new ActiveXObject("WScript.Shell");
var fso = new ActiveXObject("Scripting.FileSystemObject");
var txtstream = fso.OpenTextFile(ws.CurrentDirectory + "\\Win32_Process.aspx",
2, true, -2);
txtstream.WriteLine("<!DOCTYPE html PUBLIC ""-//W3C//DTD XHTML 1.0
Transitional//EN"" ""http://www.w3.org/TR/xhtml1/DTD/xhtml1-
transitional.dtd"">");
txtstream.WriteLine("<html xmlns='http://www.w3.org/1999/xhtml'>");
txtstream.WriteLine("<head>");
txtstream.WriteLine("<style type='text/css'>");
txtstream.WriteLine("th");
txtstream.WriteLine("{");
txtstream.WriteLine("    COLOR: darkred;");
txtstream.WriteLine("    BACKGROUND-COLOR: white;");
txtstream.WriteLine("    FONT-FAMILY:font-family: Cambria, serif;");
txtstream.WriteLine("    FONT-SIZE: 12px;");
txtstream.WriteLine("    text-align: left;");
txtstream.WriteLine("    white-Space: nowrap;");
txtstream.WriteLine("}");
txtstream.WriteLine("td");
txtstream.WriteLine("{");
txtstream.WriteLine("    COLOR: navy;");
txtstream.WriteLine("    BACKGROUND-COLOR: white;");
txtstream.WriteLine("    FONT-FAMILY: font-family: Cambria, serif;");
txtstream.WriteLine("    FONT-SIZE: 12px;");
txtstream.WriteLine("    text-align: left;");
txtstream.WriteLine("    white-Space: nowrap;");
txtstream.WriteLine("}");
txtstream.WriteLine("</style>");
```

```
txtstream.WriteLine("<title>Win32_Process</title>");
txtstream.WriteLine("</head>");
txtstream.WriteLine("<body>");
txtstream.WriteLine("<table border='1' Cellspacing='3' cellpadding = '3'>");

var Names;
var Cols;
var Rows;
var x = 0;

var v = 0;
while(v < 0)
{
    var ti = ex.NextEvent(-1);
    var obj = ti.Properties_.Item("Targetinstance").Value;
    if(v == 0)
    {
        Names = new Array[obj.Properties_.Count];
        Cols = new Array[obj.Properties_.Count];
        Rows = new Array[4];
        var propEnum = new Enumerator(obj.Properties_);
        for (; !propEnum.atEnd(); propEnum.moveNext())
        {
            var prop = propEnum.item();
            Names[x] = prop.Name;
            Cols[x] = GetValue(prop.Name, obj);
            x = x + 1;
        }
        Rows[v] = Cols;
        x = 0;
        v = v + 1;
    }
    else
    {
        var propEnum = new Enumerator(obj.Properties_);
        for (; !propEnum.atEnd(); propEnum.moveNext())
        {
            var prop = propEnum.item();
            Cols[x] = GetValue(prop.Name, obj);
            x = x + 1;
```

```
        }
        Rows[v] = Cols;
        x = 0;
        v = v + 1;
    }
}
txtstream.WriteLine("<%");
for(var a = 0;a < Names.Count; a++)
{
    txtstream.WriteLine("Response.Write(\"<tr><th align='left' nowrap>" +
Names[a] + "</th>\" + vbcrlf)");
    for(var b = 0;b < Rows.Count; b++)
    {
        var C = Rows[b];
        txtstream.WriteLine("Response.Write(\"<td style='font-family:Calibri, Sans-
Serif;font-size: 12px;color:navy;' align='left' nowrap='true'><textarea>" + C[x] +
"</textarea></td>\" + vbcrlf)");
    }
    txtstream.WriteLine("Response.Write(\"</tr>\" + vbcrlf)");
}
txtstream.WriteLine("%>");
txtstream.WriteLine("</table>");
txtstream.WriteLine("</body>");
txtstream.WriteLine("</html>");
txtstream.close();
function GetValue(Name, obj)
{
    var tempstr = new String();
    var tempstr1 = new String();
    var tName = new String();
    tempstr1 = obj.GetObjectText_();
    var re = /"/g;
    tempstr1 = tempstr1.replace(re , "");
    var pos;
    tName = Name + " = ";
    pos = tempstr1.indexOf(tName);
    if (pos > -1)
    {
        pos = pos + tName.length;
        tempstr = tempstr1.substring(pos, tempstr1.length);
```

```
pos = tempstr.indexOf(";");
tempstr = tempstr.substring(0, pos);
tempstr = tempstr.replace("{", "");
tempstr = tempstr.replace("}", "");
if (tempstr.length > 13)
{
    if (obj.Properties_(Name).CIMType == 101)
    {
        tempstr = tempstr.substr(4, 2) + "/" + tempstr.substr(6, 2) + "/" +
tempstr.substr(0, 3) + " " + tempstr.substr(8, 2) + ":" + tempstr.substr(10, 2) + ":" +
tempstr.substr(12, 2);
    }
}
return tempstr;
}
else
{
    return "";
}
}
```

Vertical Table with a textbox.

```
var locator = new ActiveXObject("WbemScripting.SWbemLocator");
var svc = locator.ConnectServer(".", "root\\cimv2");
svc.Security_.AuthenticationLevel = 6;
svc.Security_.ImpersonationLevel = 3;
var strQuery = "Select * From ___InstanceDeletionEvent WITHIN 1 where
TargetInstance ISA'Win32_Process'");
var es = svc.ExecNotificationQuery(strQuery);
var ws = new ActiveXObject("WScript.Shell");
var fso = new ActiveXObject("Scripting.FileSystemObject");
var txtstream = fso.OpenTextFile(ws.CurrentDirectory + "\\Win32_Process.aspx",
2, true, -2);
txtstream.WriteLine("<!DOCTYPE html PUBLIC ""-//W3C//DTD XHTML 1.0
Transitional//EN"" ""http://www.w3.org/TR/xhtml1/DTD/xhtml1-
transitional.dtd"">");
txtstream.WriteLine("<html xmlns='http://www.w3.org/1999/xhtml'>");
txtstream.WriteLine("<head>");
```

```
txtstream.WriteLine("<style type='text/css'>");
txtstream.WriteLine("th");
txtstream.WriteLine("{");
txtstream.WriteLine("   COLOR: darkred;");
txtstream.WriteLine("   BACKGROUND-COLOR: white;");
txtstream.WriteLine("   FONT-FAMILY:font-family: Cambria, serif;");
txtstream.WriteLine("   FONT-SIZE: 12px;");
txtstream.WriteLine("   text-align: left;");
txtstream.WriteLine("   white-Space: nowrap;");
txtstream.WriteLine("}");
txtstream.WriteLine("td");
txtstream.WriteLine("{");
txtstream.WriteLine("   COLOR: navy;");
txtstream.WriteLine("   BACKGROUND-COLOR: white;");
txtstream.WriteLine("   FONT-FAMILY: font-family: Cambria, serif;");
txtstream.WriteLine("   FONT-SIZE: 12px;");
txtstream.WriteLine("   text-align: left;");
txtstream.WriteLine("   white-Space: nowrap;");
txtstream.WriteLine("}");
txtstream.WriteLine("</style>");
txtstream.WriteLine("<title>Win32_Process</title>");
txtstream.WriteLine("</head>");
txtstream.WriteLine("<body>");
txtstream.WriteLine("<table border='1' Cellspacing='3' cellpadding = '3'>");

var Names;
var Cols;
var Rows;
var x = 0;

var v = 0;
while(v < 0)
{
   var ti = ex.NextEvent(-1);
   var obj = ti.Properties_.Item("Targetinstance").Value;
   if(v == 0)
   {
      Names = new Array[obj.Properties_.Count];
      Cols = new Array[obj.Properties_.Count];
      Rows = new Array[4];
```

```
        var propEnum = new Enumerator(obj.Properties_);
        for (; !propEnum.atEnd(); propEnum.moveNext())
        {
            var prop = propEnum.item();
            Names[x] = prop.Name;
            Cols[x] = GetValue(prop.Name, obj);
            x = x + 1;
        }
        Rows[v] = Cols;
        x = 0;
        v = v + 1;
    }
    else
    {
        var propEnum = new Enumerator(obj.Properties_);
        for (; !propEnum.atEnd(); propEnum.moveNext())
        {
            var prop = propEnum.item();
            Cols[x] = GetValue(prop.Name, obj);
            x = x + 1;
        }
        Rows[v] = Cols;
        x = 0;
        v = v + 1;
    }
}
txtstream.WriteLine("<%");
for(var a = 0;a < Names.Count; a++)
{
    txtstream.WriteLine("Response.Write(\"<tr><th align='left' nowrap>" +
Names[a] + "</th>\" + vbcrlf)");
    for(var b = 0;b < Rows.Count; b++)
    {
        var C = Rows[b];
        txtstream.WriteLine("Response.Write(\"<td style='font-family:Calibri, Sans-
Serif;font-size: 12px;color:navy;' align='left' nowrap='true'><input type=text
value=\"\"" + C[x] + "\"\"></input></td>\" + vbcrlf)");
    }
    txtstream.WriteLine("Response.Write(\"</tr>\" + vbcrlf)");
}
```

```javascript
txtstream.WriteLine("%>");
txtstream.WriteLine("</table>");
txtstream.WriteLine("</body>");
txtstream.WriteLine("</html>");
txtstream.close();
function GetValue(Name, obj)
{
    var tempstr = new String();
    var tempstr1 = new String();
    var tName = new String();
    tempstr1 = obj.GetObjectText_();
    var re = /"/g;
    tempstr1 = tempstr1.replace(re , "");
    var pos;
    tName = Name + " = ";
    pos = tempstr1.indexOf(tName);
    if (pos > -1)
    {
        pos = pos + tName.length;
        tempstr = tempstr1.substring(pos, tempstr1.length);
        pos = tempstr.indexOf(";");
        tempstr = tempstr.substring(0, pos);
        tempstr = tempstr.replace("{", "");
        tempstr = tempstr.replace("}", "");
        if (tempstr.length > 13)
        {
            if (obj.Properties_(Name).CIMType == 101)
            {
             tempstr = tempstr.substr(4, 2) + "/" + tempstr.substr(6, 2) + "/" +
tempstr.substr(0, 3) + " " + tempstr.substr(8, 2) + ":" + tempstr.substr(10, 2) + ":" +
tempstr.substr(12, 2);
            }
        }
        return tempstr;
    }
    else
    {
        return "";
    }
}
```

HTA Reports

Horizontal Report with no additional tags.

```
var locator = new ActiveXObject("WbemScripting.SWbemLocator");
var svc = locator.ConnectServer(".", "root\\cimv2");
svc.Security_.AuthenticationLevel = 6;
svc.Security_.ImpersonationLevel = 3;
var strQuery = "Select * From ___InstanceDeletionEvent WITHIN 1 where
TargetInstance ISA'Win32_Process'");
var es = svc.ExecNotificationQuery(strQuery);
var ws = new ActiveXObject("WScript.Shell");
var fso = new ActiveXObject("Scripting.FileSystemObject");
var txtstream = fso.OpenTextFile(ws.CurrentDirectory + "\\Win32_Process.hta",
2, true, -2);
txtstream.WriteLine("<html xmlns='http://www.w3.org/1999/xhtml'>");
txtstream.WriteLine("<head>");
txtstream.WriteLine("<HTA:APPLICATION ");
txtstream.WriteLine("ID = ""Process"" ");
txtstream.WriteLine("APPLICATIONNAME = ""Process"" ");
txtstream.WriteLine("SCROLL = ""yes"" ");
txtstream.WriteLine("SINGLEINSTANCE = ""yes"" ");
txtstream.WriteLine("WINDOWSTATE = ""maximize"" >");
txtstream.WriteLine("<style type='text/css'>");
txtstream.WriteLine("th");
txtstream.WriteLine("{");
txtstream.WriteLine("    COLOR: darkred;");
txtstream.WriteLine("    BACKGROUND-COLOR: white;");
txtstream.WriteLine("    FONT-FAMILY:font-family: Cambria, serif;");
txtstream.WriteLine("    FONT-SIZE: 12px;");
txtstream.WriteLine("    text-align: left;");
txtstream.WriteLine("    white-Space: nowrap;");
txtstream.WriteLine("}");
```

```
txtstream.WriteLine("td");
txtstream.WriteLine("{");
txtstream.WriteLine("    COLOR: navy;");
txtstream.WriteLine("    BACKGROUND-COLOR: white;");
txtstream.WriteLine("    FONT-FAMILY: font-family: Cambria, serif;");
txtstream.WriteLine("    FONT-SIZE: 12px;");
txtstream.WriteLine("    text-align: left;");
txtstream.WriteLine("    white-Space: nowrap;");
txtstream.WriteLine("}");
txtstream.WriteLine("</style>");
txtstream.WriteLine("<title>Win32_Process</title>");
txtstream.WriteLine("</head>");
txtstream.WriteLine("<body>");
txtstream.WriteLine("<table border='0' Cellspacing='3' cellpadding = '3'>");
var v=0;
while(v < 0)
{
   var ti = ex.NextEvent(-1);
   var obj = ti.Properties_.Item("Targetinstance").Value;
   if(v == 0)
   {
      txtstream.WriteLine("<tr>");
      var propEnum = new Enumerator(obj.Properties_);
      for (; !propEnum.atEnd(); propEnum.moveNext())
      {
         var prop = propEnum.item();
         txtstream.WriteLine("<th align='left' nowrap>" + prop.Name + "</th>");
      }
      txtstream.WriteLine("</tr>");
      propEnum.ReSet();
   }
   txtstream.WriteLine("<tr>");
   for (; !propEnum.atEnd(); propEnum.moveNext())
   {
      var prop = propEnum.item();
      txtstream.WriteLine("<td style='font-family:Calibri, Sans-Serif;font-size:
12px;color:navy;' align='left' nowrap='nowrap'>" + GetValue(prop.Name, obj) +
"</td>");
   }
   txtstream.WriteLine("</tr>");
```

```
        v = v + 1;
    }
    txtstream.WriteLine("</table>");
    txtstream.WriteLine("</body>");
    txtstream.WriteLine("</html>");
    txtstream.close();
    function GetValue(Name, obj)
    {
        var tempstr = new String();
        var tempstr1 = new String();
        var tName = new String();
        tempstr1 = obj.GetObjectText_();
        var re = /"/g;
        tempstr1 = tempstr1.replace(re , "");
        var pos;
        tName = Name + " = ";
        pos = tempstr1.indexOf(tName);
        if (pos > -1)
        {
            pos = pos + tName.length;
            tempstr = tempstr1.substring(pos, tempstr1.length);
            pos = tempstr.indexOf(";");
            tempstr = tempstr.substring(0, pos);
            tempstr = tempstr.replace("{", "");
            tempstr = tempstr.replace("}", "");
            if (tempstr.length > 13)
            {
                if (obj.Properties_(Name).CIMType == 101)
                {
                    tempstr = tempstr.substr(4, 2) + "/"  + tempstr.substr(6, 2) + "/" +
tempstr.substr(0, 3) + " " + tempstr.substr(8, 2) + ":" + tempstr.substr(10, 2) + ":" +
tempstr.substr(12, 2);
                }
            }
            return tempstr;
        }
        else
        {
            return "";
        }
```

}

Horizontal Report with a combobox.

```javascript
var locator = new ActiveXObject("WbemScripting.SWbemLocator");
var svc = locator.ConnectServer(".", "root\\cimv2");
svc.Security_.AuthenticationLevel = 6;
svc.Security_.ImpersonationLevel = 3;
var strQuery = "Select * From ___InstanceDeletionEvent WITHIN 1 where
TargetInstance ISA'Win32_Process'");
var es = svc.ExecNotificationQuery(strQuery);
var ws = new ActiveXObject("WScript.Shell");
var fso = new ActiveXObject("Scripting.FileSystemObject");
var txtstream = fso.OpenTextFile(ws.CurrentDirectory + "\\Win32_Process.hta",
2, true, -2);
txtstream.WriteLine("<html xmlns='http://www.w3.org/1999/xhtml'>");
txtstream.WriteLine("<head>");
txtstream.WriteLine("<HTA:APPLICATION ");
txtstream.WriteLine("ID = ""Process"" ");
txtstream.WriteLine("APPLICATIONNAME = ""Process"" ");
txtstream.WriteLine("SCROLL = ""yes"" ");
txtstream.WriteLine("SINGLEINSTANCE = ""yes"" ");
txtstream.WriteLine("WINDOWSTATE = ""maximize"" >");
txtstream.WriteLine("<style type='text/css'>");
txtstream.WriteLine("th");
txtstream.WriteLine("{");
txtstream.WriteLine("   COLOR: darkred;");
txtstream.WriteLine("   BACKGROUND-COLOR: white;");
txtstream.WriteLine("   FONT-FAMILY:font-family: Cambria, serif;");
txtstream.WriteLine("   FONT-SIZE: 12px;");
txtstream.WriteLine("   text-align: left;");
txtstream.WriteLine("   white-Space: nowrap;");
txtstream.WriteLine("}");
txtstream.WriteLine("td");
txtstream.WriteLine("{");
txtstream.WriteLine("   COLOR: navy;");
txtstream.WriteLine("   BACKGROUND-COLOR: white;");
txtstream.WriteLine("   FONT-FAMILY: font-family: Cambria, serif;");
txtstream.WriteLine("   FONT-SIZE: 12px;");
```

```
txtstream.WriteLine("    text-align: left;");
txtstream.WriteLine("    white-Space: nowrap;");
txtstream.WriteLine("}");
txtstream.WriteLine("</style>");
txtstream.WriteLine("<title>Win32_Process</title>");
txtstream.WriteLine("</head>");
txtstream.WriteLine("<body>");
txtstream.WriteLine("<table border='0' Cellspacing='3' cellpadding = '3'>");
var v=0;
while(v < 0)
{
    var ti = ex.NextEvent(-1);
    var obj = ti.Properties_.Item("Targetinstance").Value;
    if(v == 0)
    {
        txtstream.WriteLine("<tr>");
        var propEnum = new Enumerator(obj.Properties_);
        for (; !propEnum.atEnd(); propEnum.moveNext())
        {
            var prop = propEnum.item();
            txtstream.WriteLine("<th align='left' nowrap>" + prop.Name + "</th>");
        }
        txtstream.WriteLine("</tr>");
        propEnum.ReSet();
    }
    txtstream.WriteLine("<tr>");
    for (; !propEnum.atEnd(); propEnum.moveNext())
    {
        var prop = propEnum.item();
        txtstream.WriteLine("<td style='font-family:Calibri, Sans-Serif;font-size:
12px;color:navy;' align='left' nowrap='true'><select><option value = '" +
GetValue(prop.Name, obj) + "'>" + GetValue(prop.Name, obj) +
"</option></select></td>");
    }
    txtstream.WriteLine("</tr>");
    v = v + 1;
}
txtstream.WriteLine("</table>");
txtstream.WriteLine("</body>");
txtstream.WriteLine("</html>");
```

```
txtstream.close();
function GetValue(Name, obj)
{
    var tempstr = new String();
    var tempstr1 = new String();
    var tName = new String();
    tempstr1 = obj.GetObjectText_();
    var re = /"/g;
    tempstr1 = tempstr1.replace(re , "");
    var pos;
    tName = Name + " = ";
    pos = tempstr1.indexOf(tName);
    if (pos > -1)
    {
        pos = pos + tName.length;
        tempstr = tempstr1.substring(pos, tempstr1.length);
        pos = tempstr.indexOf(";");
        tempstr = tempstr.substring(0, pos);
        tempstr = tempstr.replace("{", "");
        tempstr = tempstr.replace("}", "");
        if (tempstr.length > 13)
        {
            if (obj.Properties_(Name).CIMType == 101)
            {
                tempstr = tempstr.substr(4, 2) + "/" + tempstr.substr(6, 2) + "/" +
tempstr.substr(0, 3) + " " + tempstr.substr(8, 2) + ":" + tempstr.substr(10, 2) + ":" +
tempstr.substr(12, 2);
            }
        }
        return tempstr;
    }
    else
    {
        return "";
    }
}
```

Horizontal Report with a link.

```
var locator = new ActiveXObject("WbemScripting.SWbemLocator");
var svc = locator.ConnectServer(".", "root\\cimv2");
svc.Security_.AuthenticationLevel = 6;
svc.Security_.ImpersonationLevel = 3;
var strQuery = "Select * From ___InstanceDeletionEvent WITHIN 1 where
TargetInstance ISA'Win32_Process'");
var es = svc.ExecNotificationQuery(strQuery);
var ws = new ActiveXObject("WScript.Shell");
var fso = new ActiveXObject("Scripting.FileSystemObject");
var txtstream = fso.OpenTextFile(ws.CurrentDirectory + "\\Win32_Process.hta",
2, true, -2);
txtstream.WriteLine("<html xmlns='http://www.w3.org/1999/xhtml'>");
txtstream.WriteLine("<head>");
txtstream.WriteLine("<HTA:APPLICATION ");
txtstream.WriteLine("ID = ""Process"" ");
txtstream.WriteLine("APPLICATIONNAME = ""Process"" ");
txtstream.WriteLine("SCROLL = ""yes"" ");
txtstream.WriteLine("SINGLEINSTANCE = ""yes"" ");
txtstream.WriteLine("WINDOWSTATE = ""maximize"" >");
txtstream.WriteLine("<style type='text/css'>");
txtstream.WriteLine("th");
txtstream.WriteLine("{");
txtstream.WriteLine("   COLOR: darkred;");
txtstream.WriteLine("   BACKGROUND-COLOR: white;");
txtstream.WriteLine("   FONT-FAMILY:font-family: Cambria, serif;");
txtstream.WriteLine("   FONT-SIZE: 12px;");
txtstream.WriteLine("   text-align: left;");
txtstream.WriteLine("   white-Space: nowrap;");
txtstream.WriteLine("}");
txtstream.WriteLine("td");
txtstream.WriteLine("{");
txtstream.WriteLine("   COLOR: navy;");
txtstream.WriteLine("   BACKGROUND-COLOR: white;");
txtstream.WriteLine("   FONT-FAMILY: font-family: Cambria, serif;");
txtstream.WriteLine("   FONT-SIZE: 12px;");
txtstream.WriteLine("   text-align: left;");
txtstream.WriteLine("   white-Space: nowrap;");
```

```javascript
txtstream.WriteLine("}");
txtstream.WriteLine("</style>");
txtstream.WriteLine("<title>Win32_Process</title>");
txtstream.WriteLine("</head>");
txtstream.WriteLine("<body>");
txtstream.WriteLine("<table border='0' Cellspacing='3' cellpadding = '3'>");
var v=0;
while(v < 0)
{
   var ti = ex.NextEvent(-1);
   var obj = ti.Properties_.Item("Targetinstance").Value;
   if(v == 0)
   {
      txtstream.WriteLine("<tr>");
      var propEnum = new Enumerator(obj.Properties_);
      for (; !propEnum.atEnd(); propEnum.moveNext())
      {
         var prop = propEnum.item();
         txtstream.WriteLine("<th align='left' nowrap>" + prop.Name + "</th>");
      }
      txtstream.WriteLine("</tr>");
      propEnum.ReSet();
   }
   txtstream.WriteLine("<tr>");
   for (; !propEnum.atEnd(); propEnum.moveNext())
   {
      var prop = propEnum.item();
      txtstream.WriteLine("<td style='font-family:Calibri, Sans-Serif;font-size:
12px;color:navy;' align='left' nowrap='true'><a href='" + GetValue(prop.Name, obj)
+ "'>" + GetValue(prop.Name, obj) + "</a></td>");
   }
   txtstream.WriteLine("</tr>");
   v = v + 1;
}
txtstream.WriteLine("</table>");
txtstream.WriteLine("</body>");
txtstream.WriteLine("</html>");
txtstream.close();
function GetValue(Name, obj)
{
```

```
var tempstr = new String();
var tempstr1 = new String();
var tName = new String();
tempstr1 = obj.GetObjectText_();
var re = /"/g;
tempstr1 = tempstr1.replace(re , "");
var pos;
tName = Name + " = ";
pos = tempstr1.indexOf(tName);
if (pos > -1)
{
    pos = pos + tName.length;
    tempstr = tempstr1.substring(pos, tempstr1.length);
    pos = tempstr.indexOf(";");
    tempstr = tempstr.substring(0, pos);
    tempstr = tempstr.replace("{", "");
    tempstr = tempstr.replace("}", "");
    if (tempstr.length > 13)
    {
        if (obj.Properties_(Name).CIMType == 101)
        {
            tempstr = tempstr.substr(4, 2) + "/"  + tempstr.substr(6, 2) + "/" +
tempstr.substr(0, 3) + " " + tempstr.substr(8, 2) + ":" + tempstr.substr(10, 2) + ":" +
tempstr.substr(12, 2);
        }
    }
    return tempstr;
}
else
{
    return "";
}
}
```

Horizontal Report with a listbox.

```
var locator = new ActiveXObject("WbemScripting.SWbemLocator");
var svc = locator.ConnectServer(".", "root\\cimv2");
svc.Security_.AuthenticationLevel = 6;
svc.Security_.ImpersonationLevel = 3;
var strQuery = "Select * From __InstanceDeletionEvent WITHIN 1 where
TargetInstance ISA'Win32_Process'");
var es = svc.ExecNotificationQuery(strQuery);
var ws = new ActiveXObject("WScript.Shell");
var fso = new ActiveXObject("Scripting.FileSystemObject");
var txtstream = fso.OpenTextFile(ws.CurrentDirectory + "\\Win32_Process.hta",
2, true, -2);
txtstream.WriteLine("<html xmlns='http://www.w3.org/1999/xhtml'>");
txtstream.WriteLine("<head>");
txtstream.WriteLine("<HTA:APPLICATION ");
txtstream.WriteLine("ID = ""Process"" ");
txtstream.WriteLine("APPLICATIONNAME = ""Process"" ");
txtstream.WriteLine("SCROLL = ""yes"" ");
txtstream.WriteLine("SINGLEINSTANCE = ""yes"" ");
txtstream.WriteLine("WINDOWSTATE = ""maximize"" >");
txtstream.WriteLine("<style type='text/css'>");
txtstream.WriteLine("th");
txtstream.WriteLine("{");
txtstream.WriteLine("    COLOR: darkred;");
txtstream.WriteLine("    BACKGROUND-COLOR: white;");
txtstream.WriteLine("    FONT-FAMILY:font-family: Cambria, serif;");
txtstream.WriteLine("    FONT-SIZE: 12px;");
txtstream.WriteLine("    text-align: left;");
txtstream.WriteLine("    white-Space: nowrap;");
txtstream.WriteLine("}");
txtstream.WriteLine("td");
txtstream.WriteLine("{");
txtstream.WriteLine("    COLOR: navy;");
txtstream.WriteLine("    BACKGROUND-COLOR: white;");
txtstream.WriteLine("    FONT-FAMILY: font-family: Cambria, serif;");
txtstream.WriteLine("    FONT-SIZE: 12px;");
txtstream.WriteLine("    text-align: left;");
txtstream.WriteLine("    white-Space: nowrap;");
```

```
txtstream.WriteLine("}");
txtstream.WriteLine("</style>");
txtstream.WriteLine("<title>Win32_Process</title>");
txtstream.WriteLine("</head>");
txtstream.WriteLine("<body>");
txtstream.WriteLine("<table border='0' Cellspacing='3' cellpadding = '3'>");
var v=0;
while(v < 0)
{
    var ti = ex.NextEvent(-1);
    var obj = ti.Properties_.Item("Targetinstance").Value;
    if(v == 0)
    {
        txtstream.WriteLine("<tr>");
        var propEnum = new Enumerator(obj.Properties_);
        for (; !propEnum.atEnd(); propEnum.moveNext())
        {
            var prop = propEnum.item();
            txtstream.WriteLine("<th align='left' nowrap>" + prop.Name + "</th>");
        }
        txtstream.WriteLine("</tr>");
        propEnum.ReSet();
    }
    txtstream.WriteLine("<tr>");
    for (; !propEnum.atEnd(); propEnum.moveNext())
    {
        var prop = propEnum.item();
        txtstream.WriteLine("<td style='font-family:Calibri, Sans-Serif;font-size:
12px;color:navy;' align='left' nowrap='true'><select multiple><option value = '" +
GetValue(prop.Name, obj) + "'>" + GetValue(prop.Name, obj) +
"</option></select></td>");
    }
    txtstream.WriteLine("</tr>");
    v = v + 1;
}
txtstream.WriteLine("</table>");
txtstream.WriteLine("</body>");
txtstream.WriteLine("</html>");
txtstream.close();
function GetValue(Name, obj)
```

```
{
    var tempstr = new String();
    var tempstr1 = new String();
    var tName = new String();
    tempstr1 = obj.GetObjectText_();
    var re = /"/g;
    tempstr1 = tempstr1.replace(re , "");
    var pos;
    tName = Name + " = ";
    pos = tempstr1.indexOf(tName);
    if (pos > -1)
    {
        pos = pos + tName.length;
        tempstr = tempstr1.substring(pos, tempstr1.length);
        pos = tempstr.indexOf(";");
        tempstr = tempstr.substring(0, pos);
        tempstr = tempstr.replace("{", "");
        tempstr = tempstr.replace("}", "");
        if (tempstr.length > 13)
        {
            if (obj.Properties_(Name).CIMType == 101)
            {
                tempstr = tempstr.substr(4, 2) + "/"  + tempstr.substr(6, 2) + "/" +
tempstr.substr(0, 3) + " " + tempstr.substr(8, 2) + ":" + tempstr.substr(10, 2) + ":" +
tempstr.substr(12, 2);
            }
        }
        return tempstr;
    }
    else
    {
        return "";
    }
}
```

Horizontal Report with a textarea.

```
var locator = new ActiveXObject("WbemScripting.SWbemLocator");
var svc = locator.ConnectServer(".", "root\\cimv2");
svc.Security_.AuthenticationLevel = 6;
svc.Security_.ImpersonationLevel = 3;
var strQuery = "Select * From __InstanceDeletionEvent WITHIN 1 where
TargetInstance ISA'Win32_Process'");
var es = svc.ExecNotificationQuery(strQuery);
var ws = new ActiveXObject("WScript.Shell");
var fso = new ActiveXObject("Scripting.FileSystemObject");
var txtstream = fso.OpenTextFile(ws.CurrentDirectory + "\\Win32_Process.hta",
2, true, -2);
txtstream.WriteLine("<html xmlns='http://www.w3.org/1999/xhtml'>");
txtstream.WriteLine("<head>");
txtstream.WriteLine("<HTA:APPLICATION ");
txtstream.WriteLine("ID = ""Process"" ");
txtstream.WriteLine("APPLICATIONNAME = ""Process"" ");
txtstream.WriteLine("SCROLL = ""yes"" ");
txtstream.WriteLine("SINGLEINSTANCE = ""yes"" ");
txtstream.WriteLine("WINDOWSTATE = ""maximize"" >");
txtstream.WriteLine("<style type='text/css'>");
txtstream.WriteLine("th");
txtstream.WriteLine("{");
txtstream.WriteLine("    COLOR: darkred;");
txtstream.WriteLine("    BACKGROUND-COLOR: white;");
txtstream.WriteLine("    FONT-FAMILY:font-family: Cambria, serif;");
txtstream.WriteLine("    FONT-SIZE: 12px;");
txtstream.WriteLine("    text-align: left;");
txtstream.WriteLine("    white-Space: nowrap;");
txtstream.WriteLine("}");
txtstream.WriteLine("td");
txtstream.WriteLine("{");
txtstream.WriteLine("    COLOR: navy;");
txtstream.WriteLine("    BACKGROUND-COLOR: white;");
txtstream.WriteLine("    FONT-FAMILY: font-family: Cambria, serif;");
txtstream.WriteLine("    FONT-SIZE: 12px;");
txtstream.WriteLine("    text-align: left;");
txtstream.WriteLine("    white-Space: nowrap;");
```

```
txtstream.WriteLine("}");
txtstream.WriteLine("</style>");
txtstream.WriteLine("<title>Win32_Process</title>");
txtstream.WriteLine("</head>");
txtstream.WriteLine("<body>");
txtstream.WriteLine("<table border='0' Cellspacing='3' cellpadding = '3'>");
var v=0;
while(v < 0)
{
   var ti = ex.NextEvent(-1);
   var obj = ti.Properties_.Item("Targetinstance").Value;
   if(v == 0)
   {
      txtstream.WriteLine("<tr>");
      var propEnum = new Enumerator(obj.Properties_);
      for (; !propEnum.atEnd(); propEnum.moveNext())
      {
         var prop = propEnum.item();
         txtstream.WriteLine("<th align='left' nowrap>" + prop.Name + "</th>");
      }
      txtstream.WriteLine("</tr>");
      propEnum.ReSet();
   }
   txtstream.WriteLine("<tr>");
   for (; !propEnum.atEnd(); propEnum.moveNext())
   {
      var prop = propEnum.item();
      txtstream.WriteLine("<td style='font-family:Calibri, Sans-Serif;font-size:
12px;color:navy;' align='left' nowrap='true'><textarea>" + GetValue(prop.Name,
obj) + "</textarea></td>");
   }
   txtstream.WriteLine("</tr>");
   v = v + 1;
}
txtstream.WriteLine("</table>");
txtstream.WriteLine("</body>");
txtstream.WriteLine("</html>");
txtstream.close();
function GetValue(Name, obj)
{
```

```
var tempstr = new String();
var tempstr1 = new String();
var tName = new String();
tempstr1 = obj.GetObjectText_();
var re = /"/g;
tempstr1 = tempstr1.replace(re , "");
var pos;
tName = Name + " = ";
pos = tempstr1.indexOf(tName);
if (pos > -1)
{
    pos = pos + tName.length;
    tempstr = tempstr1.substring(pos, tempstr1.length);
    pos = tempstr.indexOf(";");
    tempstr = tempstr.substring(0, pos);
    tempstr = tempstr.replace("{", "");
    tempstr = tempstr.replace("}", "");
    if (tempstr.length > 13)
    {
        if (obj.Properties_(Name).CIMType == 101)
        {
            tempstr = tempstr.substr(4, 2) + "/" + tempstr.substr(6, 2) + "/" +
tempstr.substr(0, 3) + " " + tempstr.substr(8, 2) + ":" + tempstr.substr(10, 2) + ":" +
tempstr.substr(12, 2);
        }
    }
    return tempstr;
}
else
{
    return "";
}
}
```

Horizontal Report with a textbox.

```
var locator = new ActiveXObject("WbemScripting.SWbemLocator");
var svc = locator.ConnectServer(".", "root\\cimv2");
svc.Security_.AuthenticationLevel = 6;
svc.Security_.ImpersonationLevel = 3;
var strQuery = "Select * From __InstanceDeletionEvent WITHIN 1 where
TargetInstance ISA'Win32_Process'");
var es = svc.ExecNotificationQuery(strQuery);
var ws = new ActiveXObject("WScript.Shell");
var fso = new ActiveXObject("Scripting.FileSystemObject");
var txtstream = fso.OpenTextFile(ws.CurrentDirectory + "\\Win32_Process.hta",
2, true, -2);
txtstream.WriteLine("<html xmlns='http://www.w3.org/1999/xhtml'>");
txtstream.WriteLine("<head>");
txtstream.WriteLine("<HTA:APPLICATION ");
txtstream.WriteLine("ID = ""Process"" ");
txtstream.WriteLine("APPLICATIONNAME = ""Process"" ");
txtstream.WriteLine("SCROLL = ""yes"" ");
txtstream.WriteLine("SINGLEINSTANCE = ""yes"" ");
txtstream.WriteLine("WINDOWSTATE = ""maximize"" >");
txtstream.WriteLine("<style type='text/css'>");
txtstream.WriteLine("th");
txtstream.WriteLine("{");
txtstream.WriteLine("    COLOR: darkred;");
txtstream.WriteLine("    BACKGROUND-COLOR: white;");
txtstream.WriteLine("    FONT-FAMILY:font-family: Cambria, serif;");
txtstream.WriteLine("    FONT-SIZE: 12px;");
txtstream.WriteLine("    text-align: left;");
txtstream.WriteLine("    white-Space: nowrap;");
txtstream.WriteLine("}");
txtstream.WriteLine("td");
txtstream.WriteLine("{");
txtstream.WriteLine("    COLOR: navy;");
txtstream.WriteLine("    BACKGROUND-COLOR: white;");
txtstream.WriteLine("    FONT-FAMILY: font-family: Cambria, serif;");
txtstream.WriteLine("    FONT-SIZE: 12px;");
txtstream.WriteLine("    text-align: left;");
txtstream.WriteLine("    white-Space: nowrap;");
```

```
txtstream.WriteLine("}");
txtstream.WriteLine("</style>");
txtstream.WriteLine("<title>Win32_Process</title>");
txtstream.WriteLine("</head>");
txtstream.WriteLine("<body>");
txtstream.WriteLine("<table border='0' Cellspacing='3' cellpadding = '3'>");
var v=0;
while(v < 0)
{
   var ti = ex.NextEvent(-1);
   var obj = ti.Properties_.Item("Targetinstance").Value;
   if(v == 0)
   {
      txtstream.WriteLine("<tr>");
      var propEnum = new Enumerator(obj.Properties_);
      for (; !propEnum.atEnd(); propEnum.moveNext())
      {
         var prop = propEnum.item();
         txtstream.WriteLine("<th align='left' nowrap>" + prop.Name + "</th>");
      }
      txtstream.WriteLine("</tr>");
      propEnum.ReSet();
   }
   txtstream.WriteLine("<tr>");
   for (; !propEnum.atEnd(); propEnum.moveNext())
   {
      var prop = propEnum.item();
      txtstream.WriteLine("<td style='font-family:Calibri, Sans-Serif;font-size:
12px;color:navy;' align='left' nowrap='true'><input type=text value='" +
GetValue(prop.Name, obj) + "'></input></td>");
   }
   txtstream.WriteLine("</tr>");
   v = v + 1;
}
txtstream.WriteLine("</table>");
txtstream.WriteLine("</body>");
txtstream.WriteLine("</html>");
txtstream.close();
function GetValue(Name, obj)
{
```

```
var tempstr = new String();
var tempstr1 = new String();
var tName = new String();
tempstr1 = obj.GetObjectText_();
var re = /"/g;
tempstr1 = tempstr1.replace(re , "");
var pos;
tName = Name + " = ";
pos = tempstr1.indexOf(tName);
if (pos > -1)
{
    pos = pos + tName.length;
    tempstr = tempstr1.substring(pos, tempstr1.length);
    pos = tempstr.indexOf(";");
    tempstr = tempstr.substring(0, pos);
    tempstr = tempstr.replace("{", "");
    tempstr = tempstr.replace("}", "");
    if (tempstr.length > 13)
    {
        if (obj.Properties_(Name).CIMType == 101)
        {
            tempstr = tempstr.substr(4, 2) + "/" + tempstr.substr(6, 2) + "/" +
tempstr.substr(0, 3) + " " + tempstr.substr(8, 2) + ":" + tempstr.substr(10, 2) + ":" +
tempstr.substr(12, 2);
        }
    }
    return tempstr;
}
else
{
    return "";
}
}
```

Vertical Report with no additional tags.

```
var locator = new ActiveXObject("WbemScripting.SWbemLocator");
var svc = locator.ConnectServer(".", "root\\cimv2");
svc.Security_.AuthenticationLevel = 6;
svc.Security_.ImpersonationLevel = 3;
var strQuery = "Select * From ___InstanceDeletionEvent WITHIN 1 where
TargetInstance ISA'Win32_Process'");
var es = svc.ExecNotificationQuery(strQuery);
var ws = new ActiveXObject("WScript.Shell");
var fso = new ActiveXObject("Scripting.FileSystemObject");
var txtstream = fso.OpenTextFile(ws.CurrentDirectory + "\\Win32_Process.hta",
2, true, -2);
txtstream.WriteLine("<html xmlns='http://www.w3.org/1999/xhtml'>");
txtstream.WriteLine("<head>");
txtstream.WriteLine("<HTA:APPLICATION ");
txtstream.WriteLine("ID = ""Process"" ");
txtstream.WriteLine("APPLICATIONNAME = ""Process"" ");
txtstream.WriteLine("SCROLL = ""yes"" ");
txtstream.WriteLine("SINGLEINSTANCE = ""yes"" ");
txtstream.WriteLine("WINDOWSTATE = ""maximize"" >");
txtstream.WriteLine("<style type='text/css'>");
txtstream.WriteLine("th");
txtstream.WriteLine("{");
txtstream.WriteLine("   COLOR: darkred;");
txtstream.WriteLine("   BACKGROUND-COLOR: white;");
txtstream.WriteLine("   FONT-FAMILY:font-family: Cambria, serif;");
txtstream.WriteLine("   FONT-SIZE: 12px;");
txtstream.WriteLine("   text-align: left;");
txtstream.WriteLine("   white-Space: nowrap;");
txtstream.WriteLine("}");
txtstream.WriteLine("td");
txtstream.WriteLine("{");
txtstream.WriteLine("   COLOR: navy;");
txtstream.WriteLine("   BACKGROUND-COLOR: white;");
txtstream.WriteLine("   FONT-FAMILY: font-family: Cambria, serif;");
txtstream.WriteLine("   FONT-SIZE: 12px;");
txtstream.WriteLine("   text-align: left;");
txtstream.WriteLine("   white-Space: nowrap;");
```

```
txtstream.WriteLine("}");
txtstream.WriteLine("</style>");
txtstream.WriteLine("<title>Win32_Process</title>");
txtstream.WriteLine("</head>");
txtstream.WriteLine("<body>");
txtstream.WriteLine("<table border='0' Cellspacing='3' cellpadding = '3'>");

var Names;
var Cols;
var Rows;
var x = 0;

var v = 0;
while(v < 0)
{
   var ti = ex.NextEvent(-1);
   var obj = ti.Properties_.Item("Targetinstance").Value;
   if(v == 0)
   {
      Names = new Array[obj.Properties_.Count];
      Cols = new Array[obj.Properties_.Count];
      Rows = new Array[4];
      var propEnum = new Enumerator(obj.Properties_);
      for (; !propEnum.atEnd(); propEnum.moveNext())
      {
         var prop = propEnum.item();
         Names[x] = prop.Name;
         Cols[x] = GetValue(prop.Name, obj);
         x = x + 1;
      }
      Rows[v] = Cols;
      x = 0;
      v = v + 1;
   }
   else
   {
      var propEnum = new Enumerator(obj.Properties_);
      for (; !propEnum.atEnd(); propEnum.moveNext())
      {
         var prop = propEnum.item();
```

```
            Cols[x] = GetValue(prop.Name, obj);
            x = x + 1;
        }
        Rows[v] = Cols;
        x = 0;
        v = v + 1;
    }
}
for(var a = 0;a < Names.Count; a++)
{
    txtstream.WriteLine("<tr><th align='left' nowrap>" + Names[a] + "</th>");
    for(var b = 0;b < Rows.Count; b++)
    {
        var C = Rows[b];
        txtstream.WriteLine("<td style='font-family:Calibri, Sans-Serif;font-size:
12px;color:navy;' align='left' nowrap='nowrap'>" + C[x] + "</td>");
    }
    txtstream.WriteLine("</tr>");
}
txtstream.WriteLine("</table>");
txtstream.WriteLine("</body>");
txtstream.WriteLine("</html>");
txtstream.close();
function GetValue(Name, obj)
{
    var tempstr = new String();
    var tempstr1 = new String();
    var tName = new String();
    tempstr1 = obj.GetObjectText_();
    var re = /"/g;
    tempstr1 = tempstr1.replace(re , "");
    var pos;
    tName = Name + " = ";
    pos = tempstr1.indexOf(tName);
    if (pos > -1)
    {
        pos = pos + tName.length;
        tempstr = tempstr1.substring(pos, tempstr1.length);
        pos = tempstr.indexOf(";");
        tempstr = tempstr.substring(0, pos);
```

```
            tempstr = tempstr.replace("{", "");
            tempstr = tempstr.replace("}", "");
            if (tempstr.length > 13)
            {
                if (obj.Properties_(Name).CIMType == 101)
                {
                tempstr = tempstr.substr(4, 2) + "/" + tempstr.substr(6, 2) + "/" +
tempstr.substr(0, 3) + " " + tempstr.substr(8, 2) + ":" + tempstr.substr(10, 2) + ":" +
tempstr.substr(12, 2);
                }
            }
            return tempstr;
        }
        else
        {
            return "";
        }
    }
```

Vertical Report with a combobox.

```
    var locator = new ActiveXObject("WbemScripting.SWbemLocator");
    var svc = locator.ConnectServer(".", "root\\cimv2");
    svc.Security_.AuthenticationLevel = 6;
    svc.Security_.ImpersonationLevel = 3;
    var strQuery = "Select * From ___InstanceDeletionEvent WITHIN 1 where
TargetInstance ISA'Win32_Process'");
    var es = svc.ExecNotificationQuery(strQuery);
    var ws = new ActiveXObject("WScript.Shell");
    var fso = new ActiveXObject("Scripting.FileSystemObject");
    var txtstream = fso.OpenTextFile(ws.CurrentDirectory + "\\Win32_Process.hta",
2, true, -2);
    txtstream.WriteLine("<html xmlns='http://www.w3.org/1999/xhtml'>");
    txtstream.WriteLine("<head>");
    txtstream.WriteLine("<HTA:APPLICATION ");
    txtstream.WriteLine("ID = ""Process"" ");
    txtstream.WriteLine("APPLICATIONNAME = ""Process"" ");
    txtstream.WriteLine("SCROLL = ""yes"" ");
    txtstream.WriteLine("SINGLEINSTANCE = ""yes"" ");
```

```
txtstream.WriteLine("WINDOWSTATE = ""maximize"" >");
txtstream.WriteLine("<style type='text/css'>");
txtstream.WriteLine("th");
txtstream.WriteLine("{");
txtstream.WriteLine("   COLOR: darkred;");
txtstream.WriteLine("   BACKGROUND-COLOR: white;");
txtstream.WriteLine("   FONT-FAMILY:font-family: Cambria, serif;");
txtstream.WriteLine("   FONT-SIZE: 12px;");
txtstream.WriteLine("   text-align: left;");
txtstream.WriteLine("   white-Space: nowrap;");
txtstream.WriteLine("}");
txtstream.WriteLine("td");
txtstream.WriteLine("{");
txtstream.WriteLine("   COLOR: navy;");
txtstream.WriteLine("   BACKGROUND-COLOR: white;");
txtstream.WriteLine("   FONT-FAMILY: font-family: Cambria, serif;");
txtstream.WriteLine("   FONT-SIZE: 12px;");
txtstream.WriteLine("   text-align: left;");
txtstream.WriteLine("   white-Space: nowrap;");
txtstream.WriteLine("}");
txtstream.WriteLine("</style>");
txtstream.WriteLine("<title>Win32_Process</title>");
txtstream.WriteLine("</head>");
txtstream.WriteLine("<body>");
txtstream.WriteLine("<table border='0' Cellspacing='3' cellpadding = '3'>");

var Names;
var Cols;
var Rows;
var x = 0;

var v = 0;
while(v < 0)
{
    var ti = ex.NextEvent(-1);
    var obj = ti.Properties_.Item("Targetinstance").Value;
    if(v == 0)
    {
        Names = new Array[obj.Properties_.Count];
        Cols = new Array[obj.Properties_.Count];
```

```
        Rows = new Array[4];
        var propEnum = new Enumerator(obj.Properties_);
        for (; !propEnum.atEnd(); propEnum.moveNext())
        {
            var prop = propEnum.item();
            Names[x] = prop.Name;
            Cols[x] = GetValue(prop.Name, obj);
            x = x + 1;
        }
        Rows[v] = Cols;
        x = 0;
        v = v + 1;
    }
    else
    {
        var propEnum = new Enumerator(obj.Properties_);
        for (; !propEnum.atEnd(); propEnum.moveNext())
        {
            var prop = propEnum.item();
            Cols[x] = GetValue(prop.Name, obj);
            x = x + 1;
        }
        Rows[v] = Cols;
        x = 0;
        v = v + 1;
    }
}
for(var a = 0;a < Names.Count; a++)
{
    txtstream.WriteLine("<tr><th align='left' nowrap>" + Names[a] + "</th>");
    for(var b = 0;b < Rows.Count; b++)
    {
        var C = Rows[b];
        txtstream.WriteLine("<td style='font-family:Calibri, Sans-Serif;font-size:
12px;color:navy;' align='left' nowrap='true'><select><option value = """ + C[x] +
""">" + C[x] + "</option></select></td>");
    }
    txtstream.WriteLine("</tr>");
}
txtstream.WriteLine("</table>");
```

```
txtstream.WriteLine("</body>");
txtstream.WriteLine("</html>");
txtstream.close();
function GetValue(Name, obj)
{
    var tempstr = new String();
    var tempstr1 = new String();
    var tName = new String();
    tempstr1 = obj.GetObjectText_();
    var re = /"/g;
    tempstr1 = tempstr1.replace(re , "");
    var pos;
    tName = Name + " = ";
    pos = tempstr1.indexOf(tName);
    if (pos > -1)
    {
        pos = pos + tName.length;
        tempstr = tempstr1.substring(pos, tempstr1.length);
        pos = tempstr.indexOf(";");
        tempstr = tempstr.substring(0, pos);
        tempstr = tempstr.replace("{", "");
        tempstr = tempstr.replace("}", "");
        if (tempstr.length > 13)
        {
            if (obj.Properties_(Name).CIMType == 101)
            {
            tempstr = tempstr.substr(4, 2) + "/"  + tempstr.substr(6, 2) + "/" +
tempstr.substr(0, 3) + " " + tempstr.substr(8, 2) + ":" + tempstr.substr(10, 2) + ":" +
tempstr.substr(12, 2);
            }
        }
        return tempstr;
    }
    else
    {
        return "";
    }
}
```

Vertical Report with a link.

```
var locator = new ActiveXObject("WbemScripting.SWbemLocator");
var svc = locator.ConnectServer(".", "root\\cimv2");
svc.Security_.AuthenticationLevel = 6;
svc.Security_.ImpersonationLevel = 3;
var strQuery = "Select * From ___InstanceDeletionEvent WITHIN 1 where
TargetInstance ISA'Win32_Process'");
var es = svc.ExecNotificationQuery(strQuery);
var ws = new ActiveXObject("WScript.Shell");
var fso = new ActiveXObject("Scripting.FileSystemObject");
var txtstream = fso.OpenTextFile(ws.CurrentDirectory + "\\Win32_Process.hta",
2, true, -2);
txtstream.WriteLine("<html xmlns='http://www.w3.org/1999/xhtml'>");
txtstream.WriteLine("<head>");
txtstream.WriteLine("<HTA:APPLICATION ");
txtstream.WriteLine("ID = ""Process"" ");
txtstream.WriteLine("APPLICATIONNAME = ""Process"" ");
txtstream.WriteLine("SCROLL = ""yes"" ");
txtstream.WriteLine("SINGLEINSTANCE = ""yes"" ");
txtstream.WriteLine("WINDOWSTATE = ""maximize"" >");
txtstream.WriteLine("<style type='text/css'>");
txtstream.WriteLine("th");
txtstream.WriteLine("{");
txtstream.WriteLine("    COLOR: darkred;");
txtstream.WriteLine("    BACKGROUND-COLOR: white;");
txtstream.WriteLine("    FONT-FAMILY:font-family: Cambria, serif;");
txtstream.WriteLine("    FONT-SIZE: 12px;");
txtstream.WriteLine("    text-align: left;");
txtstream.WriteLine("    white-Space: nowrap;");
txtstream.WriteLine("}");
txtstream.WriteLine("td");
txtstream.WriteLine("{");
txtstream.WriteLine("    COLOR: navy;");
txtstream.WriteLine("    BACKGROUND-COLOR: white;");
txtstream.WriteLine("    FONT-FAMILY: font-family: Cambria, serif;");
txtstream.WriteLine("    FONT-SIZE: 12px;");
txtstream.WriteLine("    text-align: left;");
```

```
txtstream.WriteLine("    white-Space: nowrap;");
txtstream.WriteLine("}");
txtstream.WriteLine("</style>");
txtstream.WriteLine("<title>Win32_Process</title>");
txtstream.WriteLine("</head>");
txtstream.WriteLine("<body>");
txtstream.WriteLine("<table border='0' Cellspacing='3' cellpadding = '3'>");

var Names;
var Cols;
var Rows;
var x = 0;

var v = 0;
while(v < 0)
{
    var ti = ex.NextEvent(-1);
    var obj = ti.Properties_.Item("Targetinstance").Value;
    if(v == 0)
    {
        Names = new Array[obj.Properties_.Count];
        Cols = new Array[obj.Properties_.Count];
        Rows = new Array[4];
        var propEnum = new Enumerator(obj.Properties_);
        for (; !propEnum.atEnd(); propEnum.moveNext())
        {
            var prop = propEnum.item();
            Names[x] = prop.Name;
            Cols[x] = GetValue(prop.Name, obj);
            x = x + 1;
        }
        Rows[v] = Cols;
        x = 0;
        v = v + 1;
    }
    else
    {
        var propEnum = new Enumerator(obj.Properties_);
        for (; !propEnum.atEnd(); propEnum.moveNext())
        {
```

```
            var prop = propEnum.item();
            Cols[x] = GetValue(prop.Name, obj);
            x = x + 1;
        }
        Rows[v] = Cols;
        x = 0;
        v = v + 1;
    }
}
for(var a = 0;a < Names.Count; a++)
{
    txtstream.WriteLine("<tr><th align='left' nowrap>" + Names[a] + "</th>");
    for(var b = 0;b < Rows.Count; b++)
    {
        var C = Rows[b];
        txtstream.WriteLine("<td style='font-family:Calibri, Sans-Serif;font-size:
12px;color:navy;' align='left' nowrap='true'><a href='" + C[x] + "'>" + C[x] +
"</a></td>");
    }
    txtstream.WriteLine("</tr>");
}
txtstream.WriteLine("</table>");
txtstream.WriteLine("</body>");
txtstream.WriteLine("</html>");
txtstream.close();
function GetValue(Name, obj)
{
    var tempstr = new String();
    var tempstr1 = new String();
    var tName = new String();
    tempstr1 = obj.GetObjectText_();
    var re = /"/g;
    tempstr1 = tempstr1.replace(re , "");
    var pos;
    tName = Name + " = ";
    pos = tempstr1.indexOf(tName);
    if (pos > -1)
    {
        pos = pos + tName.length;
        tempstr = tempstr1.substring(pos, tempstr1.length);
```

```
        pos = tempstr.indexOf(";");
        tempstr = tempstr.substring(0, pos);
        tempstr = tempstr.replace("{", "");
        tempstr = tempstr.replace("}", "");
        if (tempstr.length > 13)
        {
            if (obj.Properties_(Name).CIMType == 101)
            {
                tempstr = tempstr.substr(4, 2) + "/" + tempstr.substr(6, 2) + "/" +
tempstr.substr(0, 3) + " " + tempstr.substr(8, 2) + ":" + tempstr.substr(10, 2) + ":" +
tempstr.substr(12, 2);
            }
        }
        return tempstr;
    }
    else
    {
        return "";
    }
}
```

Vertical Report with a listbox.

```
    var locator = new ActiveXObject("WbemScripting.SWbemLocator");
    var svc = locator.ConnectServer(".", "root\\cimv2");
    svc.Security_.AuthenticationLevel = 6;
    svc.Security_.ImpersonationLevel = 3;
    var strQuery = "Select * From ___InstanceDeletionEvent WITHIN 1 where
TargetInstance ISA'Win32_Process'");
    var es = svc.ExecNotificationQuery(strQuery);
    var ws = new ActiveXObject("WScript.Shell");
    var fso = new ActiveXObject("Scripting.FileSystemObject");
    var txtstream = fso.OpenTextFile(ws.CurrentDirectory + "\\Win32_Process.hta",
2, true, -2);
    txtstream.WriteLine("<html xmlns='http://www.w3.org/1999/xhtml'>");
    txtstream.WriteLine("<head>");
    txtstream.WriteLine("<HTA:APPLICATION ");
    txtstream.WriteLine("ID = ""Process"" ");
    txtstream.WriteLine("APPLICATIONNAME = ""Process"" ");
```

```
txtstream.WriteLine("SCROLL = ""yes"" ");
txtstream.WriteLine("SINGLEINSTANCE = ""yes"" ");
txtstream.WriteLine("WINDOWSTATE = ""maximize"" >");
txtstream.WriteLine("<style type='text/css'>");
txtstream.WriteLine("th");
txtstream.WriteLine("{");
txtstream.WriteLine("   COLOR: darkred;");
txtstream.WriteLine("   BACKGROUND-COLOR: white;");
txtstream.WriteLine("   FONT-FAMILY:font-family: Cambria, serif;");
txtstream.WriteLine("   FONT-SIZE: 12px;");
txtstream.WriteLine("   text-align: left;");
txtstream.WriteLine("   white-Space: nowrap;");
txtstream.WriteLine("}");
txtstream.WriteLine("td");
txtstream.WriteLine("{");
txtstream.WriteLine("   COLOR: navy;");
txtstream.WriteLine("   BACKGROUND-COLOR: white;");
txtstream.WriteLine("   FONT-FAMILY: font-family: Cambria, serif;");
txtstream.WriteLine("   FONT-SIZE: 12px;");
txtstream.WriteLine("   text-align: left;");
txtstream.WriteLine("   white-Space: nowrap;");
txtstream.WriteLine("}");
txtstream.WriteLine("</style>");
txtstream.WriteLine("<title>Win32_Process</title>");
txtstream.WriteLine("</head>");
txtstream.WriteLine("<body>");
txtstream.WriteLine("<table border='0' Cellspacing='3' cellpadding = '3'>");

var Names;
var Cols;
var Rows;
var x = 0;

var v = 0;
while(v < 0)
{
   var ti = ex.NextEvent(-1);
   var obj = ti.Properties_.Item("Targetinstance").Value;
   if(v == 0)
   {
```

```
        Names = new Array[obj.Properties_.Count];
        Cols = new Array[obj.Properties_.Count];
        Rows = new Array[4];
        var propEnum = new Enumerator(obj.Properties_);
        for (; !propEnum.atEnd(); propEnum.moveNext())
        {
            var prop = propEnum.item();
            Names[x] = prop.Name;
            Cols[x] = GetValue(prop.Name, obj);
            x = x + 1;
        }
        Rows[v] = Cols;
        x = 0;
        v = v + 1;
    }
    else
    {
        var propEnum = new Enumerator(obj.Properties_);
        for (; !propEnum.atEnd(); propEnum.moveNext())
        {
            var prop = propEnum.item();
            Cols[x] = GetValue(prop.Name, obj);
            x = x + 1;
        }
        Rows[v] = Cols;
        x = 0;
        v = v + 1;
    }
}
for(var a = 0;a < Names.Count; a++)
{
    txtstream.WriteLine("<tr><th align='left' nowrap>" + Names[a] + "</th>");
    for(var b = 0;b < Rows.Count; b++)
    {
        var C = Rows[b];
        txtstream.WriteLine("<td style='font-family:Calibri, Sans-Serif;font-size:
12px;color:navy;' align='left' nowrap='true'><select multiple><option value = '''" +
C[x] + "'''>" + C[x] + "</option></select></td>");
    }
    txtstream.WriteLine("</tr>");
```

```
        }
    txtstream.WriteLine("</table>");
    txtstream.WriteLine("</body>");
    txtstream.WriteLine("</html>");
    txtstream.close();
    function GetValue(Name, obj)
    {
        var tempstr = new String();
        var tempstr1 = new String();
        var tName = new String();
        tempstr1 = obj.GetObjectText_();
        var re = /"/g;
        tempstr1 = tempstr1.replace(re , "");
        var pos;
        tName = Name + " = ";
        pos = tempstr1.indexOf(tName);
        if (pos > -1)
        {
            pos = pos + tName.length;
            tempstr = tempstr1.substring(pos, tempstr1.length);
            pos = tempstr.indexOf(";");
            tempstr = tempstr.substring(0, pos);
            tempstr = tempstr.replace("{", "");
            tempstr = tempstr.replace("}", "");
            if (tempstr.length > 13)
            {
                if (obj.Properties_(Name).CIMType == 101)
                {
                 tempstr = tempstr.substr(4, 2) + "/"  + tempstr.substr(6, 2) + "/" +
tempstr.substr(0, 3) + " " + tempstr.substr(8, 2) + ":" + tempstr.substr(10, 2) + ":" +
tempstr.substr(12, 2);
                }
            }
            return tempstr;
        }
        else
        {
            return "";
        }
    }
```

Vertical Report with a textarea.

```
var locator = new ActiveXObject("WbemScripting.SWbemLocator");
var svc = locator.ConnectServer(".", "root\\cimv2");
svc.Security_.AuthenticationLevel = 6;
svc.Security_.ImpersonationLevel = 3;
var strQuery = "Select * From __InstanceDeletionEvent WITHIN 1 where
TargetInstance ISA'Win32_Process'");
var es = svc.ExecNotificationQuery(strQuery);
var ws = new ActiveXObject("WScript.Shell");
var fso = new ActiveXObject("Scripting.FileSystemObject");
var txtstream = fso.OpenTextFile(ws.CurrentDirectory + "\\Win32_Process.hta",
2, true, -2);
txtstream.WriteLine("<html xmlns='http://www.w3.org/1999/xhtml'>");
txtstream.WriteLine("<head>");
txtstream.WriteLine("<HTA:APPLICATION ");
txtstream.WriteLine("ID = ""Process"" ");
txtstream.WriteLine("APPLICATIONNAME = ""Process"" ");
txtstream.WriteLine("SCROLL = ""yes"" ");
txtstream.WriteLine("SINGLEINSTANCE = ""yes"" ");
txtstream.WriteLine("WINDOWSTATE = ""maximize"" >");
txtstream.WriteLine("<style type='text/css'>");
txtstream.WriteLine("th");
txtstream.WriteLine("{");
txtstream.WriteLine("    COLOR: darkred;");
txtstream.WriteLine("    BACKGROUND-COLOR: white;");
txtstream.WriteLine("    FONT-FAMILY:font-family: Cambria, serif;");
txtstream.WriteLine("    FONT-SIZE: 12px;");
txtstream.WriteLine("    text-align: left;");
txtstream.WriteLine("    white-Space: nowrap;");
txtstream.WriteLine("}");
txtstream.WriteLine("td");
txtstream.WriteLine("{");
txtstream.WriteLine("    COLOR: navy;");
txtstream.WriteLine("    BACKGROUND-COLOR: white;");
txtstream.WriteLine("    FONT-FAMILY: font-family: Cambria, serif;");
txtstream.WriteLine("    FONT-SIZE: 12px;");
txtstream.WriteLine("    text-align: left;");
```

```
txtstream.WriteLine("    white-Space: nowrap;");
txtstream.WriteLine("}");
txtstream.WriteLine("</style>");
txtstream.WriteLine("<title>Win32_Process</title>");
txtstream.WriteLine("</head>");
txtstream.WriteLine("<body>");
txtstream.WriteLine("<table border='0' Cellspacing='3' cellpadding = '3'>");

var Names;
var Cols;
var Rows;
var x = 0;

var v = 0;
while(v < 0)
{
   var ti = ex.NextEvent(-1);
   var obj = ti.Properties_.Item("Targetinstance").Value;
   if(v == 0)
   {
      Names = new Array[obj.Properties_.Count];
      Cols = new Array[obj.Properties_.Count];
      Rows = new Array[4];
      var propEnum = new Enumerator(obj.Properties_);
      for (; !propEnum.atEnd(); propEnum.moveNext())
      {
         var prop = propEnum.item();
         Names[x] = prop.Name;
         Cols[x] = GetValue(prop.Name, obj);
         x = x + 1;
      }
      Rows[v] = Cols;
      x = 0;
      v = v + 1;
   }
   else
   {
      var propEnum = new Enumerator(obj.Properties_);
      for (; !propEnum.atEnd(); propEnum.moveNext())
      {
```

```
            var prop = propEnum.item();
            Cols[x] = GetValue(prop.Name, obj);
            x = x + 1;
        }
        Rows[v] = Cols;
        x = 0;
        v = v + 1;
    }
}
for(var a = 0;a < Names.Count; a++)
{
    txtstream.WriteLine("<tr><th align='left' nowrap>" + Names[a] + "</th>");
    for(var b = 0;b < Rows.Count; b++)
    {
        var C = Rows[b];
        txtstream.WriteLine("<td style='font-family:Calibri, Sans-Serif;font-size:
12px;color:navy;' align='left' nowrap='true'><textarea>" + C[x] +
"</textarea></td>");
    }
    txtstream.WriteLine("</tr>");
}
txtstream.WriteLine("</table>");
txtstream.WriteLine("</body>");
txtstream.WriteLine("</html>");
txtstream.close();
function GetValue(Name, obj)
{
    var tempstr = new String();
    var tempstr1 = new String();
    var tName = new String();
    tempstr1 = obj.GetObjectText_();
    var re = /"/g;
    tempstr1 = tempstr1.replace(re , "");
    var pos;
    tName = Name + " = ";
    pos = tempstr1.indexOf(tName);
    if (pos > -1)
    {
        pos = pos + tName.length;
        tempstr = tempstr1.substring(pos, tempstr1.length);
```

```
            pos = tempstr.indexOf(";");
            tempstr = tempstr.substring(0, pos);
            tempstr = tempstr.replace("{", "");
            tempstr = tempstr.replace("}", "");
            if (tempstr.length > 13)
            {
                if (obj.Properties_(Name).CIMType == 101)
                {
                    tempstr = tempstr.substr(4, 2) + "/" + tempstr.substr(6, 2) + "/" +
tempstr.substr(0, 3) + " " + tempstr.substr(8, 2) + ":" + tempstr.substr(10, 2) + ":" +
tempstr.substr(12, 2);
                }
            }
            return tempstr;
        }
        else
        {
            return "";
        }
    }
```

Vertical Report with a textbox.

```
    var locator = new ActiveXObject("WbemScripting.SWbemLocator");
    var svc = locator.ConnectServer(".", "root\\cimv2");
    svc.Security_.AuthenticationLevel = 6;
    svc.Security_.ImpersonationLevel = 3;
    var strQuery = "Select * From ___InstanceDeletionEvent WITHIN 1 where
TargetInstance ISA'Win32_Process'");
    var es = svc.ExecNotificationQuery(strQuery);
    var ws = new ActiveXObject("WScript.Shell");
    var fso = new ActiveXObject("Scripting.FileSystemObject");
    var txtstream = fso.OpenTextFile(ws.CurrentDirectory + "\\Win32_Process.hta",
2, true, -2);
    txtstream.WriteLine("<html xmlns='http://www.w3.org/1999/xhtml'>");
    txtstream.WriteLine("<head>");
    txtstream.WriteLine("<HTA:APPLICATION ");
    txtstream.WriteLine("ID = ""Process"" ");
    txtstream.WriteLine("APPLICATIONNAME = ""Process"" ");
```

```
txtstream.WriteLine("SCROLL = ""yes"" ");
txtstream.WriteLine("SINGLEINSTANCE = ""yes"" ");
txtstream.WriteLine("WINDOWSTATE = ""maximize"" >");
txtstream.WriteLine("<style type='text/css'>");
txtstream.WriteLine("th");
txtstream.WriteLine("{");
txtstream.WriteLine("   COLOR: darkred;");
txtstream.WriteLine("   BACKGROUND-COLOR: white;");
txtstream.WriteLine("   FONT-FAMILY:font-family: Cambria, serif;");
txtstream.WriteLine("   FONT-SIZE: 12px;");
txtstream.WriteLine("   text-align: left;");
txtstream.WriteLine("   white-Space: nowrap;");
txtstream.WriteLine("}");
txtstream.WriteLine("td");
txtstream.WriteLine("{");
txtstream.WriteLine("   COLOR: navy;");
txtstream.WriteLine("   BACKGROUND-COLOR: white;");
txtstream.WriteLine("   FONT-FAMILY: font-family: Cambria, serif;");
txtstream.WriteLine("   FONT-SIZE: 12px;");
txtstream.WriteLine("   text-align: left;");
txtstream.WriteLine("   white-Space: nowrap;");
txtstream.WriteLine("}");
txtstream.WriteLine("</style>");
txtstream.WriteLine("<title>Win32_Process</title>");
txtstream.WriteLine("</head>");
txtstream.WriteLine("<body>");
txtstream.WriteLine("<table border='0' Cellspacing='3' cellpadding = '3'>");

var Names;
var Cols;
var Rows;
var x = 0;

var v = 0;
while(v < 0)
{
    var ti = ex.NextEvent(-1);
    var obj = ti.Properties_.Item("Targetinstance").Value;
    if(v == 0)
    {
```

```
        Names = new Array[obj.Properties_.Count];
        Cols = new Array[obj.Properties_.Count];
        Rows = new Array[4];
        var propEnum = new Enumerator(obj.Properties_);
        for (; !propEnum.atEnd(); propEnum.moveNext())
        {
            var prop = propEnum.item();
            Names[x] = prop.Name;
            Cols[x] = GetValue(prop.Name, obj);
            x = x + 1;
        }
        Rows[v] = Cols;
        x = 0;
        v = v + 1;
    }
    else
    {
        var propEnum = new Enumerator(obj.Properties_);
        for (; !propEnum.atEnd(); propEnum.moveNext())
        {
            var prop = propEnum.item();
            Cols[x] = GetValue(prop.Name, obj);
            x = x + 1;
        }
        Rows[v] = Cols;
        x = 0;
        v = v + 1;
    }
}
for(var a = 0;a < Names.Count; a++)
{
    txtstream.WriteLine("<tr><th align='left' nowrap>" + Names[a] + "</th>");
    for(var b = 0;b < Rows.Count; b++)
    {
        var C = Rows[b];
        txtstream.WriteLine("<td style='font-family:Calibri, Sans-Serif;font-size:
12px;color:navy;' align='left' nowrap='true'><input type=text value='""" + C[x] +
"""'></input></td>");
    }
    txtstream.WriteLine("</tr>");
```

```
        }
        txtstream.WriteLine("</table>");
        txtstream.WriteLine("</body>");
        txtstream.WriteLine("</html>");
        txtstream.close();
        function GetValue(Name, obj)
        {
            var tempstr = new String();
            var tempstr1 = new String();
            var tName = new String();
            tempstr1 = obj.GetObjectText_();
            var re = /"/g;
            tempstr1 = tempstr1.replace(re , "");
            var pos;
            tName = Name + " = ";
            pos = tempstr1.indexOf(tName);
            if (pos > -1)
            {
                pos = pos + tName.length;
                tempstr = tempstr1.substring(pos, tempstr1.length);
                pos = tempstr.indexOf(";");
                tempstr = tempstr.substring(0, pos);
                tempstr = tempstr.replace("{", "");
                tempstr = tempstr.replace("}", "");
                if (tempstr.length > 13)
                {
                    if (obj.Properties_(Name).CIMType == 101)
                    {
                    tempstr = tempstr.substr(4, 2) + "/"  + tempstr.substr(6, 2) + "/" +
tempstr.substr(0, 3) + " " + tempstr.substr(8, 2) + ":" + tempstr.substr(10, 2) + ":" +
tempstr.substr(12, 2);
                    }
                }
                return tempstr;
            }
            else
            {
                return "";
            }
        }
```

HTA Tables

Horizontal Table with no additional tags.

```
var locator = new ActiveXObject("WbemScripting.SWbemLocator");
var svc = locator.ConnectServer(".", "root\\cimv2");
svc.Security_.AuthenticationLevel = 6;
svc.Security_.ImpersonationLevel = 3;
var strQuery = "Select * From ___InstanceDeletionEvent WITHIN 1 where
TargetInstance ISA'Win32_Process'");
var es = svc.ExecNotificationQuery(strQuery);
var ws = new ActiveXObject("WScript.Shell");
var fso = new ActiveXObject("Scripting.FileSystemObject");
var txtstream = fso.OpenTextFile(ws.CurrentDirectory + "\\Win32_Process.hta",
2, true, -2);
txtstream.WriteLine("<html xmlns='http://www.w3.org/1999/xhtml'>");
txtstream.WriteLine("<head>");
txtstream.WriteLine("<HTA:APPLICATION ");
txtstream.WriteLine("ID = ""Process"" ");
txtstream.WriteLine("APPLICATIONNAME = ""Process"" ");
txtstream.WriteLine("SCROLL = ""yes"" ");
txtstream.WriteLine("SINGLEINSTANCE = ""yes"" ");
txtstream.WriteLine("WINDOWSTATE = ""maximize"" >");
txtstream.WriteLine("<style type='text/css'>");
```

```
txtstream.WriteLine("th");
txtstream.WriteLine("{");
txtstream.WriteLine("    COLOR: darkred;");
txtstream.WriteLine("    BACKGROUND-COLOR: white;");
txtstream.WriteLine("    FONT-FAMILY:font-family: Cambria, serif;");
txtstream.WriteLine("    FONT-SIZE: 12px;");
txtstream.WriteLine("    text-align: left;");
txtstream.WriteLine("    white-Space: nowrap;");
txtstream.WriteLine("}");
txtstream.WriteLine("td");
txtstream.WriteLine("{");
txtstream.WriteLine("    COLOR: navy;");
txtstream.WriteLine("    BACKGROUND-COLOR: white;");
txtstream.WriteLine("    FONT-FAMILY: font-family: Cambria, serif;");
txtstream.WriteLine("    FONT-SIZE: 12px;");
txtstream.WriteLine("    text-align: left;");
txtstream.WriteLine("    white-Space: nowrap;");
txtstream.WriteLine("}");
txtstream.WriteLine("</style>");
txtstream.WriteLine("<title>Win32_Process</title>");
txtstream.WriteLine("</head>");
txtstream.WriteLine("<body>");
txtstream.WriteLine("<table border='1' Cellspacing='3' cellpadding = '3'>");
var v=0;
while(v < 0)
{
    var ti = ex.NextEvent(-1);
    var obj = ti.Properties_.Item("Targetinstance").Value;
    if(v == 0)
    {
        txtstream.WriteLine("<tr>");
        var propEnum = new Enumerator(obj.Properties_);
        for (; !propEnum.atEnd(); propEnum.moveNext())
        {
            var prop = propEnum.item();
            txtstream.WriteLine("<th align='left' nowrap>" + prop.Name + "</th>");
        }
        txtstream.WriteLine("</tr>");
        propEnum.ReSet();
    }
```

```
        txtstream.WriteLine("<tr>");
        for (; !propEnum.atEnd(); propEnum.moveNext())
        {
            var prop = propEnum.item();
            txtstream.WriteLine("<td style='font-family:Calibri, Sans-Serif;font-size:
12px;color:navy;' align='left' nowrap='nowrap'>" + GetValue(prop.Name, obj) +
"</td>");
        }
        txtstream.WriteLine("</tr>");
        v = v + 1;
    }
    txtstream.WriteLine("</table>");
    txtstream.WriteLine("</body>");
    txtstream.WriteLine("</html>");
    txtstream.close();
    function GetValue(Name, obj)
    {
        var tempstr = new String();
        var tempstr1 = new String();
        var tName = new String();
        tempstr1 = obj.GetObjectText_();
        var re = /"/g;
        tempstr1 = tempstr1.replace(re , "");
        var pos;
        tName = Name + " = ";
        pos = tempstr1.indexOf(tName);
        if (pos > -1)
        {
            pos = pos + tName.length;
            tempstr = tempstr1.substring(pos, tempstr1.length);
            pos = tempstr.indexOf(";");
            tempstr = tempstr.substring(0, pos);
            tempstr = tempstr.replace("{", "");
            tempstr = tempstr.replace("}", "");
            if (tempstr.length > 13)
            {
                if (obj.Properties_(Name).CIMType == 101)
                {
```

```
          tempstr = tempstr.substr(4, 2) + "/"  + tempstr.substr(6, 2) + "/" +
tempstr.substr(0, 3) + " " + tempstr.substr(8, 2) + ":" + tempstr.substr(10, 2) + ":" +
tempstr.substr(12, 2);
       }
     }
     return tempstr;
   }
   else
   {
     return "";
   }
}
```

Horizontal Table with a combobox.

```
var locator = new ActiveXObject("WbemScripting.SWbemLocator");
var svc = locator.ConnectServer(".", "root\\cimv2");
svc.Security_.AuthenticationLevel = 6;
svc.Security_.ImpersonationLevel = 3;
var strQuery = "Select * From ___InstanceDeletionEvent WITHIN 1 where
TargetInstance ISA'Win32_Process'");
var es = svc.ExecNotificationQuery(strQuery);
var ws = new ActiveXObject("WScript.Shell");
var fso = new ActiveXObject("Scripting.FileSystemObject");
var txtstream = fso.OpenTextFile(ws.CurrentDirectory + "\\Win32_Process.hta",
2, true, -2);
txtstream.WriteLine("<html xmlns='http://www.w3.org/1999/xhtml'>");
txtstream.WriteLine("<head>");
txtstream.WriteLine("<HTA:APPLICATION ");
txtstream.WriteLine("ID = ""Process"" ");
txtstream.WriteLine("APPLICATIONNAME = ""Process"" ");
txtstream.WriteLine("SCROLL = ""yes"" ");
txtstream.WriteLine("SINGLEINSTANCE = ""yes"" ");
txtstream.WriteLine("WINDOWSTATE = ""maximize"" >");
txtstream.WriteLine("<style type='text/css'>");
txtstream.WriteLine("th");
txtstream.WriteLine("{");
txtstream.WriteLine("   COLOR: darkred;");
txtstream.WriteLine("   BACKGROUND-COLOR: white;");
```

```
txtstream.WriteLine("    FONT-FAMILY:font-family: Cambria, serif;");
txtstream.WriteLine("    FONT-SIZE: 12px;");
txtstream.WriteLine("    text-align: left;");
txtstream.WriteLine("    white-Space: nowrap;");
txtstream.WriteLine("}");
txtstream.WriteLine("td");
txtstream.WriteLine("{");
txtstream.WriteLine("    COLOR: navy;");
txtstream.WriteLine("    BACKGROUND-COLOR: white;");
txtstream.WriteLine("    FONT-FAMILY: font-family: Cambria, serif;");
txtstream.WriteLine("    FONT-SIZE: 12px;");
txtstream.WriteLine("    text-align: left;");
txtstream.WriteLine("    white-Space: nowrap;");
txtstream.WriteLine("}");
txtstream.WriteLine("</style>");
txtstream.WriteLine("<title>Win32_Process</title>");
txtstream.WriteLine("</head>");
txtstream.WriteLine("<body>");
txtstream.WriteLine("<table border='1' Cellspacing='3' cellpadding = '3'>");
var v=0;
while(v < 0)
{
   var ti = ex.NextEvent(-1);
   var obj = ti.Properties_.Item("Targetinstance").Value;
   if(v == 0)
   {
      txtstream.WriteLine("<tr>");
      var propEnum = new Enumerator(obj.Properties_);
      for (; !propEnum.atEnd(); propEnum.moveNext())
      {
         var prop = propEnum.item();
         txtstream.WriteLine("<th align='left' nowrap>" + prop.Name + "</th>");
      }
      txtstream.WriteLine("</tr>");
      propEnum.ReSet();
   }
   txtstream.WriteLine("<tr>");
   for (; !propEnum.atEnd(); propEnum.moveNext())
   {
      var prop = propEnum.item();
```

```
            txtstream.WriteLine("<td style='font-family:Calibri, Sans-Serif;font-size:
12px;color:navy;' align='left' nowrap='true'><select><option value = '" +
GetValue(prop.Name, obj) + "'>" + GetValue(prop.Name, obj) +
"</option></select></td>");
            }
        txtstream.WriteLine("</tr>");
        v = v + 1;
    }
    txtstream.WriteLine("</table>");
    txtstream.WriteLine("</body>");
    txtstream.WriteLine("</html>");
    txtstream.close();
    function GetValue(Name, obj)
    {
        var tempstr = new String();
        var tempstr1 = new String();
        var tName = new String();
        tempstr1 = obj.GetObjectText_();
        var re = /"/g;
        tempstr1 = tempstr1.replace(re , "");
        var pos;
        tName = Name + " = ";
        pos = tempstr1.indexOf(tName);
        if (pos > -1)
        {
            pos = pos + tName.length;
            tempstr = tempstr1.substring(pos, tempstr1.length);
            pos = tempstr.indexOf(";");
            tempstr = tempstr.substring(0, pos);
            tempstr = tempstr.replace("{", "");
            tempstr = tempstr.replace("}", "");
            if (tempstr.length > 13)
            {
                if (obj.Properties_(Name).CIMType == 101)
                {
                    tempstr = tempstr.substr(4, 2) + "/" + tempstr.substr(6, 2) + "/" +
tempstr.substr(0, 3) + " " + tempstr.substr(8, 2) + ":" + tempstr.substr(10, 2) + ":" +
tempstr.substr(12, 2);
                }
            }
```

```
        return tempstr;
    }
    else
    {
        return "";
    }
}
```

Horizontal Table with a link.

```
    var locator = new ActiveXObject("WbemScripting.SWbemLocator");
    var svc = locator.ConnectServer(".", "root\\cimv2");
    svc.Security_.AuthenticationLevel = 6;
    svc.Security_.ImpersonationLevel = 3;
    var strQuery = "Select * From ___InstanceDeletionEvent WITHIN 1 where
TargetInstance ISA'Win32_Process'");
    var es = svc.ExecNotificationQuery(strQuery);
    var ws = new ActiveXObject("WScript.Shell");
    var fso = new ActiveXObject("Scripting.FileSystemObject");
    var txtstream = fso.OpenTextFile(ws.CurrentDirectory + "\\Win32_Process.hta",
2, true, -2);
    txtstream.WriteLine("<html xmlns='http://www.w3.org/1999/xhtml'>");
    txtstream.WriteLine("<head>");
    txtstream.WriteLine("<HTA:APPLICATION ");
    txtstream.WriteLine("ID = ""Process"" ");
    txtstream.WriteLine("APPLICATIONNAME = ""Process"" ");
    txtstream.WriteLine("SCROLL = ""yes"" ");
    txtstream.WriteLine("SINGLEINSTANCE = ""yes"" ");
    txtstream.WriteLine("WINDOWSTATE = ""maximize"" >");
    txtstream.WriteLine("<style type='text/css'>");
    txtstream.WriteLine("th");
    txtstream.WriteLine("{");
    txtstream.WriteLine("    COLOR: darkred;");
    txtstream.WriteLine("    BACKGROUND-COLOR: white;");
    txtstream.WriteLine("    FONT-FAMILY:font-family: Cambria, serif;");
    txtstream.WriteLine("    FONT-SIZE: 12px;");
    txtstream.WriteLine("    text-align: left;");
    txtstream.WriteLine("    white-Space: nowrap;");
    txtstream.WriteLine("}");
```

```
txtstream.WriteLine("td");
txtstream.WriteLine("{");
txtstream.WriteLine("   COLOR: navy;");
txtstream.WriteLine("   BACKGROUND-COLOR: white;");
txtstream.WriteLine("   FONT-FAMILY: font-family: Cambria, serif;");
txtstream.WriteLine("   FONT-SIZE: 12px;");
txtstream.WriteLine("   text-align: left;");
txtstream.WriteLine("   white-Space: nowrap;");
txtstream.WriteLine("}");
txtstream.WriteLine("</style>");
txtstream.WriteLine("<title>Win32_Process</title>");
txtstream.WriteLine("</head>");
txtstream.WriteLine("<body>");
txtstream.WriteLine("<table border='1' Cellspacing='3' cellpadding = '3'>");
var v=0;
while(v < 0)
{
   var ti = ex.NextEvent(-1);
   var obj = ti.Properties_.Item("Targetinstance").Value;
   if(v == 0)
   {
      txtstream.WriteLine("<tr>");
      var propEnum = new Enumerator(obj.Properties_);
      for (; !propEnum.atEnd(); propEnum.moveNext())
      {
         var prop = propEnum.item();
         txtstream.WriteLine("<th align='left' nowrap>" + prop.Name + "</th>");
      }
      txtstream.WriteLine("</tr>");
      propEnum.ReSet();
   }
   txtstream.WriteLine("<tr>");
   for (; !propEnum.atEnd(); propEnum.moveNext())
   {
      var prop = propEnum.item();
      txtstream.WriteLine("<td style='font-family:Calibri, Sans-Serif;font-size:
12px;color:navy;' align='left' nowrap='true'><a href='" + GetValue(prop.Name, obj)
+ "'>" + GetValue(prop.Name, obj) + "</a></td>");
   }
   txtstream.WriteLine("</tr>");
```

```
        v = v + 1;
    }
    txtstream.WriteLine("</table>");
    txtstream.WriteLine("</body>");
    txtstream.WriteLine("</html>");
    txtstream.close();
    function GetValue(Name, obj)
    {
        var tempstr = new String();
        var tempstr1 = new String();
        var tName = new String();
        tempstr1 = obj.GetObjectText_();
        var re = /"/g;
        tempstr1 = tempstr1.replace(re , "");
        var pos;
        tName = Name + " = ";
        pos = tempstr1.indexOf(tName);
        if (pos > -1)
        {
            pos = pos + tName.length;
            tempstr = tempstr1.substring(pos, tempstr1.length);
            pos = tempstr.indexOf(";");
            tempstr = tempstr.substring(0, pos);
            tempstr = tempstr.replace("{", "");
            tempstr = tempstr.replace("}", "");
            if (tempstr.length > 13)
            {
                if (obj.Properties_(Name).CIMType == 101)
                {
                    tempstr = tempstr.substr(4, 2) + "/"  + tempstr.substr(6, 2) + "/" +
tempstr.substr(0, 3) + " " + tempstr.substr(8, 2) + ":" + tempstr.substr(10, 2) + ":" +
tempstr.substr(12, 2);
                }
            }
            return tempstr;
        }
        else
        {
            return "";
        }
```

}

Horizontal Table with a listbox.

```
var locator = new ActiveXObject("WbemScripting.SWbemLocator");
var svc = locator.ConnectServer(".", "root\\cimv2");
svc.Security_.AuthenticationLevel = 6;
svc.Security_.ImpersonationLevel = 3;
var strQuery = "Select * From ___InstanceDeletionEvent WITHIN 1 where
TargetInstance ISA'Win32_Process'");
var es = svc.ExecNotificationQuery(strQuery);
var ws = new ActiveXObject("WScript.Shell");
var fso = new ActiveXObject("Scripting.FileSystemObject");
var txtstream = fso.OpenTextFile(ws.CurrentDirectory + "\\Win32_Process.hta",
2, true, -2);
txtstream.WriteLine("<html xmlns='http://www.w3.org/1999/xhtml'>");
txtstream.WriteLine("<head>");
txtstream.WriteLine("<HTA:APPLICATION ");
txtstream.WriteLine("ID = ""Process"" ");
txtstream.WriteLine("APPLICATIONNAME = ""Process"" ");
txtstream.WriteLine("SCROLL = ""yes"" ");
txtstream.WriteLine("SINGLEINSTANCE = ""yes"" ");
txtstream.WriteLine("WINDOWSTATE = ""maximize"" >");
txtstream.WriteLine("<style type='text/css'>");
txtstream.WriteLine("th");
txtstream.WriteLine("{");
txtstream.WriteLine("    COLOR: darkred;");
txtstream.WriteLine("    BACKGROUND-COLOR: white;");
txtstream.WriteLine("    FONT-FAMILY:font-family: Cambria, serif;");
txtstream.WriteLine("    FONT-SIZE: 12px;");
txtstream.WriteLine("    text-align: left;");
txtstream.WriteLine("    white-Space: nowrap;");
txtstream.WriteLine("}");
txtstream.WriteLine("td");
txtstream.WriteLine("{");
txtstream.WriteLine("    COLOR: navy;");
txtstream.WriteLine("    BACKGROUND-COLOR: white;");
txtstream.WriteLine("    FONT-FAMILY: font-family: Cambria, serif;");
txtstream.WriteLine("    FONT-SIZE: 12px;");
```

```
txtstream.WriteLine("    text-align: left;");
txtstream.WriteLine("    white-Space: nowrap;");
txtstream.WriteLine("}");
txtstream.WriteLine("</style>");
txtstream.WriteLine("<title>Win32_Process</title>");
txtstream.WriteLine("</head>");
txtstream.WriteLine("<body>");
txtstream.WriteLine("<table border='1' Cellspacing='3' cellpadding = '3'>");
var v=0;
while(v < 0)
{
    var ti = ex.NextEvent(-1);
    var obj = ti.Properties_.Item("Targetinstance").Value;
    if(v == 0)
    {
        txtstream.WriteLine("<tr>");
        var propEnum = new Enumerator(obj.Properties_);
        for (; !propEnum.atEnd(); propEnum.moveNext())
        {
            var prop = propEnum.item();
            txtstream.WriteLine("<th align='left' nowrap>" + prop.Name + "</th>");
        }
        txtstream.WriteLine("</tr>");
        propEnum.ReSet();
    }
    txtstream.WriteLine("<tr>");
    for (; !propEnum.atEnd(); propEnum.moveNext())
    {
        var prop = propEnum.item();
        txtstream.WriteLine("<td style='font-family:Calibri, Sans-Serif;font-size:
12px;color:navy;' align='left' nowrap='true'><select multiple><option value = '" +
GetValue(prop.Name, obj) + "'>" + GetValue(prop.Name, obj) +
"</option></select></td>");
    }
    txtstream.WriteLine("</tr>");
    v = v + 1;
}
txtstream.WriteLine("</table>");
txtstream.WriteLine("</body>");
txtstream.WriteLine("</html>");
```

```
txtstream.close();
function GetValue(Name, obj)
{
    var tempstr = new String();
    var tempstr1 = new String();
    var tName = new String();
    tempstr1 = obj.GetObjectText_();
    var re = /"/g;
    tempstr1 = tempstr1.replace(re , "");
    var pos;
    tName = Name + " = ";
    pos = tempstr1.indexOf(tName);
    if (pos > -1)
    {
        pos = pos + tName.length;
        tempstr = tempstr1.substring(pos, tempstr1.length);
        pos = tempstr.indexOf(";");
        tempstr = tempstr.substring(0, pos);
        tempstr = tempstr.replace("{", "");
        tempstr = tempstr.replace("}", "");
        if (tempstr.length > 13)
        {
            if (obj.Properties_(Name).CIMType == 101)
            {
                tempstr = tempstr.substr(4, 2) + "/"  + tempstr.substr(6, 2) + "/" +
tempstr.substr(0, 3) + " " + tempstr.substr(8, 2) + ":" + tempstr.substr(10, 2) + ":" +
tempstr.substr(12, 2);
            }
        }
        return tempstr;
    }
    else
    {
        return "";
    }
}
```

Horizontal Table with a textarea.

```
var locator = new ActiveXObject("WbemScripting.SWbemLocator");
var svc = locator.ConnectServer(".", "root\\cimv2");
svc.Security_.AuthenticationLevel = 6;
svc.Security_.ImpersonationLevel = 3;
var strQuery = "Select * From ___InstanceDeletionEvent WITHIN 1 where
TargetInstance ISA'Win32_Process'");
var es = svc.ExecNotificationQuery(strQuery);
var ws = new ActiveXObject("WScript.Shell");
var fso = new ActiveXObject("Scripting.FileSystemObject");
var txtstream = fso.OpenTextFile(ws.CurrentDirectory + "\\Win32_Process.hta",
2, true, -2);
txtstream.WriteLine("<html xmlns='http://www.w3.org/1999/xhtml'>");
txtstream.WriteLine("<head>");
txtstream.WriteLine("<HTA:APPLICATION ");
txtstream.WriteLine("ID = ""Process"" ");
txtstream.WriteLine("APPLICATIONNAME = ""Process"" ");
txtstream.WriteLine("SCROLL = ""yes"" ");
txtstream.WriteLine("SINGLEINSTANCE = ""yes"" ");
txtstream.WriteLine("WINDOWSTATE = ""maximize"" >");
txtstream.WriteLine("<style type='text/css'>");
txtstream.WriteLine("th");
txtstream.WriteLine("{");
txtstream.WriteLine("   COLOR: darkred;");
txtstream.WriteLine("   BACKGROUND-COLOR: white;");
txtstream.WriteLine("   FONT-FAMILY:font-family: Cambria, serif;");
txtstream.WriteLine("   FONT-SIZE: 12px;");
txtstream.WriteLine("   text-align: left;");
txtstream.WriteLine("   white-Space: nowrap;");
txtstream.WriteLine("}");
txtstream.WriteLine("td");
txtstream.WriteLine("{");
txtstream.WriteLine("   COLOR: navy;");
txtstream.WriteLine("   BACKGROUND-COLOR: white;");
txtstream.WriteLine("   FONT-FAMILY: font-family: Cambria, serif;");
txtstream.WriteLine("   FONT-SIZE: 12px;");
txtstream.WriteLine("   text-align: left;");
txtstream.WriteLine("   white-Space: nowrap;");
```

```
txtstream.WriteLine("}");
txtstream.WriteLine("</style>");
txtstream.WriteLine("<title>Win32_Process</title>");
txtstream.WriteLine("</head>");
txtstream.WriteLine("<body>");
txtstream.WriteLine("<table border='1' Cellspacing='3' cellpadding = '3'>");
var v=0;
while(v < 0)
{
    var ti = ex.NextEvent(-1);
    var obj = ti.Properties_.Item("Targetinstance").Value;
    if(v == 0)
    {
        txtstream.WriteLine("<tr>");
        var propEnum = new Enumerator(obj.Properties_);
        for (; !propEnum.atEnd(); propEnum.moveNext())
        {
            var prop = propEnum.item();
            txtstream.WriteLine("<th align='left' nowrap>" + prop.Name + "</th>");
        }
        txtstream.WriteLine("</tr>");
        propEnum.ReSet();
    }
    txtstream.WriteLine("<tr>");
    for (; !propEnum.atEnd(); propEnum.moveNext())
    {
        var prop = propEnum.item();
        txtstream.WriteLine("<td style='font-family:Calibri, Sans-Serif;font-size:
12px;color:navy;' align='left' nowrap='true'><textarea>" + GetValue(prop.Name,
obj) + "</textarea></td>");
    }
    txtstream.WriteLine("</tr>");
    v = v + 1;
}
txtstream.WriteLine("</table>");
txtstream.WriteLine("</body>");
txtstream.WriteLine("</html>");
txtstream.close();
function GetValue(Name, obj)
{
```

```
var tempstr = new String();
var tempstr1 = new String();
var tName = new String();
tempstr1 = obj.GetObjectText_();
var re = /"/g;
tempstr1 = tempstr1.replace(re , "");
var pos;
tName = Name + " = ";
pos = tempstr1.indexOf(tName);
if (pos > -1)
{
    pos = pos + tName.length;
    tempstr = tempstr1.substring(pos, tempstr1.length);
    pos = tempstr.indexOf(";");
    tempstr = tempstr.substring(0, pos);
    tempstr = tempstr.replace("{", "");
    tempstr = tempstr.replace("}", "");
    if (tempstr.length > 13)
    {
        if (obj.Properties_(Name).CIMType == 101)
        {
            tempstr = tempstr.substr(4, 2) + "/" + tempstr.substr(6, 2) + "/" +
tempstr.substr(0, 3) + " " + tempstr.substr(8, 2) + ":" + tempstr.substr(10, 2) + ":" +
tempstr.substr(12, 2);
        }
    }
    return tempstr;
}
else
{
    return "";
}
}
```

Horizontal Table with a textbox.

```
var locator = new ActiveXObject("WbemScripting.SWbemLocator");
var svc = locator.ConnectServer(".", "root\\cimv2");
svc.Security_.AuthenticationLevel = 6;
svc.Security_.ImpersonationLevel = 3;
var strQuery = "Select * From __InstanceDeletionEvent WITHIN 1 where
TargetInstance ISA'Win32_Process'");
var es = svc.ExecNotificationQuery(strQuery);
var ws = new ActiveXObject("WScript.Shell");
var fso = new ActiveXObject("Scripting.FileSystemObject");
var txtstream = fso.OpenTextFile(ws.CurrentDirectory + "\\Win32_Process.hta",
2, true, -2);
txtstream.WriteLine("<html xmlns='http://www.w3.org/1999/xhtml'>");
txtstream.WriteLine("<head>");
txtstream.WriteLine("<HTA:APPLICATION ");
txtstream.WriteLine("ID = ""Process"" ");
txtstream.WriteLine("APPLICATIONNAME = ""Process"" ");
txtstream.WriteLine("SCROLL = ""yes"" ");
txtstream.WriteLine("SINGLEINSTANCE = ""yes"" ");
txtstream.WriteLine("WINDOWSTATE = ""maximize"" >");
txtstream.WriteLine("<style type='text/css'>");
txtstream.WriteLine("th");
txtstream.WriteLine("{");
txtstream.WriteLine("   COLOR: darkred;");
txtstream.WriteLine("   BACKGROUND-COLOR: white;");
txtstream.WriteLine("   FONT-FAMILY:font-family: Cambria, serif;");
txtstream.WriteLine("   FONT-SIZE: 12px;");
txtstream.WriteLine("   text-align: left;");
txtstream.WriteLine("   white-Space: nowrap;");
txtstream.WriteLine("}");
txtstream.WriteLine("td");
txtstream.WriteLine("{");
txtstream.WriteLine("   COLOR: navy;");
txtstream.WriteLine("   BACKGROUND-COLOR: white;");
txtstream.WriteLine("   FONT-FAMILY: font-family: Cambria, serif;");
txtstream.WriteLine("   FONT-SIZE: 12px;");
txtstream.WriteLine("   text-align: left;");
txtstream.WriteLine("   white-Space: nowrap;");
```

```
txtstream.WriteLine("}");
txtstream.WriteLine("</style>");
txtstream.WriteLine("<title>Win32_Process</title>");
txtstream.WriteLine("</head>");
txtstream.WriteLine("<body>");
txtstream.WriteLine("<table border='1' Cellspacing='3' cellpadding = '3'>");
var v=0;
while(v < 0)
{
   var ti = ex.NextEvent(-1);
   var obj = ti.Properties_.Item("Targetinstance").Value;
   if(v == 0)
   {
      txtstream.WriteLine("<tr>");
      var propEnum = new Enumerator(obj.Properties_);
      for (; !propEnum.atEnd(); propEnum.moveNext())
      {
         var prop = propEnum.item();
         txtstream.WriteLine("<th align='left' nowrap>" + prop.Name + "</th>");
      }
      txtstream.WriteLine("</tr>");
      propEnum.ReSet();
   }
   txtstream.WriteLine("<tr>");
   for (; !propEnum.atEnd(); propEnum.moveNext())
   {
      var prop = propEnum.item();
      txtstream.WriteLine("<td style='font-family:Calibri, Sans-Serif;font-size:
12px;color:navy;' align='left' nowrap='true'><input type=text value='" +
GetValue(prop.Name, obj) + "'></input></td>");
   }
   txtstream.WriteLine("</tr>");
   v = v + 1;
}
txtstream.WriteLine("</table>");
txtstream.WriteLine("</body>");
txtstream.WriteLine("</html>");
txtstream.close();
function GetValue(Name, obj)
{
```

```
var tempstr = new String();
var tempstr1 = new String();
var tName = new String();
tempstr1 = obj.GetObjectText_();
var re = /"/g;
tempstr1 = tempstr1.replace(re , "");
var pos;
tName = Name + " = ";
pos = tempstr1.indexOf(tName);
if (pos > -1)
{
    pos = pos + tName.length;
    tempstr = tempstr1.substring(pos, tempstr1.length);
    pos = tempstr.indexOf(";");
    tempstr = tempstr.substring(0, pos);
    tempstr = tempstr.replace("{", "");
    tempstr = tempstr.replace("}", "");
    if (tempstr.length > 13)
    {
        if (obj.Properties_(Name).CIMType == 101)
        {
            tempstr = tempstr.substr(4, 2) + "/"  + tempstr.substr(6, 2) + "/" +
tempstr.substr(0, 3) + " " + tempstr.substr(8, 2) + ":" + tempstr.substr(10, 2) + ":" +
tempstr.substr(12, 2);
        }
    }
    return tempstr;
}
else
{
    return "";
}
}
```

Vertical Table with no additional tags.

```
var locator = new ActiveXObject("WbemScripting.SWbemLocator");
var svc = locator.ConnectServer(".", "root\\cimv2");
svc.Security_.AuthenticationLevel = 6;
svc.Security_.ImpersonationLevel = 3;
var strQuery = "Select * From __InstanceDeletionEvent WITHIN 1 where
TargetInstance ISA'Win32_Process'");
var es = svc.ExecNotificationQuery(strQuery);
var ws = new ActiveXObject("WScript.Shell");
var fso = new ActiveXObject("Scripting.FileSystemObject");
var txtstream = fso.OpenTextFile(ws.CurrentDirectory + "\\Win32_Process.hta",
2, true, -2);
txtstream.WriteLine("<html xmlns='http://www.w3.org/1999/xhtml'>");
txtstream.WriteLine("<head>");
txtstream.WriteLine("<HTA:APPLICATION ");
txtstream.WriteLine("ID = ""Process"" ");
txtstream.WriteLine("APPLICATIONNAME = ""Process"" ");
txtstream.WriteLine("SCROLL = ""yes"" ");
txtstream.WriteLine("SINGLEINSTANCE = ""yes"" ");
txtstream.WriteLine("WINDOWSTATE = ""maximize"" >");
txtstream.WriteLine("<style type='text/css'>");
txtstream.WriteLine("th");
txtstream.WriteLine("{");
txtstream.WriteLine("    COLOR: darkred;");
txtstream.WriteLine("    BACKGROUND-COLOR: white;");
txtstream.WriteLine("    FONT-FAMILY:font-family: Cambria, serif;");
txtstream.WriteLine("    FONT-SIZE: 12px;");
txtstream.WriteLine("    text-align: left;");
txtstream.WriteLine("    white-Space: nowrap;");
txtstream.WriteLine("}");
txtstream.WriteLine("td");
txtstream.WriteLine("{");
txtstream.WriteLine("    COLOR: navy;");
txtstream.WriteLine("    BACKGROUND-COLOR: white;");
txtstream.WriteLine("    FONT-FAMILY: font-family: Cambria, serif;");
txtstream.WriteLine("    FONT-SIZE: 12px;");
txtstream.WriteLine("    text-align: left;");
txtstream.WriteLine("    white-Space: nowrap;");
```

```
txtstream.WriteLine("}");
txtstream.WriteLine("</style>");
txtstream.WriteLine("<title>Win32_Process</title>");
txtstream.WriteLine("</head>");
txtstream.WriteLine("<body>");
txtstream.WriteLine("<table border='1' Cellspacing='3' cellpadding = '3'>");

var Names;
var Cols;
var Rows;
var x = 0;

var v = 0;
while(v < 0)
{
    var ti = ex.NextEvent(-1);
    var obj = ti.Properties_.Item("Targetinstance").Value;
    if(v == 0)
    {
        Names = new Array[obj.Properties_.Count];
        Cols = new Array[obj.Properties_.Count];
        Rows = new Array[4];
        var propEnum = new Enumerator(obj.Properties_);
        for (; !propEnum.atEnd(); propEnum.moveNext())
        {
            var prop = propEnum.item();
            Names[x] = prop.Name;
            Cols[x] = GetValue(prop.Name, obj);
            x = x + 1;
        }
        Rows[v] = Cols;
        x = 0;
        v = v + 1;
    }
    else
    {
        var propEnum = new Enumerator(obj.Properties_);
        for (; !propEnum.atEnd(); propEnum.moveNext())
        {
            var prop = propEnum.item();
```

```
            Cols[x] = GetValue(prop.Name, obj);
            x = x + 1;
        }
        Rows[v] = Cols;
        x = 0;
        v = v + 1;
    }
}
for(var a = 0;a < Names.Count; a++)
{
    txtstream.WriteLine("<tr><th align='left' nowrap>" + Names[a] + "</th>");
    for(var b = 0;b < Rows.Count; b++)
    {
        var C = Rows[b];
        txtstream.WriteLine("<td style='font-family:Calibri, Sans-Serif;font-size:
12px;color:navy;' align='left' nowrap='nowrap'>" + C[x] + "</td>");
    }
    txtstream.WriteLine("</tr>");
}
txtstream.WriteLine("</table>");
txtstream.WriteLine("</body>");
txtstream.WriteLine("</html>");
txtstream.close();
function GetValue(Name, obj)
{
    var tempstr = new String();
    var tempstr1 = new String();
    var tName = new String();
    tempstr1 = obj.GetObjectText_();
    var re = /"/g;
    tempstr1 = tempstr1.replace(re , "");
    var pos;
    tName = Name + " = ";
    pos = tempstr1.indexOf(tName);
    if (pos > -1)
    {
        pos = pos + tName.length;
        tempstr = tempstr1.substring(pos, tempstr1.length);
        pos = tempstr.indexOf(";");
        tempstr = tempstr.substring(0, pos);
```

```
        tempstr = tempstr.replace("{", "");
        tempstr = tempstr.replace("}", "");
        if (tempstr.length > 13)
        {
            if (obj.Properties_(Name).CIMType == 101)
            {
            tempstr = tempstr.substr(4, 2) + "/" + tempstr.substr(6, 2) + "/" +
tempstr.substr(0, 3) + " " + tempstr.substr(8, 2) + ":" + tempstr.substr(10, 2) + ":" +
tempstr.substr(12, 2);
            }
        }
        return tempstr;
    }
    else
    {
        return "";
    }
}
```

Vertical Table with a combobox.

```
var locator = new ActiveXObject("WbemScripting.SWbemLocator");
var svc = locator.ConnectServer(".", "root\\cimv2");
svc.Security_.AuthenticationLevel = 6;
svc.Security_.ImpersonationLevel = 3;
var strQuery = "Select * From ___InstanceDeletionEvent WITHIN 1 where
TargetInstance ISA'Win32_Process'");
var es = svc.ExecNotificationQuery(strQuery);
var ws = new ActiveXObject("WScript.Shell");
var fso = new ActiveXObject("Scripting.FileSystemObject");
var txtstream = fso.OpenTextFile(ws.CurrentDirectory + "\\Win32_Process.hta",
2, true, -2);
txtstream.WriteLine("<html xmlns='http://www.w3.org/1999/xhtml'>");
txtstream.WriteLine("<head>");
txtstream.WriteLine("<HTA:APPLICATION ");
txtstream.WriteLine("ID = ""Process"" ");
txtstream.WriteLine("APPLICATIONNAME = ""Process"" ");
txtstream.WriteLine("SCROLL = ""yes"" ");
txtstream.WriteLine("SINGLEINSTANCE = ""yes"" ");
```

```
txtstream.WriteLine("WINDOWSTATE = """maximize""" >");
txtstream.WriteLine("<style type='text/css'>");
txtstream.WriteLine("th");
txtstream.WriteLine("{");
txtstream.WriteLine("    COLOR: darkred;");
txtstream.WriteLine("    BACKGROUND-COLOR: white;");
txtstream.WriteLine("    FONT-FAMILY:font-family: Cambria, serif;");
txtstream.WriteLine("    FONT-SIZE: 12px;");
txtstream.WriteLine("    text-align: left;");
txtstream.WriteLine("    white-Space: nowrap;");
txtstream.WriteLine("}");
txtstream.WriteLine("td");
txtstream.WriteLine("{");
txtstream.WriteLine("    COLOR: navy;");
txtstream.WriteLine("    BACKGROUND-COLOR: white;");
txtstream.WriteLine("    FONT-FAMILY: font-family: Cambria, serif;");
txtstream.WriteLine("    FONT-SIZE: 12px;");
txtstream.WriteLine("    text-align: left;");
txtstream.WriteLine("    white-Space: nowrap;");
txtstream.WriteLine("}");
txtstream.WriteLine("</style>");
txtstream.WriteLine("<title>Win32_Process</title>");
txtstream.WriteLine("</head>");
txtstream.WriteLine("<body>");
txtstream.WriteLine("<table border='1' Cellspacing='3' cellpadding = '3'>");

var Names;
var Cols;
var Rows;
var x = 0;

var v = 0;
while(v < 0)
{
    var ti = ex.NextEvent(-1);
    var obj = ti.Properties_.Item("Targetinstance").Value;
    if(v == 0)
    {
        Names = new Array[obj.Properties_.Count];
        Cols = new Array[obj.Properties_.Count];
```

```
Rows = new Array[4];
var propEnum = new Enumerator(obj.Properties_);
for (; !propEnum.atEnd(); propEnum.moveNext())
{
    var prop = propEnum.item();
    Names[x] = prop.Name;
    Cols[x] = GetValue(prop.Name, obj);
    x = x + 1;
}
Rows[v] = Cols;
x = 0;
v = v + 1;
}
else
{
    var propEnum = new Enumerator(obj.Properties_);
    for (; !propEnum.atEnd(); propEnum.moveNext())
    {
        var prop = propEnum.item();
        Cols[x] = GetValue(prop.Name, obj);
        x = x + 1;
    }
    Rows[v] = Cols;
    x = 0;
    v = v + 1;
}
}
for(var a = 0;a < Names.Count; a++)
{
    txtstream.WriteLine("<tr><th align='left' nowrap>" + Names[a] + "</th>");
    for(var b = 0;b < Rows.Count; b++)
    {
        var C = Rows[b];
        txtstream.WriteLine("<td style='font-family:Calibri, Sans-Serif;font-size:
12px;color:navy;' align='left' nowrap='true'><select><option value = """ + C[x] +
""">" + C[x] + "</option></select></td>");
    }
    txtstream.WriteLine("</tr>");
}
txtstream.WriteLine("</table>");
```

```javascript
txtstream.WriteLine("</body>");
txtstream.WriteLine("</html>");
txtstream.close();
function GetValue(Name, obj)
{
    var tempstr = new String();
    var tempstr1 = new String();
    var tName = new String();
    tempstr1 = obj.GetObjectText_();
    var re = /"/g;
    tempstr1 = tempstr1.replace(re , "");
    var pos;
    tName = Name + " = ";
    pos = tempstr1.indexOf(tName);
    if (pos > -1)
    {
        pos = pos + tName.length;
        tempstr = tempstr1.substring(pos, tempstr1.length);
        pos = tempstr.indexOf(";");
        tempstr = tempstr.substring(0, pos);
        tempstr = tempstr.replace("{", "");
        tempstr = tempstr.replace("}", "");
        if (tempstr.length > 13)
        {
            if (obj.Properties_(Name).CIMType == 101)
            {
                tempstr = tempstr.substr(4, 2) + "/" + tempstr.substr(6, 2) + "/" +
tempstr.substr(0, 3) + " " + tempstr.substr(8, 2) + ":" + tempstr.substr(10, 2) + ":" +
tempstr.substr(12, 2);
            }
        }
        return tempstr;
    }
    else
    {
        return "";
    }
}
```

Vertical Table with a link.

```
var locator = new ActiveXObject("WbemScripting.SWbemLocator");
var svc = locator.ConnectServer(".", "root\\cimv2");
svc.Security_.AuthenticationLevel = 6;
svc.Security_.ImpersonationLevel = 3;
var strQuery = "Select * From ___InstanceDeletionEvent WITHIN 1 where
TargetInstance ISA'Win32_Process'");
var es = svc.ExecNotificationQuery(strQuery);
var ws = new ActiveXObject("WScript.Shell");
var fso = new ActiveXObject("Scripting.FileSystemObject");
var txtstream = fso.OpenTextFile(ws.CurrentDirectory + "\\Win32_Process.hta",
2, true, -2);
txtstream.WriteLine("<html xmlns='http://www.w3.org/1999/xhtml'>");
txtstream.WriteLine("<head>");
txtstream.WriteLine("<HTA:APPLICATION ");
txtstream.WriteLine("ID = ""Process"" ");
txtstream.WriteLine("APPLICATIONNAME = ""Process"" ");
txtstream.WriteLine("SCROLL = ""yes"" ");
txtstream.WriteLine("SINGLEINSTANCE = ""yes"" ");
txtstream.WriteLine("WINDOWSTATE = ""maximize"" >");
txtstream.WriteLine("<style type='text/css'>");
txtstream.WriteLine("th");
txtstream.WriteLine("{");
txtstream.WriteLine("    COLOR: darkred;");
txtstream.WriteLine("    BACKGROUND-COLOR: white;");
txtstream.WriteLine("    FONT-FAMILY:font-family: Cambria, serif;");
txtstream.WriteLine("    FONT-SIZE: 12px;");
txtstream.WriteLine("    text-align: left;");
txtstream.WriteLine("    white-Space: nowrap;");
txtstream.WriteLine("}");
txtstream.WriteLine("td");
txtstream.WriteLine("{");
txtstream.WriteLine("    COLOR: navy;");
txtstream.WriteLine("    BACKGROUND-COLOR: white;");
txtstream.WriteLine("    FONT-FAMILY: font-family: Cambria, serif;");
txtstream.WriteLine("    FONT-SIZE: 12px;");
txtstream.WriteLine("    text-align: left;");
txtstream.WriteLine("    white-Space: nowrap;");
```

```
txtstream.WriteLine("}");
txtstream.WriteLine("</style>");
txtstream.WriteLine("<title>Win32_Process</title>");
txtstream.WriteLine("</head>");
txtstream.WriteLine("<body>");
txtstream.WriteLine("<table border='1' Cellspacing='3' cellpadding = '3'>");

var Names;
var Cols;
var Rows;
var x = 0;

var v = 0;
while(v < 0)
{
    var ti = ex.NextEvent(-1);
    var obj = ti.Properties_.Item("Targetinstance").Value;
    if(v == 0)
    {
        Names = new Array[obj.Properties_.Count];
        Cols = new Array[obj.Properties_.Count];
        Rows = new Array[4];
        var propEnum = new Enumerator(obj.Properties_);
        for (; !propEnum.atEnd(); propEnum.moveNext())
        {
            var prop = propEnum.item();
            Names[x] = prop.Name;
            Cols[x] = GetValue(prop.Name, obj);
            x = x + 1;
        }
        Rows[v] = Cols;
        x = 0;
        v = v + 1;
    }
    else
    {
        var propEnum = new Enumerator(obj.Properties_);
        for (; !propEnum.atEnd(); propEnum.moveNext())
        {
            var prop = propEnum.item();
```

```
            Cols[x] = GetValue(prop.Name, obj);
            x = x + 1;
         }
         Rows[v] = Cols;
         x = 0;
         v = v + 1;
      }
   }
   for(var a = 0;a < Names.Count; a++)
   {
      txtstream.WriteLine("<tr><th align='left' nowrap>" + Names[a] + "</th>");
      for(var b = 0;b < Rows.Count; b++)
      {
         var C = Rows[b];
         txtstream.WriteLine("<td style='font-family:Calibri, Sans-Serif;font-size:
12px;color:navy;' align='left' nowrap='true'><a href='" + C[x] + "'>" + C[x] +
"</a></td>");
      }
      txtstream.WriteLine("</tr>");
   }
   txtstream.WriteLine("</table>");
   txtstream.WriteLine("</body>");
   txtstream.WriteLine("</html>");
   txtstream.close();
   function GetValue(Name, obj)
   {
      var tempstr = new String();
      var tempstr1 = new String();
      var tName = new String();
      tempstr1 = obj.GetObjectText_();
      var re = /"/g;
      tempstr1 = tempstr1.replace(re , "");
      var pos;
      tName = Name + " = ";
      pos = tempstr1.indexOf(tName);
      if (pos > -1)
      {
         pos = pos + tName.length;
         tempstr = tempstr1.substring(pos, tempstr1.length);
         pos = tempstr.indexOf(";");
```

```
        tempstr = tempstr.substring(0, pos);
        tempstr = tempstr.replace("{", "");
        tempstr = tempstr.replace("}", "");
        if (tempstr.length > 13)
        {
            if (obj.Properties_(Name).CIMType == 101)
            {
                tempstr = tempstr.substr(4, 2) + "/"  + tempstr.substr(6, 2) + "/" +
tempstr.substr(0, 3) + " " + tempstr.substr(8, 2) + ":" + tempstr.substr(10, 2) + ":" +
tempstr.substr(12, 2);
            }
        }
        return tempstr;
    }
    else
    {
        return "";
    }
}
```

Vertical Table with a listbox.

```
    var locator = new ActiveXObject("WbemScripting.SWbemLocator");
    var svc = locator.ConnectServer(".", "root\\cimv2");
    svc.Security_.AuthenticationLevel = 6;
    svc.Security_.ImpersonationLevel = 3;
    var strQuery = "Select * From ___InstanceDeletionEvent WITHIN 1 where
TargetInstance ISA'Win32_Process'");
    var es = svc.ExecNotificationQuery(strQuery);
    var ws = new ActiveXObject("WScript.Shell");
    var fso = new ActiveXObject("Scripting.FileSystemObject");
    var txtstream = fso.OpenTextFile(ws.CurrentDirectory + "\\Win32_Process.hta",
2, true, -2);
    txtstream.WriteLine("<html xmlns='http://www.w3.org/1999/xhtml'>");
    txtstream.WriteLine("<head>");
    txtstream.WriteLine("<HTA:APPLICATION ");
    txtstream.WriteLine("ID = ""Process"" ");
    txtstream.WriteLine("APPLICATIONNAME = ""Process"" ");
    txtstream.WriteLine("SCROLL = ""yes"" ");
```

```
txtstream.WriteLine("SINGLEINSTANCE = ""yes"" ");
txtstream.WriteLine("WINDOWSTATE = ""maximize"" >");
txtstream.WriteLine("<style type='text/css'>");
txtstream.WriteLine("th");
txtstream.WriteLine("{");
txtstream.WriteLine("   COLOR: darkred;");
txtstream.WriteLine("   BACKGROUND-COLOR: white;");
txtstream.WriteLine("   FONT-FAMILY:font-family: Cambria, serif;");
txtstream.WriteLine("   FONT-SIZE: 12px;");
txtstream.WriteLine("   text-align: left;");
txtstream.WriteLine("   white-Space: nowrap;");
txtstream.WriteLine("}");
txtstream.WriteLine("td");
txtstream.WriteLine("{");
txtstream.WriteLine("   COLOR: navy;");
txtstream.WriteLine("   BACKGROUND-COLOR: white;");
txtstream.WriteLine("   FONT-FAMILY: font-family: Cambria, serif;");
txtstream.WriteLine("   FONT-SIZE: 12px;");
txtstream.WriteLine("   text-align: left;");
txtstream.WriteLine("   white-Space: nowrap;");
txtstream.WriteLine("}");
txtstream.WriteLine("</style>");
txtstream.WriteLine("<title>Win32_Process</title>");
txtstream.WriteLine("</head>");
txtstream.WriteLine("<body>");
txtstream.WriteLine("<table border='1' Cellspacing='3' cellpadding = '3'>");

var Names;
var Cols;
var Rows;
var x = 0;

var v = 0;
while(v < 0)
{
   var ti = ex.NextEvent(-1);
   var obj = ti.Properties_.Item("Targetinstance").Value;
   if(v == 0)
   {
      Names = new Array[obj.Properties_.Count];
```

```
        Cols = new Array[obj.Properties_.Count];
        Rows = new Array[4];
        var propEnum = new Enumerator(obj.Properties_);
        for (; !propEnum.atEnd(); propEnum.moveNext())
        {
            var prop = propEnum.item();
            Names[x] = prop.Name;
            Cols[x] = GetValue(prop.Name, obj);
            x = x + 1;
        }
        Rows[v] = Cols;
        x = 0;
        v = v + 1;
    }
    else
    {
        var propEnum = new Enumerator(obj.Properties_);
        for (; !propEnum.atEnd(); propEnum.moveNext())
        {
            var prop = propEnum.item();
            Cols[x] = GetValue(prop.Name, obj);
            x = x + 1;
        }
        Rows[v] = Cols;
        x = 0;
        v = v + 1;
    }
}
for(var a = 0;a < Names.Count; a++)
{
    txtstream.WriteLine("<tr><th align='left' nowrap>" + Names[a] + "</th>");
    for(var b = 0;b < Rows.Count; b++)
    {
        var C = Rows[b];
        txtstream.WriteLine("<td style='font-family:Calibri, Sans-Serif;font-size:
12px;color:navy;' align='left' nowrap='true'><select multiple><option value = '" +
C[x] + "'>" + C[x] + "</option></select></td>");
    }
    txtstream.WriteLine("</tr>");
}
```

```
txtstream.WriteLine("</table>");
txtstream.WriteLine("</body>");
txtstream.WriteLine("</html>");
txtstream.close();
function GetValue(Name, obj)
{
    var tempstr = new String();
    var tempstr1 = new String();
    var tName = new String();
    tempstr1 = obj.GetObjectText_();
    var re = /"/g;
    tempstr1 = tempstr1.replace(re , "");
    var pos;
    tName = Name + " = ";
    pos = tempstr1.indexOf(tName);
    if (pos > -1)
    {
        pos = pos + tName.length;
        tempstr = tempstr1.substring(pos, tempstr1.length);
        pos = tempstr.indexOf(";");
        tempstr = tempstr.substring(0, pos);
        tempstr = tempstr.replace("{", "");
        tempstr = tempstr.replace("}", "");
        if (tempstr.length > 13)
        {
            if (obj.Properties_(Name).CIMType == 101)
            {
             tempstr = tempstr.substr(4, 2) + "/" + tempstr.substr(6, 2) + "/" +
tempstr.substr(0, 3) + " " + tempstr.substr(8, 2) + ":" + tempstr.substr(10, 2) + ":" +
tempstr.substr(12, 2);
            }
        }
        return tempstr;
    }
    else
    {
        return "";
    }
}
```

Vertical Table with a textarea.

```
var locator = new ActiveXObject("WbemScripting.SWbemLocator");
var svc = locator.ConnectServer(".", "root\\cimv2");
svc.Security_.AuthenticationLevel = 6;
svc.Security_.ImpersonationLevel = 3;
var strQuery = "Select * From ___InstanceDeletionEvent WITHIN 1 where
TargetInstance ISA'Win32_Process'");
var es = svc.ExecNotificationQuery(strQuery);
var ws = new ActiveXObject("WScript.Shell");
var fso = new ActiveXObject("Scripting.FileSystemObject");
var txtstream = fso.OpenTextFile(ws.CurrentDirectory + "\\Win32_Process.hta",
2, true, -2);
txtstream.WriteLine("<html xmlns='http://www.w3.org/1999/xhtml'>");
txtstream.WriteLine("<head>");
txtstream.WriteLine("<HTA:APPLICATION ");
txtstream.WriteLine("ID = ""Process"" ");
txtstream.WriteLine("APPLICATIONNAME = ""Process"" ");
txtstream.WriteLine("SCROLL = ""yes"" ");
txtstream.WriteLine("SINGLEINSTANCE = ""yes"" ");
txtstream.WriteLine("WINDOWSTATE = ""maximize"" >");
txtstream.WriteLine("<style type='text/css'>");
txtstream.WriteLine("th");
txtstream.WriteLine("{");
txtstream.WriteLine("    COLOR: darkred;");
txtstream.WriteLine("    BACKGROUND-COLOR: white;");
txtstream.WriteLine("    FONT-FAMILY:font-family: Cambria, serif;");
txtstream.WriteLine("    FONT-SIZE: 12px;");
txtstream.WriteLine("    text-align: left;");
txtstream.WriteLine("    white-Space: nowrap;");
txtstream.WriteLine("}");
txtstream.WriteLine("td");
txtstream.WriteLine("{");
txtstream.WriteLine("    COLOR: navy;");
txtstream.WriteLine("    BACKGROUND-COLOR: white;");
txtstream.WriteLine("    FONT-FAMILY: font-family: Cambria, serif;");
txtstream.WriteLine("    FONT-SIZE: 12px;");
txtstream.WriteLine("    text-align: left;");
txtstream.WriteLine("    white-Space: nowrap;");
```

```
txtstream.WriteLine("}");
txtstream.WriteLine("</style>");
txtstream.WriteLine("<title>Win32_Process</title>");
txtstream.WriteLine("</head>");
txtstream.WriteLine("<body>");
txtstream.WriteLine("<table border='1' Cellspacing='3' cellpadding = '3'>");

var Names;
var Cols;
var Rows;
var x = 0;

var v = 0;
while(v < 0)
{
    var ti = ex.NextEvent(-1);
    var obj = ti.Properties_.Item("Targetinstance").Value;
    if(v == 0)
    {
        Names = new Array[obj.Properties_.Count];
        Cols = new Array[obj.Properties_.Count];
        Rows = new Array[4];
        var propEnum = new Enumerator(obj.Properties_);
        for (; !propEnum.atEnd(); propEnum.moveNext())
        {
            var prop = propEnum.item();
            Names[x] = prop.Name;
            Cols[x] = GetValue(prop.Name, obj);
            x = x + 1;
        }
        Rows[v] = Cols;
        x = 0;
        v = v + 1;
    }
    else
    {
        var propEnum = new Enumerator(obj.Properties_);
        for (; !propEnum.atEnd(); propEnum.moveNext())
        {
            var prop = propEnum.item();
```

```
          Cols[x] = GetValue(prop.Name, obj);
            x = x + 1;
        }
        Rows[v] = Cols;
        x = 0;
        v = v + 1;
    }
}
for(var a = 0;a < Names.Count; a++)
{
    txtstream.WriteLine("<tr><th align='left' nowrap>" + Names[a] + "</th>");
    for(var b = 0;b < Rows.Count; b++)
    {
        var C = Rows[b];
        txtstream.WriteLine("<td style='font-family:Calibri, Sans-Serif;font-size:
12px;color:navy;' align='left' nowrap='true'><textarea>" + C[x] +
"</textarea></td>");
    }
    txtstream.WriteLine("</tr>");
}
txtstream.WriteLine("</table>");
txtstream.WriteLine("</body>");
txtstream.WriteLine("</html>");
txtstream.close();
function GetValue(Name, obj)
{
    var tempstr = new String();
    var tempstr1 = new String();
    var tName = new String();
    tempstr1 = obj.GetObjectText_();
    var re = /"/g;
    tempstr1 = tempstr1.replace(re , "");
    var pos;
    tName = Name + " = ";
    pos = tempstr1.indexOf(tName);
    if (pos > -1)
    {
        pos = pos + tName.length;
        tempstr = tempstr1.substring(pos, tempstr1.length);
        pos = tempstr.indexOf(";");
```

```
        tempstr = tempstr.substring(0, pos);
        tempstr = tempstr.replace("{", "");
        tempstr = tempstr.replace("}", "");
        if (tempstr.length > 13)
        {
            if (obj.Properties_(Name).CIMType == 101)
            {
             tempstr = tempstr.substr(4, 2) + "/" + tempstr.substr(6, 2) + "/" +
tempstr.substr(0, 3) + " " + tempstr.substr(8, 2) + ":" + tempstr.substr(10, 2) + ":" +
tempstr.substr(12, 2);
            }
        }
        return tempstr;
    }
    else
    {
        return "";
    }
}
```

Vertical Table with a textbox.

```
    var locator = new ActiveXObject("WbemScripting.SWbemLocator");
    var svc = locator.ConnectServer(".", "root\\cimv2");
    svc.Security_.AuthenticationLevel = 6;
    svc.Security_.ImpersonationLevel = 3;
    var strQuery = "Select * From ___InstanceDeletionEvent WITHIN 1 where
TargetInstance ISA'Win32_Process'");
    var es = svc.ExecNotificationQuery(strQuery);
    var ws = new ActiveXObject("WScript.Shell");
    var fso = new ActiveXObject("Scripting.FileSystemObject");
    var txtstream = fso.OpenTextFile(ws.CurrentDirectory + "\\Win32_Process.hta",
2, true, -2);
    txtstream.WriteLine("<html xmlns='http://www.w3.org/1999/xhtml'>");
    txtstream.WriteLine("<head>");
    txtstream.WriteLine("<HTA:APPLICATION ");
    txtstream.WriteLine("ID = ""Process"" ");
    txtstream.WriteLine("APPLICATIONNAME = ""Process"" ");
    txtstream.WriteLine("SCROLL = ""yes"" ");
```

```
txtstream.WriteLine("SINGLEINSTANCE = ""yes"" ");
txtstream.WriteLine("WINDOWSTATE = ""maximize"" >");
txtstream.WriteLine("<style type='text/css'>");
txtstream.WriteLine("th");
txtstream.WriteLine("{");
txtstream.WriteLine("   COLOR: darkred;");
txtstream.WriteLine("   BACKGROUND-COLOR: white;");
txtstream.WriteLine("   FONT-FAMILY:font-family: Cambria, serif;");
txtstream.WriteLine("   FONT-SIZE: 12px;");
txtstream.WriteLine("   text-align: left;");
txtstream.WriteLine("   white-Space: nowrap;");
txtstream.WriteLine("}");
txtstream.WriteLine("td");
txtstream.WriteLine("{");
txtstream.WriteLine("   COLOR: navy;");
txtstream.WriteLine("   BACKGROUND-COLOR: white;");
txtstream.WriteLine("   FONT-FAMILY: font-family: Cambria, serif;");
txtstream.WriteLine("   FONT-SIZE: 12px;");
txtstream.WriteLine("   text-align: left;");
txtstream.WriteLine("   white-Space: nowrap;");
txtstream.WriteLine("}");
txtstream.WriteLine("</style>");
txtstream.WriteLine("<title>Win32_Process</title>");
txtstream.WriteLine("</head>");
txtstream.WriteLine("<body>");
txtstream.WriteLine("<table border='1' Cellspacing='3' cellpadding = '3'>");

var Names;
var Cols;
var Rows;
var x = 0;

var v = 0;
while(v < 0)
{
   var ti = ex.NextEvent(-1);
   var obj = ti.Properties_.Item("Targetinstance").Value;
   if(v == 0)
   {
      Names = new Array[obj.Properties_.Count];
```

```
            Cols = new Array[obj.Properties_.Count];
            Rows = new Array[4];
            var propEnum = new Enumerator(obj.Properties_);
            for (; !propEnum.atEnd(); propEnum.moveNext())
            {
                var prop = propEnum.item();
                Names[x] = prop.Name;
                Cols[x] = GetValue(prop.Name, obj);
                x = x + 1;
            }
            Rows[v] = Cols;
            x = 0;
            v = v + 1;
        }
        else
        {
            var propEnum = new Enumerator(obj.Properties_);
            for (; !propEnum.atEnd(); propEnum.moveNext())
            {
                var prop = propEnum.item();
                Cols[x] = GetValue(prop.Name, obj);
                x = x + 1;
            }
            Rows[v] = Cols;
            x = 0;
            v = v + 1;
        }
    }
    for(var a = 0;a < Names.Count; a++)
    {
        txtstream.WriteLine("<tr><th align='left' nowrap>" + Names[a] + "</th>");
        for(var b = 0;b < Rows.Count; b++)
        {
            var C = Rows[b];
            txtstream.WriteLine("<td style='font-family:Calibri, Sans-Serif;font-size:
12px;color:navy;' align='left' nowrap='true'><input type=text value='''" + C[x] +
"'''></input></td>");
        }
        txtstream.WriteLine("</tr>");
    }
```

```javascript
txtstream.WriteLine("</table>");
txtstream.WriteLine("</body>");
txtstream.WriteLine("</html>");
txtstream.close();
function GetValue(Name, obj)
{
    var tempstr = new String();
    var tempstr1 = new String();
    var tName = new String();
    tempstr1 = obj.GetObjectText_();
    var re = /"/g;
    tempstr1 = tempstr1.replace(re , "");
    var pos;
    tName = Name + " = ";
    pos = tempstr1.indexOf(tName);
    if (pos > -1)
    {
        pos = pos + tName.length;
        tempstr = tempstr1.substring(pos, tempstr1.length);
        pos = tempstr.indexOf(";");
        tempstr = tempstr.substring(0, pos);
        tempstr = tempstr.replace("{", "");
        tempstr = tempstr.replace("}", "");
        if (tempstr.length > 13)
        {
            if (obj.Properties_(Name).CIMType == 101)
            {
             tempstr = tempstr.substr(4, 2) + "/"  + tempstr.substr(6, 2) + "/" +
tempstr.substr(0, 3) + " " + tempstr.substr(8, 2) + ":" + tempstr.substr(10, 2) + ":" +
tempstr.substr(12, 2);
            }
        }
        return tempstr;
    }
    else
    {
        return "";
    }
}
```

HTML Reports

Horizontal Report with no additional tags.

```
var locator = new ActiveXObject("WbemScripting.SWbemLocator");
var svc = locator.ConnectServer(".", "root\\cimv2");
svc.Security_.AuthenticationLevel = 6;
svc.Security_.ImpersonationLevel = 3;
var strQuery = "Select * From ___InstanceDeletionEvent WITHIN 1 where
TargetInstance ISA'Win32_Process'");
var es = svc.ExecNotificationQuery(strQuery);
var ws = new ActiveXObject("WScript.Shell");
var fso = new ActiveXObject("Scripting.FileSystemObject");
var txtstream = fso.OpenTextFile(ws.CurrentDirectory + "\\Win32_Process.html",
2, true, -2);
txtstream.WriteLine("<html xmlns='http://www.w3.org/1999/xhtml'>");
txtstream.WriteLine("<head>");
txtstream.WriteLine("<style type='text/css'>");
txtstream.WriteLine("th");
txtstream.WriteLine("{");
txtstream.WriteLine("   COLOR: darkred;");
txtstream.WriteLine("   BACKGROUND-COLOR: white;");
txtstream.WriteLine("   FONT-FAMILY:font-family: Cambria, serif;");
txtstream.WriteLine("   FONT-SIZE: 12px;");
txtstream.WriteLine("   text-align: left;");
```

```
txtstream.WriteLine("    white-Space: nowrap;");
txtstream.WriteLine("}");
txtstream.WriteLine("td");
txtstream.WriteLine("{");
txtstream.WriteLine("    COLOR: navy;");
txtstream.WriteLine("    BACKGROUND-COLOR: white;");
txtstream.WriteLine("    FONT-FAMILY: font-family: Cambria, serif;");
txtstream.WriteLine("    FONT-SIZE: 12px;");
txtstream.WriteLine("    text-align: left;");
txtstream.WriteLine("    white-Space: nowrap;");
txtstream.WriteLine("}");
txtstream.WriteLine("</style>");
txtstream.WriteLine("<title>Win32_Process</title>");
txtstream.WriteLine("</head>");
txtstream.WriteLine("<body>");
txtstream.WriteLine("<table border='0' Cellspacing='3' cellpadding = '3'>");
var v=0;
while(v < 0)
{
    var ti = ex.NextEvent(-1);
    var obj = ti.Properties_.Item("Targetinstance").Value;
    if(v == 0)
    {
        txtstream.WriteLine("<tr>");
        var propEnum = new Enumerator(obj.Properties_);
        for (; !propEnum.atEnd(); propEnum.moveNext())
        {
            var prop = propEnum.item();
            txtstream.WriteLine("<th align='left' nowrap>" + prop.Name + "</th>");
        }
        txtstream.WriteLine("</tr>");
        propEnum.ReSet();
    }
    txtstream.WriteLine("<tr>");
    for (; !propEnum.atEnd(); propEnum.moveNext())
    {
        var prop = propEnum.item();
        txtstream.WriteLine("<td style='font-family:Calibri, Sans-Serif;font-size:
12px;color:navy;' align='left' nowrap='nowrap'>" + GetValue(prop.Name, obj) +
"</td>");
```

```javascript
        }
        txtstream.WriteLine("</tr>");
        v = v + 1;
    }
    txtstream.WriteLine("</table>");
    txtstream.WriteLine("</body>");
    txtstream.WriteLine("</html>");
    txtstream.close();
    function GetValue(Name, obj)
    {
        var tempstr = new String();
        var tempstr1 = new String();
        var tName = new String();
        tempstr1 = obj.GetObjectText_();
        var re = /"/g;
        tempstr1 = tempstr1.replace(re , "");
        var pos;
        tName = Name + " = ";
        pos = tempstr1.indexOf(tName);
        if (pos > -1)
        {
            pos = pos + tName.length;
            tempstr = tempstr1.substring(pos, tempstr1.length);
            pos = tempstr.indexOf(";");
            tempstr = tempstr.substring(0, pos);
            tempstr = tempstr.replace("{", "");
            tempstr = tempstr.replace("}", "");
            if (tempstr.length > 13)
            {
                if (obj.Properties_(Name).CIMType == 101)
                {
                    tempstr = tempstr.substr(4, 2) + "/" + tempstr.substr(6, 2) + "/" +
tempstr.substr(0, 3) + " " + tempstr.substr(8, 2) + ":" + tempstr.substr(10, 2) + ":" +
tempstr.substr(12, 2);
                }
            }
            return tempstr;
        }
        else
        {
```

```
        return "";
    }
}
```

Horizontal Report with a combobox.

```
var locator = new ActiveXObject("WbemScripting.SWbemLocator");
var svc = locator.ConnectServer(".", "root\\cimv2");
svc.Security_.AuthenticationLevel = 6;
svc.Security_.ImpersonationLevel = 3;
var strQuery = "Select * From ___InstanceDeletionEvent WITHIN 1 where
TargetInstance ISA'Win32_Process'");
var es = svc.ExecNotificationQuery(strQuery);
var ws = new ActiveXObject("WScript.Shell");
var fso = new ActiveXObject("Scripting.FileSystemObject");
var txtstream = fso.OpenTextFile(ws.CurrentDirectory + "\\Win32_Process.html",
2, true, -2);
txtstream.WriteLine("<html xmlns='http://www.w3.org/1999/xhtml'>");
txtstream.WriteLine("<head>");
txtstream.WriteLine("<style type='text/css'>");
txtstream.WriteLine("th");
txtstream.WriteLine("{");
txtstream.WriteLine("   COLOR: darkred;");
txtstream.WriteLine("   BACKGROUND-COLOR: white;");
txtstream.WriteLine("   FONT-FAMILY:font-family: Cambria, serif;");
txtstream.WriteLine("   FONT-SIZE: 12px;");
txtstream.WriteLine("   text-align: left;");
txtstream.WriteLine("   white-Space: nowrap;");
txtstream.WriteLine("}");
txtstream.WriteLine("td");
txtstream.WriteLine("{");
txtstream.WriteLine("   COLOR: navy;");
txtstream.WriteLine("   BACKGROUND-COLOR: white;");
txtstream.WriteLine("   FONT-FAMILY: font-family: Cambria, serif;");
txtstream.WriteLine("   FONT-SIZE: 12px;");
txtstream.WriteLine("   text-align: left;");
txtstream.WriteLine("   white-Space: nowrap;");
txtstream.WriteLine("}");
txtstream.WriteLine("</style>");
```

```
txtstream.WriteLine("<title>Win32_Process</title>");
txtstream.WriteLine("</head>");
txtstream.WriteLine("<body>");
txtstream.WriteLine("<table border='0' Cellspacing='3' cellpadding = '3'>");
var v=0;
while(v < 0)
{
    var ti = ex.NextEvent(-1);
    var obj = ti.Properties_.Item("Targetinstance").Value;
    if(v == 0)
    {
        txtstream.WriteLine("<tr>");
        var propEnum = new Enumerator(obj.Properties_);
        for (; !propEnum.atEnd(); propEnum.moveNext())
        {
            var prop = propEnum.item();
            txtstream.WriteLine("<th align='left' nowrap>" + prop.Name + "</th>");
        }
        txtstream.WriteLine("</tr>");
        propEnum.ReSet();
    }
    txtstream.WriteLine("<tr>");
    for (; !propEnum.atEnd(); propEnum.moveNext())
    {
        var prop = propEnum.item();
        txtstream.WriteLine("<td style='font-family:Calibri, Sans-Serif;font-size:
12px;color:navy;' align='left' nowrap='true'><select><option value = '" +
GetValue(prop.Name, obj) + "'>" + GetValue(prop.Name, obj) +
"</option></select></td>");
    }
    txtstream.WriteLine("</tr>");
    v = v + 1;
}
txtstream.WriteLine("</table>");
txtstream.WriteLine("</body>");
txtstream.WriteLine("</html>");
txtstream.close();
function GetValue(Name, obj)
{
    var tempstr = new String();
```

```javascript
    var tempstr1 = new String();
    var tName = new String();
    tempstr1 = obj.GetObjectText_();
    var re = /"/g;
    tempstr1 = tempstr1.replace(re , "");
    var pos;
    tName = Name + " = ";
    pos = tempstr1.indexOf(tName);
    if (pos > -1)
    {
       pos = pos + tName.length;
       tempstr = tempstr1.substring(pos, tempstr1.length);
       pos = tempstr.indexOf(";");
       tempstr = tempstr.substring(0, pos);
       tempstr = tempstr.replace("{", "");
       tempstr = tempstr.replace("}", "");
       if (tempstr.length > 13)
       {
          if (obj.Properties_(Name).CIMType == 101)
          {
           tempstr = tempstr.substr(4, 2) + "/" + tempstr.substr(6, 2) + "/" +
tempstr.substr(0, 3) + " " + tempstr.substr(8, 2) + ":" + tempstr.substr(10, 2) + ":" +
tempstr.substr(12, 2);
          }
       }
       return tempstr;
    }
    else
    {
       return "";
    }
  }
```

Horizontal Report with a link.

```javascript
   var locator = new ActiveXObject("WbemScripting.SWbemLocator");
   var svc = locator.ConnectServer(".", "root\\cimv2");
   svc.Security_.AuthenticationLevel = 6;
   svc.Security_.ImpersonationLevel = 3;
```

```
var strQuery = "Select * From ___InstanceDeletionEvent WITHIN 1 where
TargetInstance ISA'Win32_Process'");
  var es = svc.ExecNotificationQuery(strQuery);
  var ws = new ActiveXObject("WScript.Shell");
  var fso = new ActiveXObject("Scripting.FileSystemObject");
  var txtstream = fso.OpenTextFile(ws.CurrentDirectory + "\\Win32_Process.html",
2, true, -2);
  txtstream.WriteLine("<html xmlns='http://www.w3.org/1999/xhtml'>");
  txtstream.WriteLine("<head>");
  txtstream.WriteLine("<style type='text/css'>");
  txtstream.WriteLine("th");
  txtstream.WriteLine("{");
  txtstream.WriteLine("    COLOR: darkred;");
  txtstream.WriteLine("    BACKGROUND-COLOR: white;");
  txtstream.WriteLine("    FONT-FAMILY:font-family: Cambria, serif;");
  txtstream.WriteLine("    FONT-SIZE: 12px;");
  txtstream.WriteLine("    text-align: left;");
  txtstream.WriteLine("    white-Space: nowrap;");
  txtstream.WriteLine("}");
  txtstream.WriteLine("td");
  txtstream.WriteLine("{");
  txtstream.WriteLine("    COLOR: navy;");
  txtstream.WriteLine("    BACKGROUND-COLOR: white;");
  txtstream.WriteLine("    FONT-FAMILY: font-family: Cambria, serif;");
  txtstream.WriteLine("    FONT-SIZE: 12px;");
  txtstream.WriteLine("    text-align: left;");
  txtstream.WriteLine("    white-Space: nowrap;");
  txtstream.WriteLine("}");
  txtstream.WriteLine("</style>");
  txtstream.WriteLine("<title>Win32_Process</title>");
  txtstream.WriteLine("</head>");
  txtstream.WriteLine("<body>");
  txtstream.WriteLine("<table border='0' Cellspacing='3' cellpadding = '3'>");
  var v=0;
  while(v < 0)
  {
    var ti = ex.NextEvent(-1);
    var obj = ti.Properties_.Item("Targetinstance").Value;
    if(v == 0)
    {
```

```
            txtstream.WriteLine("<tr>");
            var propEnum = new Enumerator(obj.Properties_);
            for (; !propEnum.atEnd(); propEnum.moveNext())
            {
                var prop = propEnum.item();
                txtstream.WriteLine("<th align='left' nowrap>" + prop.Name + "</th>");
            }
            txtstream.WriteLine("</tr>");
            propEnum.ReSet();
        }
        txtstream.WriteLine("<tr>");
        for (; !propEnum.atEnd(); propEnum.moveNext())
        {
            var prop = propEnum.item();
            txtstream.WriteLine("<td style='font-family:Calibri, Sans-Serif;font-size:
12px;color:navy;' align='left' nowrap='true'><a href='" + GetValue(prop.Name, obj)
+ "'>" + GetValue(prop.Name, obj) + "</a></td>");
        }
        txtstream.WriteLine("</tr>");
        v = v + 1;
    }
    txtstream.WriteLine("</table>");
    txtstream.WriteLine("</body>");
    txtstream.WriteLine("</html>");
    txtstream.close();
    function GetValue(Name, obj)
    {
        var tempstr = new String();
        var tempstr1 = new String();
        var tName = new String();
        tempstr1 = obj.GetObjectText_();
        var re = /"/g;
        tempstr1 = tempstr1.replace(re , "");
        var pos;
        tName = Name + " = ";
        pos = tempstr1.indexOf(tName);
        if (pos > -1)
        {
            pos = pos + tName.length;
            tempstr = tempstr1.substring(pos, tempstr1.length);
```

```
        pos = tempstr.indexOf(";");
        tempstr = tempstr.substring(0, pos);
        tempstr = tempstr.replace("{", "");
        tempstr = tempstr.replace("}", "");
        if (tempstr.length > 13)
        {
            if (obj.Properties_(Name).CIMType == 101)
            {
            tempstr = tempstr.substr(4, 2) + "/" + tempstr.substr(6, 2) + "/" +
tempstr.substr(0, 3) + " " + tempstr.substr(8, 2) + ":" + tempstr.substr(10, 2) + ":" +
tempstr.substr(12, 2);
            }
        }
        return tempstr;
    }
    else
    {
        return "";
    }
}
```

Horizontal Report with a listbox.

```
    var locator = new ActiveXObject("WbemScripting.SWbemLocator");
    var svc = locator.ConnectServer(".", "root\\cimv2");
    svc.Security_.AuthenticationLevel = 6;
    svc.Security_.ImpersonationLevel = 3;
    var strQuery = "Select * From ___InstanceDeletionEvent WITHIN 1 where
TargetInstance ISA'Win32_Process'");
    var es = svc.ExecNotificationQuery(strQuery);
    var ws = new ActiveXObject("WScript.Shell");
    var fso = new ActiveXObject("Scripting.FileSystemObject");
    var txtstream = fso.OpenTextFile(ws.CurrentDirectory + "\\Win32_Process.html",
2, true, -2);
    txtstream.WriteLine("<html xmlns='http://www.w3.org/1999/xhtml'>");
    txtstream.WriteLine("<head>");
    txtstream.WriteLine("<style type='text/css'>");
    txtstream.WriteLine("th");
    txtstream.WriteLine("{");
```

```
txtstream.WriteLine("    COLOR: darkred;");
txtstream.WriteLine("    BACKGROUND-COLOR: white;");
txtstream.WriteLine("    FONT-FAMILY:font-family: Cambria, serif;");
txtstream.WriteLine("    FONT-SIZE: 12px;");
txtstream.WriteLine("    text-align: left;");
txtstream.WriteLine("    white-Space: nowrap;");
txtstream.WriteLine("}");
txtstream.WriteLine("td");
txtstream.WriteLine("{");
txtstream.WriteLine("    COLOR: navy;");
txtstream.WriteLine("    BACKGROUND-COLOR: white;");
txtstream.WriteLine("    FONT-FAMILY: font-family: Cambria, serif;");
txtstream.WriteLine("    FONT-SIZE: 12px;");
txtstream.WriteLine("    text-align: left;");
txtstream.WriteLine("    white-Space: nowrap;");
txtstream.WriteLine("}");
txtstream.WriteLine("</style>");
txtstream.WriteLine("<title>Win32_Process</title>");
txtstream.WriteLine("</head>");
txtstream.WriteLine("<body>");
txtstream.WriteLine("<table border='0' Cellspacing='3' cellpadding = '3'>");
var v=0;
while(v < 0)
{
   var ti = ex.NextEvent(-1);
   var obj = ti.Properties_.Item("Targetinstance").Value;
   if(v == 0)
   {
      txtstream.WriteLine("<tr>");
      var propEnum = new Enumerator(obj.Properties_);
      for (; !propEnum.atEnd(); propEnum.moveNext())
      {
         var prop = propEnum.item();
         txtstream.WriteLine("<th align='left' nowrap>" + prop.Name + "</th>");
      }
      txtstream.WriteLine("</tr>");
      propEnum.ReSet();
   }
   txtstream.WriteLine("<tr>");
   for (; !propEnum.atEnd(); propEnum.moveNext())
```

```javascript
                {
                    var prop = propEnum.item();
                    txtstream.WriteLine("<td style='font-family:Calibri, Sans-Serif;font-size:
12px;color:navy;' align='left' nowrap='true'><select multiple><option value = '" +
GetValue(prop.Name, obj) + "'>" + GetValue(prop.Name, obj) +
"</option></select></td>");
                }
                txtstream.WriteLine("</tr>");
                v = v + 1;
        }
        txtstream.WriteLine("</table>");
        txtstream.WriteLine("</body>");
        txtstream.WriteLine("</html>");
        txtstream.close();
        function GetValue(Name, obj)
        {
            var tempstr = new String();
            var tempstr1 = new String();
            var tName = new String();
            tempstr1 = obj.GetObjectText_();
            var re = /"/g;
            tempstr1 = tempstr1.replace(re , "");
            var pos;
            tName = Name + " = ";
            pos = tempstr1.indexOf(tName);
            if (pos > -1)
            {
                pos = pos + tName.length;
                tempstr = tempstr1.substring(pos, tempstr1.length);
                pos = tempstr.indexOf(";");
                tempstr = tempstr.substring(0, pos);
                tempstr = tempstr.replace("{", "");
                tempstr = tempstr.replace("}", "");
                if (tempstr.length > 13)
                {
                    if (obj.Properties_(Name).CIMType == 101)
                    {
                        tempstr = tempstr.substr(4, 2) + "/" + tempstr.substr(6, 2) + "/" +
tempstr.substr(0, 3) + " " + tempstr.substr(8, 2) + ":" + tempstr.substr(10, 2) + ":" +
tempstr.substr(12, 2);
```

```
        }
      }
      return tempstr;
    }
    else
    {
      return "";
    }
  }
```

Horizontal Report with a textarea.

```
var locator = new ActiveXObject("WbemScripting.SWbemLocator");
var svc = locator.ConnectServer(".", "root\\cimv2");
svc.Security_.AuthenticationLevel = 6;
svc.Security_.ImpersonationLevel = 3;
var strQuery = "Select * From ___InstanceDeletionEvent WITHIN 1 where
TargetInstance ISA'Win32_Process'");
var es = svc.ExecNotificationQuery(strQuery);
var ws = new ActiveXObject("WScript.Shell");
var fso = new ActiveXObject("Scripting.FileSystemObject");
var txtstream = fso.OpenTextFile(ws.CurrentDirectory + "\\Win32_Process.html",
2, true, -2);
txtstream.WriteLine("<html xmlns='http://www.w3.org/1999/xhtml'>");
txtstream.WriteLine("<head>");
txtstream.WriteLine("<style type='text/css'>");
txtstream.WriteLine("th");
txtstream.WriteLine("{");
txtstream.WriteLine("   COLOR: darkred;");
txtstream.WriteLine("   BACKGROUND-COLOR: white;");
txtstream.WriteLine("   FONT-FAMILY:font-family: Cambria, serif;");
txtstream.WriteLine("   FONT-SIZE: 12px;");
txtstream.WriteLine("   text-align: left;");
txtstream.WriteLine("   white-Space: nowrap;");
txtstream.WriteLine("}");
txtstream.WriteLine("td");
txtstream.WriteLine("{");
txtstream.WriteLine("   COLOR: navy;");
txtstream.WriteLine("   BACKGROUND-COLOR: white;");
```

```
txtstream.WriteLine("    FONT-FAMILY: font-family: Cambria, serif;");
txtstream.WriteLine("    FONT-SIZE: 12px;");
txtstream.WriteLine("    text-align: left;");
txtstream.WriteLine("    white-Space: nowrap;");
txtstream.WriteLine("}");
txtstream.WriteLine("</style>");
txtstream.WriteLine("<title>Win32_Process</title>");
txtstream.WriteLine("</head>");
txtstream.WriteLine("<body>");
txtstream.WriteLine("<table border='0' Cellspacing='3' cellpadding = '3'>");
var v=0;
while(v < 0)
{
    var ti = ex.NextEvent(-1);
    var obj = ti.Properties_.Item("Targetinstance").Value;
    if(v == 0)
    {
        txtstream.WriteLine("<tr>");
        var propEnum = new Enumerator(obj.Properties_);
        for (; !propEnum.atEnd(); propEnum.moveNext())
        {
            var prop = propEnum.item();
            txtstream.WriteLine("<th align='left' nowrap>" + prop.Name + "</th>");
        }
        txtstream.WriteLine("</tr>");
        propEnum.ReSet();
    }
    txtstream.WriteLine("<tr>");
    for (; !propEnum.atEnd(); propEnum.moveNext())
    {
        var prop = propEnum.item();
        txtstream.WriteLine("<td style='font-family:Calibri, Sans-Serif;font-size:
12px;color:navy;' align='left' nowrap='true'><textarea>" + GetValue(prop.Name,
obj) + "</textarea></td>");
    }
    txtstream.WriteLine("</tr>");
    v = v + 1;
}
txtstream.WriteLine("</table>");
txtstream.WriteLine("</body>");
```

```
txtstream.WriteLine("</html>");
txtstream.close();
function GetValue(Name, obj)
{
    var tempstr = new String();
    var tempstr1 = new String();
    var tName = new String();
    tempstr1 = obj.GetObjectText_();
    var re = /"/g;
    tempstr1 = tempstr1.replace(re , "");
    var pos;
    tName = Name + " = ";
    pos = tempstr1.indexOf(tName);
    if (pos > -1)
    {
        pos = pos + tName.length;
        tempstr = tempstr1.substring(pos, tempstr1.length);
        pos = tempstr.indexOf(";");
        tempstr = tempstr.substring(0, pos);
        tempstr = tempstr.replace("{", "");
        tempstr = tempstr.replace("}", "");
        if (tempstr.length > 13)
        {
            if (obj.Properties_(Name).CIMType == 101)
            {
                tempstr = tempstr.substr(4, 2) + "/" + tempstr.substr(6, 2) + "/" +
tempstr.substr(0, 3) + " " + tempstr.substr(8, 2) + ":" + tempstr.substr(10, 2) + ":" +
tempstr.substr(12, 2);
            }
        }
        return tempstr;
    }
    else
    {
        return "";
    }
}
```

Horizontal Report with a textbox.

```
var locator = new ActiveXObject("WbemScripting.SWbemLocator");
var svc = locator.ConnectServer(".", "root\\cimv2");
svc.Security_.AuthenticationLevel = 6;
svc.Security_.ImpersonationLevel = 3;
var strQuery = "Select * From __InstanceDeletionEvent WITHIN 1 where
TargetInstance ISA'Win32_Process'");
var es = svc.ExecNotificationQuery(strQuery);
var ws = new ActiveXObject("WScript.Shell");
var fso = new ActiveXObject("Scripting.FileSystemObject");
var txtstream = fso.OpenTextFile(ws.CurrentDirectory + "\\Win32_Process.html",
2, true, -2);
txtstream.WriteLine("<html xmlns='http://www.w3.org/1999/xhtml'>");
txtstream.WriteLine("<head>");
txtstream.WriteLine("<style type='text/css'>");
txtstream.WriteLine("th");
txtstream.WriteLine("{");
txtstream.WriteLine("   COLOR: darkred;");
txtstream.WriteLine("   BACKGROUND-COLOR: white;");
txtstream.WriteLine("   FONT-FAMILY:font-family: Cambria, serif;");
txtstream.WriteLine("   FONT-SIZE: 12px;");
txtstream.WriteLine("   text-align: left;");
txtstream.WriteLine("   white-Space: nowrap;");
txtstream.WriteLine("}");
txtstream.WriteLine("td");
txtstream.WriteLine("{");
txtstream.WriteLine("   COLOR: navy;");
txtstream.WriteLine("   BACKGROUND-COLOR: white;");
txtstream.WriteLine("   FONT-FAMILY: font-family: Cambria, serif;");
txtstream.WriteLine("   FONT-SIZE: 12px;");
txtstream.WriteLine("   text-align: left;");
txtstream.WriteLine("   white-Space: nowrap;");
txtstream.WriteLine("}");
txtstream.WriteLine("</style>");
txtstream.WriteLine("<title>Win32_Process</title>");
txtstream.WriteLine("</head>");
txtstream.WriteLine("<body>");
txtstream.WriteLine("<table border='0' Cellspacing='3' cellpadding = '3'>");
```

```
var v=0;
while(v < 0)
{
   var ti = ex.NextEvent(-1);
   var obj = ti.Properties_.Item("Targetinstance").Value;
   if(v == 0)
   {
      txtstream.WriteLine("<tr>");
      var propEnum = new Enumerator(obj.Properties_);
      for (; !propEnum.atEnd(); propEnum.moveNext())
      {
         var prop = propEnum.item();
         txtstream.WriteLine("<th align='left' nowrap>" + prop.Name + "</th>");
      }
      txtstream.WriteLine("</tr>");
      propEnum.ReSet();
   }
   txtstream.WriteLine("<tr>");
   for (; !propEnum.atEnd(); propEnum.moveNext())
   {
      var prop = propEnum.item();
      txtstream.WriteLine("<td style='font-family:Calibri, Sans-Serif;font-size:
12px;color:navy;' align='left' nowrap='true'><input type=text value='" +
GetValue(prop.Name, obj) + "'></input></td>");
   }
   txtstream.WriteLine("</tr>");
   v = v + 1;
}
txtstream.WriteLine("</table>");
txtstream.WriteLine("</body>");
txtstream.WriteLine("</html>");
txtstream.close();
function GetValue(Name, obj)
{
   var tempstr = new String();
   var tempstr1 = new String();
   var tName = new String();
   tempstr1 = obj.GetObjectText_();
   var re = /"/g;
   tempstr1 = tempstr1.replace(re , "");
```

```
var pos;
tName = Name + " = ";
pos = tempstr1.indexOf(tName);
if (pos > -1)
{
    pos = pos + tName.length;
    tempstr = tempstr1.substring(pos, tempstr1.length);
    pos = tempstr.indexOf(";");
    tempstr = tempstr.substring(0, pos);
    tempstr = tempstr.replace("{", "");
    tempstr = tempstr.replace("}", "");
    if (tempstr.length > 13)
    {
        if (obj.Properties_(Name).CIMType == 101)
        {
            tempstr = tempstr.substr(4, 2) + "/" + tempstr.substr(6, 2) + "/" +
tempstr.substr(0, 3) + " " + tempstr.substr(8, 2) + ":" + tempstr.substr(10, 2) + ":" +
tempstr.substr(12, 2);
        }
    }
    return tempstr;
}
else
{
    return "";
}
}
```

Vertical Report with no additional tags.

```
var locator = new ActiveXObject("WbemScripting.SWbemLocator");
var svc = locator.ConnectServer(".", "root\\cimv2");
svc.Security_.AuthenticationLevel = 6;
svc.Security_.ImpersonationLevel = 3;
var strQuery = "Select * From ___InstanceDeletionEvent WITHIN 1 where
TargetInstance ISA'Win32_Process'");
var es = svc.ExecNotificationQuery(strQuery);
var ws = new ActiveXObject("WScript.Shell");
var fso = new ActiveXObject("Scripting.FileSystemObject");
```

```javascript
var txtstream = fso.OpenTextFile(ws.CurrentDirectory + "\\Win32_Process.html",
2, true, -2);
    txtstream.WriteLine("<html xmlns='http://www.w3.org/1999/xhtml'>");
    txtstream.WriteLine("<head>");
    txtstream.WriteLine("<style type='text/css'>");
    txtstream.WriteLine("th");
    txtstream.WriteLine("{");
    txtstream.WriteLine("   COLOR: darkred;");
    txtstream.WriteLine("   BACKGROUND-COLOR: white;");
    txtstream.WriteLine("   FONT-FAMILY:font-family: Cambria, serif;");
    txtstream.WriteLine("   FONT-SIZE: 12px;");
    txtstream.WriteLine("   text-align: left;");
    txtstream.WriteLine("   white-Space: nowrap;");
    txtstream.WriteLine("}");
    txtstream.WriteLine("td");
    txtstream.WriteLine("{");
    txtstream.WriteLine("   COLOR: navy;");
    txtstream.WriteLine("   BACKGROUND-COLOR: white;");
    txtstream.WriteLine("   FONT-FAMILY: font-family: Cambria, serif;");
    txtstream.WriteLine("   FONT-SIZE: 12px;");
    txtstream.WriteLine("   text-align: left;");
    txtstream.WriteLine("   white-Space: nowrap;");
    txtstream.WriteLine("}");
    txtstream.WriteLine("</style>");
    txtstream.WriteLine("<title>Win32_Process</title>");
    txtstream.WriteLine("</head>");
    txtstream.WriteLine("<body>");
    txtstream.WriteLine("<table border='0' Cellspacing='3' cellpadding = '3'>");

    var Names;
    var Cols;
    var Rows;
    var x = 0;

    var v = 0;
    while(v < 0)
    {
        var ti = ex.NextEvent(-1);
        var obj = ti.Properties_.Item("Targetinstance").Value;
        if(v == 0)
```

```
{
    Names = new Array[obj.Properties_.Count];
    Cols = new Array[obj.Properties_.Count];
    Rows = new Array[4];
    var propEnum = new Enumerator(obj.Properties_);
    for (; !propEnum.atEnd(); propEnum.moveNext())
    {
        var prop = propEnum.item();
        Names[x] = prop.Name;
        Cols[x] = GetValue(prop.Name, obj);
        x = x + 1;
    }
    Rows[v] = Cols;
    x = 0;
    v = v + 1;
}
else
{
    var propEnum = new Enumerator(obj.Properties_);
    for (; !propEnum.atEnd(); propEnum.moveNext())
    {
        var prop = propEnum.item();
        Cols[x] = GetValue(prop.Name, obj);
        x = x + 1;
    }
    Rows[v] = Cols;
    x = 0;
    v = v + 1;
}
}
for(var a = 0;a < Names.Count; a++)
{
    txtstream.WriteLine("<tr><th align='left' nowrap>" + Names[a] + "</th>");
    for(var b = 0;b < Rows.Count; b++)
    {
        var C = Rows[b];
        txtstream.WriteLine("<td style='font-family:Calibri, Sans-Serif;font-size:
12px;color:navy;' align='left' nowrap='nowrap'>" + C[x] + "</td>");
    }
    txtstream.WriteLine("</tr>");
```

```
   }
   txtstream.WriteLine("</table>");
   txtstream.WriteLine("</body>");
   txtstream.WriteLine("</html>");
   txtstream.close();
   function GetValue(Name, obj)
   {
      var tempstr = new String();
      var tempstr1 = new String();
      var tName = new String();
      tempstr1 = obj.GetObjectText_();
      var re = /"/g;
      tempstr1 = tempstr1.replace(re , "");
      var pos;
      tName = Name + " = ";
      pos = tempstr1.indexOf(tName);
      if (pos > -1)
      {
         pos = pos + tName.length;
         tempstr = tempstr1.substring(pos, tempstr1.length);
         pos = tempstr.indexOf(";");
         tempstr = tempstr.substring(0, pos);
         tempstr = tempstr.replace("{", "");
         tempstr = tempstr.replace("}", "");
         if (tempstr.length > 13)
         {
            if (obj.Properties_(Name).CIMType == 101)
            {
              tempstr = tempstr.substr(4, 2) + "/" + tempstr.substr(6, 2) + "/" +
tempstr.substr(0, 3) + " " + tempstr.substr(8, 2) + ":" + tempstr.substr(10, 2) + ":" +
tempstr.substr(12, 2);
            }
         }
         return tempstr;
      }
      else
      {
         return "";
      }
   }
```

Vertical Report with a combobox.

```
var locator = new ActiveXObject("WbemScripting.SWbemLocator");
var svc = locator.ConnectServer(".", "root\\cimv2");
svc.Security_.AuthenticationLevel = 6;
svc.Security_.ImpersonationLevel = 3;
var strQuery = "Select * From ___InstanceDeletionEvent WITHIN 1 where
TargetInstance ISA'Win32_Process'");
var es = svc.ExecNotificationQuery(strQuery);
var ws = new ActiveXObject("WScript.Shell");
var fso = new ActiveXObject("Scripting.FileSystemObject");
var txtstream = fso.OpenTextFile(ws.CurrentDirectory + "\\Win32_Process.html",
2, true, -2);
txtstream.WriteLine("<html xmlns='http://www.w3.org/1999/xhtml'>");
txtstream.WriteLine("<head>");
txtstream.WriteLine("<style type='text/css'>");
txtstream.WriteLine("th");
txtstream.WriteLine("{");
txtstream.WriteLine("   COLOR: darkred;");
txtstream.WriteLine("   BACKGROUND-COLOR: white;");
txtstream.WriteLine("   FONT-FAMILY:font-family: Cambria, serif;");
txtstream.WriteLine("   FONT-SIZE: 12px;");
txtstream.WriteLine("   text-align: left;");
txtstream.WriteLine("   white-Space: nowrap;");
txtstream.WriteLine("}");
txtstream.WriteLine("td");
txtstream.WriteLine("{");
txtstream.WriteLine("   COLOR: navy;");
txtstream.WriteLine("   BACKGROUND-COLOR: white;");
txtstream.WriteLine("   FONT-FAMILY: font-family: Cambria, serif;");
txtstream.WriteLine("   FONT-SIZE: 12px;");
txtstream.WriteLine("   text-align: left;");
txtstream.WriteLine("   white-Space: nowrap;");
txtstream.WriteLine("}");
txtstream.WriteLine("</style>");
txtstream.WriteLine("<title>Win32_Process</title>");
txtstream.WriteLine("</head>");
txtstream.WriteLine("<body>");
```

```
txtstream.WriteLine("<table border='0' Cellspacing='3' cellpadding = '3'>");

var Names;
var Cols;
var Rows;
var x = 0;

var v = 0;
while(v < 0)
{
    var ti = ex.NextEvent(-1);
    var obj = ti.Properties_.Item("Targetinstance").Value;
    if(v == 0)
    {
        Names = new Array[obj.Properties_.Count];
        Cols = new Array[obj.Properties_.Count];
        Rows = new Array[4];
        var propEnum = new Enumerator(obj.Properties_);
        for (; !propEnum.atEnd(); propEnum.moveNext())
        {
            var prop = propEnum.item();
            Names[x] = prop.Name;
            Cols[x] = GetValue(prop.Name, obj);
            x = x + 1;
        }
        Rows[v] = Cols;
        x = 0;
        v = v + 1;
    }
    else
    {
        var propEnum = new Enumerator(obj.Properties_);
        for (; !propEnum.atEnd(); propEnum.moveNext())
        {
            var prop = propEnum.item();
            Cols[x] = GetValue(prop.Name, obj);
            x = x + 1;
        }
        Rows[v] = Cols;
        x = 0;
```

```
        v = v + 1;
    }
}
for(var a = 0;a < Names.Count; a++)
{
    txtstream.WriteLine("<tr><th align='left' nowrap>" + Names[a] + "</th>");
    for(var b = 0;b < Rows.Count; b++)
    {
        var C = Rows[b];
        txtstream.WriteLine("<td style='font-family:Calibri, Sans-Serif;font-size:
12px;color:navy;' align='left' nowrap='true'><select><option value = """ + C[x] +
""">" + C[x] + "</option></select></td>");
    }
    txtstream.WriteLine("</tr>");
}
txtstream.WriteLine("</table>");
txtstream.WriteLine("</body>");
txtstream.WriteLine("</html>");
txtstream.close();
function GetValue(Name, obj)
{
    var tempstr = new String();
    var tempstr1 = new String();
    var tName = new String();
    tempstr1 = obj.GetObjectText_();
    var re = /"/g;
    tempstr1 = tempstr1.replace(re , "");
    var pos;
    tName = Name + " = ";
    pos = tempstr1.indexOf(tName);
    if (pos > -1)
    {
        pos = pos + tName.length;
        tempstr = tempstr1.substring(pos, tempstr1.length);
        pos = tempstr.indexOf(";");
        tempstr = tempstr.substring(0, pos);
        tempstr = tempstr.replace("{", "");
        tempstr = tempstr.replace("}", "");
        if (tempstr.length > 13)
        {
```

```
        if (obj.Properties_(Name).CIMType == 101)
        {
            tempstr = tempstr.substr(4, 2) + "/" + tempstr.substr(6, 2) + "/" +
tempstr.substr(0, 3) + " " + tempstr.substr(8, 2) + ":" + tempstr.substr(10, 2) + ":" +
tempstr.substr(12, 2);
        }
    }
    return tempstr;
}
else
{
    return "";
}
}
```

Vertical Report with a link.

```
var locator = new ActiveXObject("WbemScripting.SWbemLocator");
var svc = locator.ConnectServer(".", "root\\cimv2");
svc.Security_.AuthenticationLevel = 6;
svc.Security_.ImpersonationLevel = 3;
var strQuery = "Select * From ___InstanceDeletionEvent WITHIN 1 where
TargetInstance ISA'Win32_Process'");
var es = svc.ExecNotificationQuery(strQuery);
var ws = new ActiveXObject("WScript.Shell");
var fso = new ActiveXObject("Scripting.FileSystemObject");
var txtstream = fso.OpenTextFile(ws.CurrentDirectory + "\\Win32_Process.html",
2, true, -2);
txtstream.WriteLine("<html xmlns='http://www.w3.org/1999/xhtml'>");
txtstream.WriteLine("<head>");
txtstream.WriteLine("<style type='text/css'>");
txtstream.WriteLine("th");
txtstream.WriteLine("{");
txtstream.WriteLine("   COLOR: darkred;");
txtstream.WriteLine("   BACKGROUND-COLOR: white;");
txtstream.WriteLine("   FONT-FAMILY:font-family: Cambria, serif;");
txtstream.WriteLine("   FONT-SIZE: 12px;");
txtstream.WriteLine("   text-align: left;");
txtstream.WriteLine("   white-Space: nowrap;");
```

```
txtstream.WriteLine("}");
txtstream.WriteLine("td");
txtstream.WriteLine("{");
txtstream.WriteLine("    COLOR: navy;");
txtstream.WriteLine("    BACKGROUND-COLOR: white;");
txtstream.WriteLine("    FONT-FAMILY: font-family: Cambria, serif;");
txtstream.WriteLine("    FONT-SIZE: 12px;");
txtstream.WriteLine("    text-align: left;");
txtstream.WriteLine("    white-Space: nowrap;");
txtstream.WriteLine("}");
txtstream.WriteLine("</style>");
txtstream.WriteLine("<title>Win32_Process</title>");
txtstream.WriteLine("</head>");
txtstream.WriteLine("<body>");
txtstream.WriteLine("<table border='0' Cellspacing='3' cellpadding = '3'>");

var Names;
var Cols;
var Rows;
var x = 0;

var v = 0;
while(v < 0)
{
   var ti = ex.NextEvent(-1);
   var obj = ti.Properties_.Item("Targetinstance").Value;
   if(v == 0)
   {
      Names = new Array[obj.Properties_.Count];
      Cols = new Array[obj.Properties_.Count];
      Rows = new Array[4];
      var propEnum = new Enumerator(obj.Properties_);
      for (; !propEnum.atEnd(); propEnum.moveNext())
      {
         var prop = propEnum.item();
         Names[x] = prop.Name;
         Cols[x] = GetValue(prop.Name, obj);
         x = x + 1;
      }
      Rows[v] = Cols;
```

```
        x = 0;
        v = v + 1;
    }
    else
    {
        var propEnum = new Enumerator(obj.Properties_);
        for (; !propEnum.atEnd(); propEnum.moveNext())
        {
            var prop = propEnum.item();
            Cols[x] = GetValue(prop.Name, obj);
            x = x + 1;
        }
        Rows[v] = Cols;
        x = 0;
        v = v + 1;
    }
}
for(var a = 0;a < Names.Count; a++)
{
    txtstream.WriteLine("<tr><th align='left' nowrap>" + Names[a] + "</th>");
    for(var b = 0;b < Rows.Count; b++)
    {
        var C = Rows[b];
        txtstream.WriteLine("<td style='font-family:Calibri, Sans-Serif;font-size:
12px;color:navy;' align='left' nowrap='true'><a href='" + C[x] + "'>" + C[x] +
"</a></td>");
    }
    txtstream.WriteLine("</tr>");
}
txtstream.WriteLine("</table>");
txtstream.WriteLine("</body>");
txtstream.WriteLine("</html>");
txtstream.close();
function GetValue(Name, obj)
{
    var tempstr = new String();
    var tempstr1 = new String();
    var tName = new String();
    tempstr1 = obj.GetObjectText_();
    var re = /"/g;
```

```
tempstr1 = tempstr1.replace(re , "");
var pos;
tName = Name + " = ";
pos = tempstr1.indexOf(tName);
if (pos > -1)
{
    pos = pos + tName.length;
    tempstr = tempstr1.substring(pos, tempstr1.length);
    pos = tempstr.indexOf(";");
    tempstr = tempstr.substring(0, pos);
    tempstr = tempstr.replace("{", "");
    tempstr = tempstr.replace("}", "");
    if (tempstr.length > 13)
    {
        if (obj.Properties_(Name).CIMType == 101)
        {
        tempstr = tempstr.substr(4, 2) + "/"  + tempstr.substr(6, 2) + "/" +
tempstr.substr(0, 3) + " " + tempstr.substr(8, 2) + ":" + tempstr.substr(10, 2) + ":" +
tempstr.substr(12, 2);
        }
    }
    return tempstr;
}
else
{
    return "";
}
}
```

Vertical Report with a listbox.

```
var locator = new ActiveXObject("WbemScripting.SWbemLocator");
var svc = locator.ConnectServer(".", "root\\cimv2");
svc.Security_.AuthenticationLevel = 6;
svc.Security_.ImpersonationLevel = 3;
var strQuery = "Select * From ___InstanceDeletionEvent WITHIN 1 where
TargetInstance ISA'Win32_Process'");
var es = svc.ExecNotificationQuery(strQuery);
var ws = new ActiveXObject("WScript.Shell");
```

```
var fso = new ActiveXObject("Scripting.FileSystemObject");
var txtstream = fso.OpenTextFile(ws.CurrentDirectory + "\\Win32_Process.html",
2, true, -2);
txtstream.WriteLine("<html xmlns='http://www.w3.org/1999/xhtml'>");
txtstream.WriteLine("<head>");
txtstream.WriteLine("<style type='text/css'>");
txtstream.WriteLine("th");
txtstream.WriteLine("{");
txtstream.WriteLine("    COLOR: darkred;");
txtstream.WriteLine("    BACKGROUND-COLOR: white;");
txtstream.WriteLine("    FONT-FAMILY:font-family: Cambria, serif;");
txtstream.WriteLine("    FONT-SIZE: 12px;");
txtstream.WriteLine("    text-align: left;");
txtstream.WriteLine("    white-Space: nowrap;");
txtstream.WriteLine("}");
txtstream.WriteLine("td");
txtstream.WriteLine("{");
txtstream.WriteLine("    COLOR: navy;");
txtstream.WriteLine("    BACKGROUND-COLOR: white;");
txtstream.WriteLine("    FONT-FAMILY: font-family: Cambria, serif;");
txtstream.WriteLine("    FONT-SIZE: 12px;");
txtstream.WriteLine("    text-align: left;");
txtstream.WriteLine("    white-Space: nowrap;");
txtstream.WriteLine("}");
txtstream.WriteLine("</style>");
txtstream.WriteLine("<title>Win32_Process</title>");
txtstream.WriteLine("</head>");
txtstream.WriteLine("<body>");
txtstream.WriteLine("<table border='0' Cellspacing='3' cellpadding = '3'>");

var Names;
var Cols;
var Rows;
var x = 0;

var v = 0;
while(v < 0)
{
    var ti = ex.NextEvent(-1);
    var obj = ti.Properties_.Item("Targetinstance").Value;
```

```
if(v == 0)
{
    Names = new Array[obj.Properties_.Count];
    Cols = new Array[obj.Properties_.Count];
    Rows = new Array[4];
    var propEnum = new Enumerator(obj.Properties_);
    for (; !propEnum.atEnd(); propEnum.moveNext())
    {
        var prop = propEnum.item();
        Names[x] = prop.Name;
        Cols[x] = GetValue(prop.Name, obj);
        x = x + 1;
    }
    Rows[v] = Cols;
    x = 0;
    v = v + 1;
}
else
{
    var propEnum = new Enumerator(obj.Properties_);
    for (; !propEnum.atEnd(); propEnum.moveNext())
    {
        var prop = propEnum.item();
        Cols[x] = GetValue(prop.Name, obj);
        x = x + 1;
    }
    Rows[v] = Cols;
    x = 0;
    v = v + 1;
}
}
for(var a = 0;a < Names.Count; a++)
{
    txtstream.WriteLine("<tr><th align='left' nowrap>" + Names[a] + "</th>");
    for(var b = 0;b < Rows.Count; b++)
    {
        var C = Rows[b];
        txtstream.WriteLine("<td style='font-family:Calibri, Sans-Serif;font-size:
12px;color:navy;' align='left' nowrap='true'><select multiple><option value = """ +
C[x] + """>" + C[x] + "</option></select></td>");
```

```javascript
      }
      txtstream.WriteLine("</tr>");
   }
   txtstream.WriteLine("</table>");
   txtstream.WriteLine("</body>");
   txtstream.WriteLine("</html>");
   txtstream.close();
   function GetValue(Name, obj)
   {
      var tempstr = new String();
      var tempstr1 = new String();
      var tName = new String();
      tempstr1 = obj.GetObjectText_();
      var re = /"/g;
      tempstr1 = tempstr1.replace(re , "");
      var pos;
      tName = Name + " = ";
      pos = tempstr1.indexOf(tName);
      if (pos > -1)
      {
         pos = pos + tName.length;
         tempstr = tempstr1.substring(pos, tempstr1.length);
         pos = tempstr.indexOf(";");
         tempstr = tempstr.substring(0, pos);
         tempstr = tempstr.replace("{", "");
         tempstr = tempstr.replace("}", "");
         if (tempstr.length > 13)
         {
            if (obj.Properties_(Name).CIMType == 101)
            {
               tempstr = tempstr.substr(4, 2) + "/" + tempstr.substr(6, 2) + "/" +
tempstr.substr(0, 3) + " " + tempstr.substr(8, 2) + ":" + tempstr.substr(10, 2) + ":" +
tempstr.substr(12, 2);
            }
         }
         return tempstr;
      }
      else
      {
         return "";
```

```
        }
    }
```

Vertical Report with a textarea.

```
var locator = new ActiveXObject("WbemScripting.SWbemLocator");
var svc = locator.ConnectServer(".", "root\\cimv2");
svc.Security_.AuthenticationLevel = 6;
svc.Security_.ImpersonationLevel = 3;
var strQuery = "Select * From ___InstanceDeletionEvent WITHIN 1 where
TargetInstance ISA'Win32_Process'");
var es = svc.ExecNotificationQuery(strQuery);
var ws = new ActiveXObject("WScript.Shell");
var fso = new ActiveXObject("Scripting.FileSystemObject");
var txtstream = fso.OpenTextFile(ws.CurrentDirectory + "\\Win32_Process.html",
2, true, -2);
txtstream.WriteLine("<html xmlns='http://www.w3.org/1999/xhtml'>");
txtstream.WriteLine("<head>");
txtstream.WriteLine("<style type='text/css'>");
txtstream.WriteLine("th");
txtstream.WriteLine("{");
txtstream.WriteLine("    COLOR: darkred;");
txtstream.WriteLine("    BACKGROUND-COLOR: white;");
txtstream.WriteLine("    FONT-FAMILY:font-family: Cambria, serif;");
txtstream.WriteLine("    FONT-SIZE: 12px;");
txtstream.WriteLine("    text-align: left;");
txtstream.WriteLine("    white-Space: nowrap;");
txtstream.WriteLine("}");
txtstream.WriteLine("td");
txtstream.WriteLine("{");
txtstream.WriteLine("    COLOR: navy;");
txtstream.WriteLine("    BACKGROUND-COLOR: white;");
txtstream.WriteLine("    FONT-FAMILY: font-family: Cambria, serif;");
txtstream.WriteLine("    FONT-SIZE: 12px;");
txtstream.WriteLine("    text-align: left;");
txtstream.WriteLine("    white-Space: nowrap;");
txtstream.WriteLine("}");
txtstream.WriteLine("</style>");
txtstream.WriteLine("<title>Win32_Process</title>");
```

```
txtstream.WriteLine("</head>");
txtstream.WriteLine("<body>");
txtstream.WriteLine("<table border='0' Cellspacing='3' cellpadding = '3'>");

var Names;
var Cols;
var Rows;
var x = 0;

var v = 0;
while(v < 0)
{
    var ti = ex.NextEvent(-1);
    var obj = ti.Properties_.Item("Targetinstance").Value;
    if(v == 0)
    {
        Names = new Array[obj.Properties_.Count];
        Cols = new Array[obj.Properties_.Count];
        Rows = new Array[4];
        var propEnum = new Enumerator(obj.Properties_);
        for (; !propEnum.atEnd(); propEnum.moveNext())
        {
            var prop = propEnum.item();
            Names[x] = prop.Name;
            Cols[x] = GetValue(prop.Name, obj);
            x = x + 1;
        }
        Rows[v] = Cols;
        x = 0;
        v = v + 1;
    }
    else
    {
        var propEnum = new Enumerator(obj.Properties_);
        for (; !propEnum.atEnd(); propEnum.moveNext())
        {
            var prop = propEnum.item();
            Cols[x] = GetValue(prop.Name, obj);
            x = x + 1;
        }
```

```
        Rows[v] = Cols;
        x = 0;
        v = v + 1;
      }
    }
    for(var a = 0;a < Names.Count; a++)
    {
        txtstream.WriteLine("<tr><th align='left' nowrap>" + Names[a] + "</th>");
        for(var b = 0;b < Rows.Count; b++)
        {
            var C = Rows[b];
            txtstream.WriteLine("<td style='font-family:Calibri, Sans-Serif;font-size:
12px;color:navy;' align='left' nowrap='true'><textarea>" + C[x] +
"</textarea></td>");
        }
        txtstream.WriteLine("</tr>");
    }
    txtstream.WriteLine("</table>");
    txtstream.WriteLine("</body>");
    txtstream.WriteLine("</html>");
    txtstream.close();
    function GetValue(Name, obj)
    {
        var tempstr = new String();
        var tempstr1 = new String();
        var tName = new String();
        tempstr1 = obj.GetObjectText_();
        var re = /"/g;
        tempstr1 = tempstr1.replace(re , "");
        var pos;
        tName = Name + " = ";
        pos = tempstr1.indexOf(tName);
        if (pos > -1)
        {
            pos = pos + tName.length;
            tempstr = tempstr1.substring(pos, tempstr1.length);
            pos = tempstr.indexOf(";");
            tempstr = tempstr.substring(0, pos);
            tempstr = tempstr.replace("{", "");
            tempstr = tempstr.replace("}", "");
```

```
        if (tempstr.length > 13)
        {
            if (obj.Properties_(Name).CIMType == 101)
            {
            tempstr = tempstr.substr(4, 2) + "/"  + tempstr.substr(6, 2) + "/" +
tempstr.substr(0, 3) + " " + tempstr.substr(8, 2) + ":" + tempstr.substr(10, 2) + ":" +
tempstr.substr(12, 2);
            }
        }
        return tempstr;
    }
    else
    {
        return "";
    }
}
```

Vertical Report with a textbox.

```
var locator = new ActiveXObject("WbemScripting.SWbemLocator");
var svc = locator.ConnectServer(".", "root\\cimv2");
svc.Security_.AuthenticationLevel = 6;
svc.Security_.ImpersonationLevel = 3;
var strQuery = "Select * From ___InstanceDeletionEvent WITHIN 1 where
TargetInstance ISA'Win32_Process'");
var es = svc.ExecNotificationQuery(strQuery);
var ws = new ActiveXObject("WScript.Shell");
var fso = new ActiveXObject("Scripting.FileSystemObject");
var txtstream = fso.OpenTextFile(ws.CurrentDirectory + "\\Win32_Process.html",
2, true, -2);
txtstream.WriteLine("<html xmlns='http://www.w3.org/1999/xhtml'>");
txtstream.WriteLine("<head>");
txtstream.WriteLine("<style type='text/css'>");
txtstream.WriteLine("th");
txtstream.WriteLine("{");
txtstream.WriteLine("    COLOR: darkred;");
txtstream.WriteLine("    BACKGROUND-COLOR: white;");
txtstream.WriteLine("    FONT-FAMILY:font-family: Cambria, serif;");
txtstream.WriteLine("    FONT-SIZE: 12px;");
```

```
txtstream.WriteLine("   text-align: left;");
txtstream.WriteLine("   white-Space: nowrap;");
txtstream.WriteLine("}");
txtstream.WriteLine("td");
txtstream.WriteLine("{");
txtstream.WriteLine("   COLOR: navy;");
txtstream.WriteLine("   BACKGROUND-COLOR: white;");
txtstream.WriteLine("   FONT-FAMILY: font-family: Cambria, serif;");
txtstream.WriteLine("   FONT-SIZE: 12px;");
txtstream.WriteLine("   text-align: left;");
txtstream.WriteLine("   white-Space: nowrap;");
txtstream.WriteLine("}");
txtstream.WriteLine("</style>");
txtstream.WriteLine("<title>Win32_Process</title>");
txtstream.WriteLine("</head>");
txtstream.WriteLine("<body>");
txtstream.WriteLine("<table border='0' Cellspacing='3' cellpadding = '3'>");

var Names;
var Cols;
var Rows;
var x = 0;

var v = 0;
while(v < 0)
{
    var ti = ex.NextEvent(-1);
    var obj = ti.Properties_.Item("Targetinstance").Value;
    if(v == 0)
    {
        Names = new Array[obj.Properties_.Count];
        Cols = new Array[obj.Properties_.Count];
        Rows = new Array[4];
        var propEnum = new Enumerator(obj.Properties_);
        for (; !propEnum.atEnd(); propEnum.moveNext())
        {
            var prop = propEnum.item();
            Names[x] = prop.Name;
            Cols[x] = GetValue(prop.Name, obj);
            x = x + 1;
```

```
            }
            Rows[v] = Cols;
            x = 0;
            v = v + 1;
        }
        else
        {
            var propEnum = new Enumerator(obj.Properties_);
            for (; !propEnum.atEnd(); propEnum.moveNext())
            {
                var prop = propEnum.item();
                Cols[x] = GetValue(prop.Name, obj);
                x = x + 1;
            }
            Rows[v] = Cols;
            x = 0;
            v = v + 1;
        }
    }
    for(var a = 0;a < Names.Count; a++)
    {
        txtstream.WriteLine("<tr><th align='left' nowrap>" + Names[a] + "</th>");
        for(var b = 0;b < Rows.Count; b++)
        {
            var C = Rows[b];
            txtstream.WriteLine("<td style='font-family:Calibri, Sans-Serif;font-size:
12px;color:navy;' align='left' nowrap='true'><input type=text value='"" + C[x] +
"'"></input></td>");
        }
        txtstream.WriteLine("</tr>");
    }
    txtstream.WriteLine("</table>");
    txtstream.WriteLine("</body>");
    txtstream.WriteLine("</html>");
    txtstream.close();
    function GetValue(Name, obj)
    {
        var tempstr = new String();
        var tempstr1 = new String();
        var tName = new String();
```

```
tempstr1 = obj.GetObjectText_();
var re = /"/g;
tempstr1 = tempstr1.replace(re , "");
var pos;
tName = Name + " = ";
pos = tempstr1.indexOf(tName);
if (pos > -1)
{
    pos = pos + tName.length;
    tempstr = tempstr1.substring(pos, tempstr1.length);
    pos = tempstr.indexOf(";");
    tempstr = tempstr.substring(0, pos);
    tempstr = tempstr.replace("{", "");
    tempstr = tempstr.replace("}", "");
    if (tempstr.length > 13)
    {
        if (obj.Properties_(Name).CIMType == 101)
        {
            tempstr = tempstr.substr(4, 2) + "/" + tempstr.substr(6, 2) + "/" +
tempstr.substr(0, 3) + " " + tempstr.substr(8, 2) + ":" + tempstr.substr(10, 2) + ":" +
tempstr.substr(12, 2);
        }
    }
    return tempstr;
}
else
{
    return "";
}
}
```

HTML Tables

Horizontal Table with no additional tags.

```
var locator = new ActiveXObject("WbemScripting.SWbemLocator");
var svc = locator.ConnectServer(".", "root\\cimv2");
svc.Security_.AuthenticationLevel = 6;
svc.Security_.ImpersonationLevel = 3;
var strQuery = "Select * From ___InstanceDeletionEvent WITHIN 1 where
TargetInstance ISA'Win32_Process'");
var es = svc.ExecNotificationQuery(strQuery);
var ws = new ActiveXObject("WScript.Shell");
var fso = new ActiveXObject("Scripting.FileSystemObject");
var txtstream = fso.OpenTextFile(ws.CurrentDirectory + "\\Win32_Process.html",
2, true, -2);
txtstream.WriteLine("<html xmlns='http://www.w3.org/1999/xhtml'>");
txtstream.WriteLine("<head>");
txtstream.WriteLine("<style type='text/css'>");
txtstream.WriteLine("th");
txtstream.WriteLine("{");
txtstream.WriteLine("    COLOR: darkred;");
```

```
txtstream.WriteLine("   BACKGROUND-COLOR: white;");
txtstream.WriteLine("   FONT-FAMILY:font-family: Cambria, serif;");
txtstream.WriteLine("   FONT-SIZE: 12px;");
txtstream.WriteLine("   text-align: left;");
txtstream.WriteLine("   white-Space: nowrap;");
txtstream.WriteLine("}");
txtstream.WriteLine("td");
txtstream.WriteLine("{");
txtstream.WriteLine("   COLOR: navy;");
txtstream.WriteLine("   BACKGROUND-COLOR: white;");
txtstream.WriteLine("   FONT-FAMILY: font-family: Cambria, serif;");
txtstream.WriteLine("   FONT-SIZE: 12px;");
txtstream.WriteLine("   text-align: left;");
txtstream.WriteLine("   white-Space: nowrap;");
txtstream.WriteLine("}");
txtstream.WriteLine("</style>");
txtstream.WriteLine("<title>Win32_Process</title>");
txtstream.WriteLine("</head>");
txtstream.WriteLine("<body>");
txtstream.WriteLine("<table border='1' Cellspacing='3' cellpadding = '3'>");
var v=0;
while(v < 0)
{
   var ti = ex.NextEvent(-1);
   var obj = ti.Properties_.Item("Targetinstance").Value;
   if(v == 0)
   {
      txtstream.WriteLine("<tr>");
      var propEnum = new Enumerator(obj.Properties_);
      for (; !propEnum.atEnd(); propEnum.moveNext())
      {
         var prop = propEnum.item();
         txtstream.WriteLine("<th align='left' nowrap>" + prop.Name + "</th>");
      }
      txtstream.WriteLine("</tr>");
      propEnum.ReSet();
   }
   txtstream.WriteLine("<tr>");
   for (; !propEnum.atEnd(); propEnum.moveNext())
   {
```

```
        var prop = propEnum.item();
        txtstream.WriteLine("<td style='font-family:Calibri, Sans-Serif;font-size:
12px;color:navy;' align='left' nowrap='nowrap'>" + GetValue(prop.Name, obj) +
"</td>");
    }
    txtstream.WriteLine("</tr>");
    v = v + 1;
}
txtstream.WriteLine("</table>");
txtstream.WriteLine("</body>");
txtstream.WriteLine("</html>");
txtstream.close();
function GetValue(Name, obj)
{
    var tempstr = new String();
    var tempstr1 = new String();
    var tName = new String();
    tempstr1 = obj.GetObjectText_();
    var re = /"/g;
    tempstr1 = tempstr1.replace(re , "");
    var pos;
    tName = Name + " = ";
    pos = tempstr1.indexOf(tName);
    if (pos > -1)
    {
        pos = pos + tName.length;
        tempstr = tempstr1.substring(pos, tempstr1.length);
        pos = tempstr.indexOf(";");
        tempstr = tempstr.substring(0, pos);
        tempstr = tempstr.replace("{", "");
        tempstr = tempstr.replace("}", "");
        if (tempstr.length > 13)
        {
            if (obj.Properties_(Name).CIMType == 101)
            {
                tempstr = tempstr.substr(4, 2) + "/" + tempstr.substr(6, 2) + "/" +
tempstr.substr(0, 3) + " " + tempstr.substr(8, 2) + ":" + tempstr.substr(10, 2) + ":" +
tempstr.substr(12, 2);
            }
        }
```

```
        return tempstr;
    }
    else
    {
        return "";
    }
}
```

Horizontal Table with a combobox.

```
var locator = new ActiveXObject("WbemScripting.SWbemLocator");
var svc = locator.ConnectServer(".", "root\\cimv2");
svc.Security_.AuthenticationLevel = 6;
svc.Security_.ImpersonationLevel = 3;
var strQuery = "Select * From ___InstanceDeletionEvent WITHIN 1 where
TargetInstance ISA'Win32_Process'");
var es = svc.ExecNotificationQuery(strQuery);
var ws = new ActiveXObject("WScript.Shell");
var fso = new ActiveXObject("Scripting.FileSystemObject");
var txtstream = fso.OpenTextFile(ws.CurrentDirectory + "\\Win32_Process.html",
2, true, -2);
txtstream.WriteLine("<html xmlns='http://www.w3.org/1999/xhtml'>");
txtstream.WriteLine("<head>");
txtstream.WriteLine("<style type='text/css'>");
txtstream.WriteLine("th");
txtstream.WriteLine("{");
txtstream.WriteLine("    COLOR: darkred;");
txtstream.WriteLine("    BACKGROUND-COLOR: white;");
txtstream.WriteLine("    FONT-FAMILY:font-family: Cambria, serif;");
txtstream.WriteLine("    FONT-SIZE: 12px;");
txtstream.WriteLine("    text-align: left;");
txtstream.WriteLine("    white-Space: nowrap;");
txtstream.WriteLine("}");
txtstream.WriteLine("td");
txtstream.WriteLine("{");
txtstream.WriteLine("    COLOR: navy;");
txtstream.WriteLine("    BACKGROUND-COLOR: white;");
txtstream.WriteLine("    FONT-FAMILY: font-family: Cambria, serif;");
txtstream.WriteLine("    FONT-SIZE: 12px;");
```

```
txtstream.WriteLine("    text-align: left;");
txtstream.WriteLine("    white-Space: nowrap;");
txtstream.WriteLine("}");
txtstream.WriteLine("</style>");
txtstream.WriteLine("<title>Win32_Process</title>");
txtstream.WriteLine("</head>");
txtstream.WriteLine("<body>");
txtstream.WriteLine("<table border='1' Cellspacing='3' cellpadding = '3'>");
var v=0;
while(v < 0)
{
   var ti = ex.NextEvent(-1);
   var obj = ti.Properties_.Item("Targetinstance").Value;
   if(v == 0)
   {
      txtstream.WriteLine("<tr>");
      var propEnum = new Enumerator(obj.Properties_);
      for (; !propEnum.atEnd(); propEnum.moveNext())
      {
         var prop = propEnum.item();
         txtstream.WriteLine("<th align='left' nowrap>" + prop.Name + "</th>");
      }
      txtstream.WriteLine("</tr>");
      propEnum.ReSet();
   }
   txtstream.WriteLine("<tr>");
   for (; !propEnum.atEnd(); propEnum.moveNext())
   {
      var prop = propEnum.item();
      txtstream.WriteLine("<td style='font-family:Calibri, Sans-Serif;font-size:
12px;color:navy;' align='left' nowrap='true'><select><option value = '" +
GetValue(prop.Name, obj) + "'>" + GetValue(prop.Name, obj) +
"</option></select></td>");
   }
   txtstream.WriteLine("</tr>");
   v = v + 1;
}
txtstream.WriteLine("</table>");
txtstream.WriteLine("</body>");
txtstream.WriteLine("</html>");
```

```
txtstream.close();
function GetValue(Name, obj)
{
    var tempstr = new String();
    var tempstr1 = new String();
    var tName = new String();
    tempstr1 = obj.GetObjectText_();
    var re = /"/g;
    tempstr1 = tempstr1.replace(re , "");
    var pos;
    tName = Name + " = ";
    pos = tempstr1.indexOf(tName);
    if (pos > -1)
    {
        pos = pos + tName.length;
        tempstr = tempstr1.substring(pos, tempstr1.length);
        pos = tempstr.indexOf(";");
        tempstr = tempstr.substring(0, pos);
        tempstr = tempstr.replace("{", "");
        tempstr = tempstr.replace("}", "");
        if (tempstr.length > 13)
        {
            if (obj.Properties_(Name).CIMType == 101)
            {
                tempstr = tempstr.substr(4, 2) + "/"  + tempstr.substr(6, 2) + "/" +
tempstr.substr(0, 3) + " " + tempstr.substr(8, 2) + ":" + tempstr.substr(10, 2) + ":" +
tempstr.substr(12, 2);
            }
        }
        return tempstr;
    }
    else
    {
        return "";
    }
}
```

Horizontal Table with a link.

```
var locator = new ActiveXObject("WbemScripting.SWbemLocator");
var svc = locator.ConnectServer(".", "root\\cimv2");
svc.Security_.AuthenticationLevel = 6;
svc.Security_.ImpersonationLevel = 3;
var strQuery = "Select * From ___InstanceDeletionEvent WITHIN 1 where
TargetInstance ISA'Win32_Process'");
var es = svc.ExecNotificationQuery(strQuery);
var ws = new ActiveXObject("WScript.Shell");
var fso = new ActiveXObject("Scripting.FileSystemObject");
var txtstream = fso.OpenTextFile(ws.CurrentDirectory + "\\Win32_Process.html",
2, true, -2);
txtstream.WriteLine("<html xmlns='http://www.w3.org/1999/xhtml'>");
txtstream.WriteLine("<head>");
txtstream.WriteLine("<style type='text/css'>");
txtstream.WriteLine("th");
txtstream.WriteLine("{");
txtstream.WriteLine("    COLOR: darkred;");
txtstream.WriteLine("    BACKGROUND-COLOR: white;");
txtstream.WriteLine("    FONT-FAMILY:font-family: Cambria, serif;");
txtstream.WriteLine("    FONT-SIZE: 12px;");
txtstream.WriteLine("    text-align: left;");
txtstream.WriteLine("    white-Space: nowrap;");
txtstream.WriteLine("}");
txtstream.WriteLine("td");
txtstream.WriteLine("{");
txtstream.WriteLine("    COLOR: navy;");
txtstream.WriteLine("    BACKGROUND-COLOR: white;");
txtstream.WriteLine("    FONT-FAMILY: font-family: Cambria, serif;");
txtstream.WriteLine("    FONT-SIZE: 12px;");
txtstream.WriteLine("    text-align: left;");
txtstream.WriteLine("    white-Space: nowrap;");
txtstream.WriteLine("}");
txtstream.WriteLine("</style>");
txtstream.WriteLine("<title>Win32_Process</title>");
txtstream.WriteLine("</head>");
txtstream.WriteLine("<body>");
txtstream.WriteLine("<table border='1' Cellspacing='3' cellpadding = '3'>");
```

```
var v=0;
while(v < 0)
{
    var ti = ex.NextEvent(-1);
    var obj = ti.Properties_.Item("Targetinstance").Value;
    if(v == 0)
    {
        txtstream.WriteLine("<tr>");
        var propEnum = new Enumerator(obj.Properties_);
        for (; !propEnum.atEnd(); propEnum.moveNext())
        {
            var prop = propEnum.item();
            txtstream.WriteLine("<th align='left' nowrap>" + prop.Name + "</th>");
        }
        txtstream.WriteLine("</tr>");
        propEnum.ReSet();
    }
    txtstream.WriteLine("<tr>");
    for (; !propEnum.atEnd(); propEnum.moveNext())
    {
        var prop = propEnum.item();
        txtstream.WriteLine("<td style='font-family:Calibri, Sans-Serif;font-size:
12px;color:navy;' align='left' nowrap='true'><a href='" + GetValue(prop.Name, obj)
+ "'>" + GetValue(prop.Name, obj) + "</a></td>");
    }
    txtstream.WriteLine("</tr>");
    v = v + 1;
}
txtstream.WriteLine("</table>");
txtstream.WriteLine("</body>");
txtstream.WriteLine("</html>");
txtstream.close();
function GetValue(Name, obj)
{
    var tempstr = new String();
    var tempstr1 = new String();
    var tName = new String();
    tempstr1 = obj.GetObjectText_();
    var re = /"/g;
    tempstr1 = tempstr1.replace(re , "");
```

```
    var pos;
    tName = Name + " = ";
    pos = tempstr1.indexOf(tName);
    if (pos > -1)
    {
        pos = pos + tName.length;
        tempstr = tempstr1.substring(pos, tempstr1.length);
        pos = tempstr.indexOf(";");
        tempstr = tempstr.substring(0, pos);
        tempstr = tempstr.replace("{", "");
        tempstr = tempstr.replace("}", "");
        if (tempstr.length > 13)
        {
            if (obj.Properties_(Name).CIMType == 101)
            {
                tempstr = tempstr.substr(4, 2) + "/"  + tempstr.substr(6, 2) + "/" +
tempstr.substr(0, 3) + " " + tempstr.substr(8, 2) + ":" + tempstr.substr(10, 2) + ":" +
tempstr.substr(12, 2);
            }
        }
        return tempstr;
    }
    else
    {
        return "";
    }
}
```

Horizontal Table with a listbox.

```
var locator = new ActiveXObject("WbemScripting.SWbemLocator");
var svc = locator.ConnectServer(".", "root\\cimv2");
svc.Security_.AuthenticationLevel = 6;
svc.Security_.ImpersonationLevel = 3;
var strQuery = "Select * From ___InstanceDeletionEvent WITHIN 1 where
TargetInstance ISA'Win32_Process'");
var es = svc.ExecNotificationQuery(strQuery);
var ws = new ActiveXObject("WScript.Shell");
var fso = new ActiveXObject("Scripting.FileSystemObject");
```

```
var txtstream = fso.OpenTextFile(ws.CurrentDirectory + "\\Win32_Process.html",
2, true, -2);
txtstream.WriteLine("<html xmlns='http://www.w3.org/1999/xhtml'>");
txtstream.WriteLine("<head>");
txtstream.WriteLine("<style type='text/css'>");
txtstream.WriteLine("th");
txtstream.WriteLine("{");
txtstream.WriteLine("    COLOR: darkred;");
txtstream.WriteLine("    BACKGROUND-COLOR: white;");
txtstream.WriteLine("    FONT-FAMILY:font-family: Cambria, serif;");
txtstream.WriteLine("    FONT-SIZE: 12px;");
txtstream.WriteLine("    text-align: left;");
txtstream.WriteLine("    white-Space: nowrap;");
txtstream.WriteLine("}");
txtstream.WriteLine("td");
txtstream.WriteLine("{");
txtstream.WriteLine("    COLOR: navy;");
txtstream.WriteLine("    BACKGROUND-COLOR: white;");
txtstream.WriteLine("    FONT-FAMILY: font-family: Cambria, serif;");
txtstream.WriteLine("    FONT-SIZE: 12px;");
txtstream.WriteLine("    text-align: left;");
txtstream.WriteLine("    white-Space: nowrap;");
txtstream.WriteLine("}");
txtstream.WriteLine("</style>");
txtstream.WriteLine("<title>Win32_Process</title>");
txtstream.WriteLine("</head>");
txtstream.WriteLine("<body>");
txtstream.WriteLine("<table border='1' Cellspacing='3' cellpadding = '3'>");
var v=0;
while(v < 0)
{
    var ti = ex.NextEvent(-1);
    var obj = ti.Properties_.Item("Targetinstance").Value;
    if(v == 0)
    {
        txtstream.WriteLine("<tr>");
        var propEnum = new Enumerator(obj.Properties_);
        for (; !propEnum.atEnd(); propEnum.moveNext())
        {
            var prop = propEnum.item();
```

```
      txtstream.WriteLine("<th align='left' nowrap>" + prop.Name + "</th>");
   }
   txtstream.WriteLine("</tr>");
   propEnum.ReSet();
}
txtstream.WriteLine("<tr>");
for (; !propEnum.atEnd(); propEnum.moveNext())
{
   var prop = propEnum.item();
   txtstream.WriteLine("<td style='font-family:Calibri, Sans-Serif;font-size:
12px;color:navy;' align='left' nowrap='true'><select multiple><option value = '" +
GetValue(prop.Name, obj) + "'>" + GetValue(prop.Name, obj) +
"</option></select></td>");
}
txtstream.WriteLine("</tr>");
v = v + 1;
}
txtstream.WriteLine("</table>");
txtstream.WriteLine("</body>");
txtstream.WriteLine("</html>");
txtstream.close();
function GetValue(Name, obj)
{
   var tempstr = new String();
   var tempstr1 = new String();
   var tName = new String();
   tempstr1 = obj.GetObjectText_();
   var re = /"/g;
   tempstr1 = tempstr1.replace(re , "");
   var pos;
   tName = Name + " = ";
   pos = tempstr1.indexOf(tName);
   if (pos > -1)
   {
      pos = pos + tName.length;
      tempstr = tempstr1.substring(pos, tempstr1.length);
      pos = tempstr.indexOf(";");
      tempstr = tempstr.substring(0, pos);
      tempstr = tempstr.replace("{", "");
      tempstr = tempstr.replace("}", "");
```

```javascript
        if (tempstr.length > 13)
        {
            if (obj.Properties_(Name).CIMType == 101)
            {
                tempstr = tempstr.substr(4, 2) + "/" + tempstr.substr(6, 2) + "/" +
tempstr.substr(0, 3) + " " + tempstr.substr(8, 2) + ":" + tempstr.substr(10, 2) + ":" +
tempstr.substr(12, 2);
            }
        }
        return tempstr;
    }
    else
    {
        return "";
    }
}
```

Horizontal Table with a textarea.

```javascript
var locator = new ActiveXObject("WbemScripting.SWbemLocator");
var svc = locator.ConnectServer(".", "root\\cimv2");
svc.Security_.AuthenticationLevel = 6;
svc.Security_.ImpersonationLevel = 3;
var strQuery = "Select * From ___InstanceDeletionEvent WITHIN 1 where
TargetInstance ISA'Win32_Process'");
var es = svc.ExecNotificationQuery(strQuery);
var ws = new ActiveXObject("WScript.Shell");
var fso = new ActiveXObject("Scripting.FileSystemObject");
var txtstream = fso.OpenTextFile(ws.CurrentDirectory + "\\Win32_Process.html",
2, true, -2);
txtstream.WriteLine("<html xmlns='http://www.w3.org/1999/xhtml'>");
txtstream.WriteLine("<head>");
txtstream.WriteLine("<style type='text/css'>");
txtstream.WriteLine("th");
txtstream.WriteLine("{");
txtstream.WriteLine("   COLOR: darkred;");
txtstream.WriteLine("   BACKGROUND-COLOR: white;");
txtstream.WriteLine("   FONT-FAMILY:font-family: Cambria, serif;");
txtstream.WriteLine("   FONT-SIZE: 12px;");
```

```
txtstream.WriteLine("    text-align: left;");
txtstream.WriteLine("    white-Space: nowrap;");
txtstream.WriteLine("}");
txtstream.WriteLine("td");
txtstream.WriteLine("{");
txtstream.WriteLine("    COLOR: navy;");
txtstream.WriteLine("    BACKGROUND-COLOR: white;");
txtstream.WriteLine("    FONT-FAMILY: font-family: Cambria, serif;");
txtstream.WriteLine("    FONT-SIZE: 12px;");
txtstream.WriteLine("    text-align: left;");
txtstream.WriteLine("    white-Space: nowrap;");
txtstream.WriteLine("}");
txtstream.WriteLine("</style>");
txtstream.WriteLine("<title>Win32_Process</title>");
txtstream.WriteLine("</head>");
txtstream.WriteLine("<body>");
txtstream.WriteLine("<table border='1' Cellspacing='3' cellpadding = '3'>");
var v=0;
while(v < 0)
{
   var ti = ex.NextEvent(-1);
   var obj = ti.Properties_.Item("Targetinstance").Value;
   if(v == 0)
   {
      txtstream.WriteLine("<tr>");
      var propEnum = new Enumerator(obj.Properties_);
      for (; !propEnum.atEnd(); propEnum.moveNext())
      {
         var prop = propEnum.item();
         txtstream.WriteLine("<th align='left' nowrap>" + prop.Name + "</th>");
      }
      txtstream.WriteLine("</tr>");
      propEnum.ReSet();
   }
   txtstream.WriteLine("<tr>");
   for (; !propEnum.atEnd(); propEnum.moveNext())
   {
      var prop = propEnum.item();
```

```
        txtstream.WriteLine("<td style='font-family:Calibri, Sans-Serif;font-size:
12px;color:navy;' align='left' nowrap='true'><textarea>" + GetValue(prop.Name,
obj) + "</textarea></td>");
    }
    txtstream.WriteLine("</tr>");
    v = v + 1;
}
txtstream.WriteLine("</table>");
txtstream.WriteLine("</body>");
txtstream.WriteLine("</html>");
txtstream.close();
function GetValue(Name, obj)
{
    var tempstr = new String();
    var tempstr1 = new String();
    var tName = new String();
    tempstr1 = obj.GetObjectText_();
    var re = /"/g;
    tempstr1 = tempstr1.replace(re , "");
    var pos;
    tName = Name + " = ";
    pos = tempstr1.indexOf(tName);
    if (pos > -1)
    {
        pos = pos + tName.length;
        tempstr = tempstr1.substring(pos, tempstr1.length);
        pos = tempstr.indexOf(";");
        tempstr = tempstr.substring(0, pos);
        tempstr = tempstr.replace("{", "");
        tempstr = tempstr.replace("}", "");
        if (tempstr.length > 13)
        {
            if (obj.Properties_(Name).CIMType == 101)
            {
                tempstr = tempstr.substr(4, 2) + "/" + tempstr.substr(6, 2) + "/" +
tempstr.substr(0, 3) + " " + tempstr.substr(8, 2) + ":" + tempstr.substr(10, 2) + ":" +
tempstr.substr(12, 2);
            }
        }
        return tempstr;
```

```
    }
    else
    {
      return "";
    }
  }
```

Horizontal Table with a textbox.

```
  var locator = new ActiveXObject("WbemScripting.SWbemLocator");
  var svc = locator.ConnectServer(".", "root\\cimv2");
  svc.Security_.AuthenticationLevel = 6;
  svc.Security_.ImpersonationLevel = 3;
  var strQuery = "Select * From ___InstanceDeletionEvent WITHIN 1 where
TargetInstance ISA'Win32_Process'");
  var es = svc.ExecNotificationQuery(strQuery);
  var ws = new ActiveXObject("WScript.Shell");
  var fso = new ActiveXObject("Scripting.FileSystemObject");
  var txtstream = fso.OpenTextFile(ws.CurrentDirectory + "\\Win32_Process.html",
2, true, -2);
  txtstream.WriteLine("<html xmlns='http://www.w3.org/1999/xhtml'>");
  txtstream.WriteLine("<head>");
  txtstream.WriteLine("<style type='text/css'>");
  txtstream.WriteLine("th");
  txtstream.WriteLine("{");
  txtstream.WriteLine("    COLOR: darkred;");
  txtstream.WriteLine("    BACKGROUND-COLOR: white;");
  txtstream.WriteLine("    FONT-FAMILY:font-family: Cambria, serif;");
  txtstream.WriteLine("    FONT-SIZE: 12px;");
  txtstream.WriteLine("    text-align: left;");
  txtstream.WriteLine("    white-Space: nowrap;");
  txtstream.WriteLine("}");
  txtstream.WriteLine("td");
  txtstream.WriteLine("{");
  txtstream.WriteLine("    COLOR: navy;");
  txtstream.WriteLine("    BACKGROUND-COLOR: white;");
  txtstream.WriteLine("    FONT-FAMILY: font-family: Cambria, serif;");
  txtstream.WriteLine("    FONT-SIZE: 12px;");
  txtstream.WriteLine("    text-align: left;");
```

```
txtstream.WriteLine("    white-Space: nowrap;");
txtstream.WriteLine("}");
txtstream.WriteLine("</style>");
txtstream.WriteLine("<title>Win32_Process</title>");
txtstream.WriteLine("</head>");
txtstream.WriteLine("<body>");
txtstream.WriteLine("<table border='1' Cellspacing='3' cellpadding = '3'>");
var v=0;
while(v < 0)
{
    var ti = ex.NextEvent(-1);
    var obj = ti.Properties_.Item("Targetinstance").Value;
    if(v == 0)
    {
        txtstream.WriteLine("<tr>");
        var propEnum = new Enumerator(obj.Properties_);
        for (; !propEnum.atEnd(); propEnum.moveNext())
        {
            var prop = propEnum.item();
            txtstream.WriteLine("<th align='left' nowrap>" + prop.Name + "</th>");
        }
        txtstream.WriteLine("</tr>");
        propEnum.ReSet();
    }
    txtstream.WriteLine("<tr>");
    for (; !propEnum.atEnd(); propEnum.moveNext())
    {
        var prop = propEnum.item();
        txtstream.WriteLine("<td style='font-family:Calibri, Sans-Serif;font-size:
12px;color:navy;' align='left' nowrap='true'><input type=text value='" +
GetValue(prop.Name, obj) + "'></input></td>");
    }
    txtstream.WriteLine("</tr>");
    v = v + 1;
}
txtstream.WriteLine("</table>");
txtstream.WriteLine("</body>");
txtstream.WriteLine("</html>");
txtstream.close();
function GetValue(Name, obj)
```

```
    {
      var tempstr = new String();
      var tempstr1 = new String();
      var tName = new String();
      tempstr1 = obj.GetObjectText_();
      var re = /"/g;
      tempstr1 = tempstr1.replace(re , "");
      var pos;
      tName = Name + " = ";
      pos = tempstr1.indexOf(tName);
      if (pos > -1)
      {
        pos = pos + tName.length;
        tempstr = tempstr1.substring(pos, tempstr1.length);
        pos = tempstr.indexOf(";");
        tempstr = tempstr.substring(0, pos);
        tempstr = tempstr.replace("{", "");
        tempstr = tempstr.replace("}", "");
        if (tempstr.length > 13)
        {
          if (obj.Properties_(Name).CIMType == 101)
          {
            tempstr = tempstr.substr(4, 2) + "/" + tempstr.substr(6, 2) + "/" +
tempstr.substr(0, 3) + " " + tempstr.substr(8, 2) + ":" + tempstr.substr(10, 2) + ":" +
tempstr.substr(12, 2);
          }
        }
        return tempstr;
      }
      else
      {
        return "";
      }
    }
```

Vertical Table with no additional tags.

```
  var locator = new ActiveXObject("WbemScripting.SWbemLocator");
  var svc = locator.ConnectServer(".", "root\\cimv2");
```

```javascript
svc.Security_.AuthenticationLevel = 6;
svc.Security_.ImpersonationLevel = 3;
var strQuery = "Select * From ___InstanceDeletionEvent WITHIN 1 where
TargetInstance ISA'Win32_Process'");
var es = svc.ExecNotificationQuery(strQuery);
var ws = new ActiveXObject("WScript.Shell");
var fso = new ActiveXObject("Scripting.FileSystemObject");
var txtstream = fso.OpenTextFile(ws.CurrentDirectory + "\\Win32_Process.html",
2, true, -2);
txtstream.WriteLine("<html xmlns='http://www.w3.org/1999/xhtml'>");
txtstream.WriteLine("<head>");
txtstream.WriteLine("<style type='text/css'>");
txtstream.WriteLine("th");
txtstream.WriteLine("{");
txtstream.WriteLine("    COLOR: darkred;");
txtstream.WriteLine("    BACKGROUND-COLOR: white;");
txtstream.WriteLine("    FONT-FAMILY:font-family: Cambria, serif;");
txtstream.WriteLine("    FONT-SIZE: 12px;");
txtstream.WriteLine("    text-align: left;");
txtstream.WriteLine("    white-Space: nowrap;");
txtstream.WriteLine("}");
txtstream.WriteLine("td");
txtstream.WriteLine("{");
txtstream.WriteLine("    COLOR: navy;");
txtstream.WriteLine("    BACKGROUND-COLOR: white;");
txtstream.WriteLine("    FONT-FAMILY: font-family: Cambria, serif;");
txtstream.WriteLine("    FONT-SIZE: 12px;");
txtstream.WriteLine("    text-align: left;");
txtstream.WriteLine("    white-Space: nowrap;");
txtstream.WriteLine("}");
txtstream.WriteLine("</style>");
txtstream.WriteLine("<title>Win32_Process</title>");
txtstream.WriteLine("</head>");
txtstream.WriteLine("<body>");
txtstream.WriteLine("<table border='1' Cellspacing='3' cellpadding = '3'>");

var Names;
var Cols;
var Rows;
var x = 0;
```

```
var v = 0;
while(v < 0)
{
   var ti = ex.NextEvent(-1);
   var obj = ti.Properties_.Item("Targetinstance").Value;
   if(v == 0)
   {
      Names = new Array[obj.Properties_.Count];
      Cols = new Array[obj.Properties_.Count];
      Rows = new Array[4];
      var propEnum = new Enumerator(obj.Properties_);
      for (; !propEnum.atEnd(); propEnum.moveNext())
      {
         var prop = propEnum.item();
         Names[x] = prop.Name;
         Cols[x] = GetValue(prop.Name, obj);
         x = x + 1;
      }
      Rows[v] = Cols;
      x = 0;
      v = v + 1;
   }
   else
   {
      var propEnum = new Enumerator(obj.Properties_);
      for (; !propEnum.atEnd(); propEnum.moveNext())
      {
         var prop = propEnum.item();
         Cols[x] = GetValue(prop.Name, obj);
         x = x + 1;
      }
      Rows[v] = Cols;
      x = 0;
      v = v + 1;
   }
}
for(var a = 0;a < Names.Count; a++)
{
   txtstream.WriteLine("<tr><th align='left' nowrap>" + Names[a] + "</th>");
```

```javascript
    for(var b = 0;b < Rows.Count; b++)
    {
        var C = Rows[b];
        txtstream.WriteLine("<td style='font-family:Calibri, Sans-Serif;font-size:
12px;color:navy;' align='left' nowrap='nowrap'>" + C[x] + "</td>");
    }
    txtstream.WriteLine("</tr>");
}
txtstream.WriteLine("</table>");
txtstream.WriteLine("</body>");
txtstream.WriteLine("</html>");
txtstream.close();
function GetValue(Name, obj)
{
    var tempstr = new String();
    var tempstr1 = new String();
    var tName = new String();
    tempstr1 = obj.GetObjectText_();
    var re = /"/g;
    tempstr1 = tempstr1.replace(re , "");
    var pos;
    tName = Name + " = ";
    pos = tempstr1.indexOf(tName);
    if (pos > -1)
    {
        pos = pos + tName.length;
        tempstr = tempstr1.substring(pos, tempstr1.length);
        pos = tempstr.indexOf(";");
        tempstr = tempstr.substring(0, pos);
        tempstr = tempstr.replace("{", "");
        tempstr = tempstr.replace("}", "");
        if (tempstr.length > 13)
        {
            if (obj.Properties_(Name).CIMType == 101)
            {
                tempstr = tempstr.substr(4, 2) + "/"  + tempstr.substr(6, 2) + "/" +
tempstr.substr(0, 3) + " " + tempstr.substr(8, 2) + ":" + tempstr.substr(10, 2) + ":" +
tempstr.substr(12, 2);
            }
        }
```

```
      return tempstr;
   }
   else
   {
      return "";
   }
}
```

Vertical Table with a combobox.

```
   var locator = new ActiveXObject("WbemScripting.SWbemLocator");
   var svc = locator.ConnectServer(".", "root\\cimv2");
   svc.Security_.AuthenticationLevel = 6;
   svc.Security_.ImpersonationLevel = 3;
   var strQuery = "Select * From ___InstanceDeletionEvent WITHIN 1 where
TargetInstance ISA'Win32_Process'");
   var es = svc.ExecNotificationQuery(strQuery);
   var ws = new ActiveXObject("WScript.Shell");
   var fso = new ActiveXObject("Scripting.FileSystemObject");
   var txtstream = fso.OpenTextFile(ws.CurrentDirectory + "\\Win32_Process.html",
2, true, -2);
   txtstream.WriteLine("<html xmlns='http://www.w3.org/1999/xhtml'>");
   txtstream.WriteLine("<head>");
   txtstream.WriteLine("<style type='text/css'>");
   txtstream.WriteLine("th");
   txtstream.WriteLine("{");
   txtstream.WriteLine("   COLOR: darkred;");
   txtstream.WriteLine("   BACKGROUND-COLOR: white;");
   txtstream.WriteLine("   FONT-FAMILY:font-family: Cambria, serif;");
   txtstream.WriteLine("   FONT-SIZE: 12px;");
   txtstream.WriteLine("   text-align: left;");
   txtstream.WriteLine("   white-Space: nowrap;");
   txtstream.WriteLine("}");
   txtstream.WriteLine("td");
   txtstream.WriteLine("{");
   txtstream.WriteLine("   COLOR: navy;");
   txtstream.WriteLine("   BACKGROUND-COLOR: white;");
   txtstream.WriteLine("   FONT-FAMILY: font-family: Cambria, serif;");
   txtstream.WriteLine("   FONT-SIZE: 12px;");
```

```
txtstream.WriteLine("   text-align: left;");
txtstream.WriteLine("   white-Space: nowrap;");
txtstream.WriteLine("}");
txtstream.WriteLine("</style>");
txtstream.WriteLine("<title>Win32_Process</title>");
txtstream.WriteLine("</head>");
txtstream.WriteLine("<body>");
txtstream.WriteLine("<table border='1' Cellspacing='3' cellpadding = '3'>");

var Names;
var Cols;
var Rows;
var x = 0;

var v = 0;
while(v < 0)
{
   var ti = ex.NextEvent(-1);
   var obj = ti.Properties_.Item("Targetinstance").Value;
   if(v == 0)
   {
      Names = new Array[obj.Properties_.Count];
      Cols = new Array[obj.Properties_.Count];
      Rows = new Array[4];
      var propEnum = new Enumerator(obj.Properties_);
      for (; !propEnum.atEnd(); propEnum.moveNext())
      {
         var prop = propEnum.item();
         Names[x] = prop.Name;
         Cols[x] = GetValue(prop.Name, obj);
         x = x + 1;
      }
      Rows[v] = Cols;
      x = 0;
      v = v + 1;
   }
   else
   {
      var propEnum = new Enumerator(obj.Properties_);
      for (; !propEnum.atEnd(); propEnum.moveNext())
```

```
        {
           var prop = propEnum.item();
           Cols[x] = GetValue(prop.Name, obj);
           x = x + 1;
        }
        Rows[v] = Cols;
        x = 0;
        v = v + 1;
     }
  }
  for(var a = 0;a < Names.Count; a++)
  {
     txtstream.WriteLine("<tr><th align='left' nowrap>" + Names[a] + "</th>");
     for(var b = 0;b < Rows.Count; b++)
     {
        var C = Rows[b];
        txtstream.WriteLine("<td style='font-family:Calibri, Sans-Serif;font-size:
12px;color:navy;' align='left' nowrap='true'><select><option value = "'" + C[x] +
"'">" + C[x] + "</option></select></td>");
     }
     txtstream.WriteLine("</tr>");
  }
  txtstream.WriteLine("</table>");
  txtstream.WriteLine("</body>");
  txtstream.WriteLine("</html>");
  txtstream.close();
  function GetValue(Name, obj)
  {
     var tempstr = new String();
     var tempstr1 = new String();
     var tName = new String();
     tempstr1 = obj.GetObjectText_();
     var re = /"/g;
     tempstr1 = tempstr1.replace(re , "");
     var pos;
     tName = Name + " = ";
     pos = tempstr1.indexOf(tName);
     if (pos > -1)
     {
        pos = pos + tName.length;
```

```
    tempstr = tempstr1.substring(pos, tempstr1.length);
    pos = tempstr.indexOf(";");
    tempstr = tempstr.substring(0, pos);
    tempstr = tempstr.replace("{", "");
    tempstr = tempstr.replace("}", "");
    if (tempstr.length > 13)
    {
        if (obj.Properties_(Name).CIMType == 101)
        {
        tempstr = tempstr.substr(4, 2) + "/" + tempstr.substr(6, 2) + "/" +
tempstr.substr(0, 3) + " " + tempstr.substr(8, 2) + ":" + tempstr.substr(10, 2) + ":" +
tempstr.substr(12, 2);
        }
    }
    return tempstr;
    }
    else
    {
        return "";
    }
}
```

Vertical Table with a link.

```
var locator = new ActiveXObject("WbemScripting.SWbemLocator");
var svc = locator.ConnectServer(".", "root\\cimv2");
svc.Security_.AuthenticationLevel = 6;
svc.Security_.ImpersonationLevel = 3;
var strQuery = "Select * From ___InstanceDeletionEvent WITHIN 1 where
TargetInstance ISA'Win32_Process'");
var es = svc.ExecNotificationQuery(strQuery);
var ws = new ActiveXObject("WScript.Shell");
var fso = new ActiveXObject("Scripting.FileSystemObject");
var txtstream = fso.OpenTextFile(ws.CurrentDirectory + "\\Win32_Process.html",
2, true, -2);
txtstream.WriteLine("<html xmlns='http://www.w3.org/1999/xhtml'>");
txtstream.WriteLine("<head>");
txtstream.WriteLine("<style type='text/css'>");
txtstream.WriteLine("th");
```

```
txtstream.WriteLine("{");
txtstream.WriteLine("    COLOR: darkred;");
txtstream.WriteLine("    BACKGROUND-COLOR: white;");
txtstream.WriteLine("    FONT-FAMILY:font-family: Cambria, serif;");
txtstream.WriteLine("    FONT-SIZE: 12px;");
txtstream.WriteLine("    text-align: left;");
txtstream.WriteLine("    white-Space: nowrap;");
txtstream.WriteLine("}");
txtstream.WriteLine("td");
txtstream.WriteLine("{");
txtstream.WriteLine("    COLOR: navy;");
txtstream.WriteLine("    BACKGROUND-COLOR: white;");
txtstream.WriteLine("    FONT-FAMILY: font-family: Cambria, serif;");
txtstream.WriteLine("    FONT-SIZE: 12px;");
txtstream.WriteLine("    text-align: left;");
txtstream.WriteLine("    white-Space: nowrap;");
txtstream.WriteLine("}");
txtstream.WriteLine("</style>");
txtstream.WriteLine("<title>Win32_Process</title>");
txtstream.WriteLine("</head>");
txtstream.WriteLine("<body>");
txtstream.WriteLine("<table border='1' Cellspacing='3' cellpadding = '3'>");

var Names;
var Cols;
var Rows;
var x = 0;

var v = 0;
while(v < 0)
{
    var ti = ex.NextEvent(-1);
    var obj = ti.Properties_.Item("Targetinstance").Value;
    if(v == 0)
    {
        Names = new Array[obj.Properties_.Count];
        Cols = new Array[obj.Properties_.Count];
        Rows = new Array[4];
        var propEnum = new Enumerator(obj.Properties_);
        for (; !propEnum.atEnd(); propEnum.moveNext())
```

```
        {
            var prop = propEnum.item();
            Names[x] = prop.Name;
            Cols[x] = GetValue(prop.Name, obj);
            x = x + 1;
        }
        Rows[v] = Cols;
        x = 0;
        v = v + 1;
    }
    else
    {
        var propEnum = new Enumerator(obj.Properties_);
        for (; !propEnum.atEnd(); propEnum.moveNext())
        {
            var prop = propEnum.item();
            Cols[x] = GetValue(prop.Name, obj);
            x = x + 1;
        }
        Rows[v] = Cols;
        x = 0;
        v = v + 1;
    }
}
for(var a = 0;a < Names.Count; a++)
{
    txtstream.WriteLine("<tr><th align='left' nowrap>" + Names[a] + "</th>");
    for(var b = 0;b < Rows.Count; b++)
    {
        var C = Rows[b];
        txtstream.WriteLine("<td style='font-family:Calibri, Sans-Serif;font-size:
12px;color:navy;' align='left' nowrap='true'><a href='" + C[x] + "'>" + C[x] +
"</a></td>");
    }
    txtstream.WriteLine("</tr>");
}
txtstream.WriteLine("</table>");
txtstream.WriteLine("</body>");
txtstream.WriteLine("</html>");
txtstream.close();
```

```
function GetValue(Name, obj)
{
    var tempstr = new String();
    var tempstr1 = new String();
    var tName = new String();
    tempstr1 = obj.GetObjectText_();
    var re = /"/g;
    tempstr1 = tempstr1.replace(re , "");
    var pos;
    tName = Name + " = ";
    pos = tempstr1.indexOf(tName);
    if (pos > -1)
    {
        pos = pos + tName.length;
        tempstr = tempstr1.substring(pos, tempstr1.length);
        pos = tempstr.indexOf(";");
        tempstr = tempstr.substring(0, pos);
        tempstr = tempstr.replace("{", "");
        tempstr = tempstr.replace("}", "");
        if (tempstr.length > 13)
        {
            if (obj.Properties_(Name).CIMType == 101)
            {
                tempstr = tempstr.substr(4, 2) + "/"  + tempstr.substr(6, 2) + "/" +
tempstr.substr(0, 3) + " " + tempstr.substr(8, 2) + ":" + tempstr.substr(10, 2) + ":" +
tempstr.substr(12, 2);
            }
        }
        return tempstr;
    }
    else
    {
        return "";
    }
}
```

Vertical Table with a listbox.

```
var locator = new ActiveXObject("WbemScripting.SWbemLocator");
```

```
var svc = locator.ConnectServer(".", "root\\cimv2");
svc.Security_.AuthenticationLevel = 6;
svc.Security_.ImpersonationLevel = 3;
var strQuery = "Select * From ___InstanceDeletionEvent WITHIN 1 where
TargetInstance ISA'Win32_Process'");
var es = svc.ExecNotificationQuery(strQuery);
var ws = new ActiveXObject("WScript.Shell");
var fso = new ActiveXObject("Scripting.FileSystemObject");
var txtstream = fso.OpenTextFile(ws.CurrentDirectory + "\\Win32_Process.html",
2, true, -2);
txtstream.WriteLine("<html xmlns='http://www.w3.org/1999/xhtml'>");
txtstream.WriteLine("<head>");
txtstream.WriteLine("<style type='text/css'>");
txtstream.WriteLine("th");
txtstream.WriteLine("{");
txtstream.WriteLine("    COLOR: darkred;");
txtstream.WriteLine("    BACKGROUND-COLOR: white;");
txtstream.WriteLine("    FONT-FAMILY:font-family: Cambria, serif;");
txtstream.WriteLine("    FONT-SIZE: 12px;");
txtstream.WriteLine("    text-align: left;");
txtstream.WriteLine("    white-Space: nowrap;");
txtstream.WriteLine("}");
txtstream.WriteLine("td");
txtstream.WriteLine("{");
txtstream.WriteLine("    COLOR: navy;");
txtstream.WriteLine("    BACKGROUND-COLOR: white;");
txtstream.WriteLine("    FONT-FAMILY: font-family: Cambria, serif;");
txtstream.WriteLine("    FONT-SIZE: 12px;");
txtstream.WriteLine("    text-align: left;");
txtstream.WriteLine("    white-Space: nowrap;");
txtstream.WriteLine("}");
txtstream.WriteLine("</style>");
txtstream.WriteLine("<title>Win32_Process</title>");
txtstream.WriteLine("</head>");
txtstream.WriteLine("<body>");
txtstream.WriteLine("<table border='1' Cellspacing='3' cellpadding = '3'>");

var Names;
var Cols;
var Rows;
```

```
var x = 0;

var v = 0;
while(v < 0)
{
   var ti = ex.NextEvent(-1);
   var obj = ti.Properties_.Item("Targetinstance").Value;
   if(v == 0)
   {
      Names = new Array[obj.Properties_.Count];
      Cols = new Array[obj.Properties_.Count];
      Rows = new Array[4];
      var propEnum = new Enumerator(obj.Properties_);
      for (; !propEnum.atEnd(); propEnum.moveNext())
      {
         var prop = propEnum.item();
         Names[x] = prop.Name;
         Cols[x] = GetValue(prop.Name, obj);
         x = x + 1;
      }
      Rows[v] = Cols;
      x = 0;
      v = v + 1;
   }
   else
   {
      var propEnum = new Enumerator(obj.Properties_);
      for (; !propEnum.atEnd(); propEnum.moveNext())
      {
         var prop = propEnum.item();
         Cols[x] = GetValue(prop.Name, obj);
         x = x + 1;
      }
      Rows[v] = Cols;
      x = 0;
      v = v + 1;
   }
}
for(var a = 0;a < Names.Count; a++)
{
```

```
        txtstream.WriteLine("<tr><th align='left' nowrap>" + Names[a] + "</th>");
        for(var b = 0;b < Rows.Count; b++)
        {
            var C = Rows[b];
            txtstream.WriteLine("<td style='font-family:Calibri, Sans-Serif;font-size:
12px;color:navy;' align='left' nowrap='true'><select multiple><option value = """ +
C[x] + """>" + C[x] + "</option></select></td>");
        }
        txtstream.WriteLine("</tr>");
    }
    txtstream.WriteLine("</table>");
    txtstream.WriteLine("</body>");
    txtstream.WriteLine("</html>");
    txtstream.close();
    function GetValue(Name, obj)
    {
        var tempstr = new String();
        var tempstr1 = new String();
        var tName = new String();
        tempstr1 = obj.GetObjectText_();
        var re = /"/g;
        tempstr1 = tempstr1.replace(re , "");
        var pos;
        tName = Name + " = ";
        pos = tempstr1.indexOf(tName);
        if (pos > -1)
        {
            pos = pos + tName.length;
            tempstr = tempstr1.substring(pos, tempstr1.length);
            pos = tempstr.indexOf(";");
            tempstr = tempstr.substring(0, pos);
            tempstr = tempstr.replace("{", "");
            tempstr = tempstr.replace("}", "");
            if (tempstr.length > 13)
            {
                if (obj.Properties_(Name).CIMType == 101)
                {
                    tempstr = tempstr.substr(4, 2) + "/" + tempstr.substr(6, 2) + "/" +
tempstr.substr(0, 3) + " " + tempstr.substr(8, 2) + ":" + tempstr.substr(10, 2) + ":" +
tempstr.substr(12, 2);
```

```
        }
    }
    return tempstr;
}
else
{
    return "";
}
}
```

Vertical Table with a textarea.

```
var locator = new ActiveXObject("WbemScripting.SWbemLocator");
var svc = locator.ConnectServer(".", "root\\cimv2");
svc.Security_.AuthenticationLevel = 6;
svc.Security_.ImpersonationLevel = 3;
var strQuery = "Select * From ___InstanceDeletionEvent WITHIN 1 where
TargetInstance ISA'Win32_Process'");
var es = svc.ExecNotificationQuery(strQuery);
var ws = new ActiveXObject("WScript.Shell");
var fso = new ActiveXObject("Scripting.FileSystemObject");
var txtstream = fso.OpenTextFile(ws.CurrentDirectory + "\\Win32_Process.html",
2, true, -2);
txtstream.WriteLine("<html xmlns='http://www.w3.org/1999/xhtml'>");
txtstream.WriteLine("<head>");
txtstream.WriteLine("<style type='text/css'>");
txtstream.WriteLine("th");
txtstream.WriteLine("{");
txtstream.WriteLine("   COLOR: darkred;");
txtstream.WriteLine("   BACKGROUND-COLOR: white;");
txtstream.WriteLine("   FONT-FAMILY:font-family: Cambria, serif;");
txtstream.WriteLine("   FONT-SIZE: 12px;");
txtstream.WriteLine("   text-align: left;");
txtstream.WriteLine("   white-Space: nowrap;");
txtstream.WriteLine("}");
txtstream.WriteLine("td");
txtstream.WriteLine("{");
txtstream.WriteLine("   COLOR: navy;");
txtstream.WriteLine("   BACKGROUND-COLOR: white;");
```

```
txtstream.WriteLine("    FONT-FAMILY: font-family: Cambria, serif;");
txtstream.WriteLine("    FONT-SIZE: 12px;");
txtstream.WriteLine("    text-align: left;");
txtstream.WriteLine("    white-Space: nowrap;");
txtstream.WriteLine("}");
txtstream.WriteLine("</style>");
txtstream.WriteLine("<title>Win32_Process</title>");
txtstream.WriteLine("</head>");
txtstream.WriteLine("<body>");
txtstream.WriteLine("<table border='1' Cellspacing='3' cellpadding = '3'>");

var Names;
var Cols;
var Rows;
var x = 0;

var v = 0;
while(v < 0)
{
    var ti = ex.NextEvent(-1);
    var obj = ti.Properties_.Item("Targetinstance").Value;
    if(v == 0)
    {
        Names = new Array[obj.Properties_.Count];
        Cols = new Array[obj.Properties_.Count];
        Rows = new Array[4];
        var propEnum = new Enumerator(obj.Properties_);
        for (; !propEnum.atEnd(); propEnum.moveNext())
        {
            var prop = propEnum.item();
            Names[x] = prop.Name;
            Cols[x] = GetValue(prop.Name, obj);
            x = x + 1;
        }
        Rows[v] = Cols;
        x = 0;
        v = v + 1;
    }
    else
    {
```

```
      var propEnum = new Enumerator(obj.Properties_);
      for (; !propEnum.atEnd(); propEnum.moveNext())
      {
         var prop = propEnum.item();
         Cols[x] = GetValue(prop.Name, obj);
         x = x + 1;
      }
      Rows[v] = Cols;
      x = 0;
      v = v + 1;
   }
}
for(var a = 0;a < Names.Count; a++)
{
   txtstream.WriteLine("<tr><th align='left' nowrap>" + Names[a] + "</th>");
   for(var b = 0;b < Rows.Count; b++)
   {
      var C = Rows[b];
      txtstream.WriteLine("<td style='font-family:Calibri, Sans-Serif;font-size:
12px;color:navy;' align='left' nowrap='true'><textarea>" + C[x] +
"</textarea></td>");
   }
   txtstream.WriteLine("</tr>");
}
txtstream.WriteLine("</table>");
txtstream.WriteLine("</body>");
txtstream.WriteLine("</html>");
txtstream.close();
function GetValue(Name, obj)
{
   var tempstr = new String();
   var tempstr1 = new String();
   var tName = new String();
   tempstr1 = obj.GetObjectText_();
   var re = /"/g;
   tempstr1 = tempstr1.replace(re , "");
   var pos;
   tName = Name + " = ";
   pos = tempstr1.indexOf(tName);
   if (pos > -1)
```

```
    {
        pos = pos + tName.length;
        tempstr = tempstr1.substring(pos, tempstr1.length);
        pos = tempstr.indexOf(";");
        tempstr = tempstr.substring(0, pos);
        tempstr = tempstr.replace("{", "");
        tempstr = tempstr.replace("}", "");
        if (tempstr.length > 13)
        {
            if (obj.Properties_(Name).CIMType == 101)
            {
                tempstr = tempstr.substr(4, 2) + "/"  + tempstr.substr(6, 2) + "/" +
tempstr.substr(0, 3) + " " + tempstr.substr(8, 2) + ":" + tempstr.substr(10, 2) + ":" +
tempstr.substr(12, 2);
            }
        }
        return tempstr;
    }
    else
    {
        return "";
    }
}
```

Vertical Table with a textbox.

```
    var locator = new ActiveXObject("WbemScripting.SWbemLocator");
    var svc = locator.ConnectServer(".", "root\\cimv2");
    svc.Security_.AuthenticationLevel = 6;
    svc.Security_.ImpersonationLevel = 3;
    var strQuery = "Select * From ___InstanceDeletionEvent WITHIN 1 where
TargetInstance ISA'Win32_Process'");
    var es = svc.ExecNotificationQuery(strQuery);
    var ws = new ActiveXObject("WScript.Shell");
    var fso = new ActiveXObject("Scripting.FileSystemObject");
    var txtstream = fso.OpenTextFile(ws.CurrentDirectory + "\\Win32_Process.html",
2, true, -2);
    txtstream.WriteLine("<html xmlns='http://www.w3.org/1999/xhtml'>");
    txtstream.WriteLine("<head>");
```

```
txtstream.WriteLine("<style type='text/css'>");
txtstream.WriteLine("th");
txtstream.WriteLine("{");
txtstream.WriteLine("    COLOR: darkred;");
txtstream.WriteLine("    BACKGROUND-COLOR: white;");
txtstream.WriteLine("    FONT-FAMILY:font-family: Cambria, serif;");
txtstream.WriteLine("    FONT-SIZE: 12px;");
txtstream.WriteLine("    text-align: left;");
txtstream.WriteLine("    white-Space: nowrap;");
txtstream.WriteLine("}");
txtstream.WriteLine("td");
txtstream.WriteLine("{");
txtstream.WriteLine("    COLOR: navy;");
txtstream.WriteLine("    BACKGROUND-COLOR: white;");
txtstream.WriteLine("    FONT-FAMILY: font-family: Cambria, serif;");
txtstream.WriteLine("    FONT-SIZE: 12px;");
txtstream.WriteLine("    text-align: left;");
txtstream.WriteLine("    white-Space: nowrap;");
txtstream.WriteLine("}");
txtstream.WriteLine("</style>");
txtstream.WriteLine("<title>Win32_Process</title>");
txtstream.WriteLine("</head>");
txtstream.WriteLine("<body>");
txtstream.WriteLine("<table border='1' Cellspacing='3' cellpadding = '3'>");

var Names;
var Cols;
var Rows;
var x = 0;

var v = 0;
while(v < 0)
{
    var ti = ex.NextEvent(-1);
    var obj = ti.Properties_.Item("Targetinstance").Value;
    if(v == 0)
    {
        Names = new Array[obj.Properties_.Count];
        Cols = new Array[obj.Properties_.Count];
        Rows = new Array[4];
```

```
        var propEnum = new Enumerator(obj.Properties_);
        for (; !propEnum.atEnd(); propEnum.moveNext())
        {
            var prop = propEnum.item();
            Names[x] = prop.Name;
            Cols[x] = GetValue(prop.Name, obj);
            x = x + 1;
        }
        Rows[v] = Cols;
        x = 0;
        v = v + 1;
    }
    else
    {
        var propEnum = new Enumerator(obj.Properties_);
        for (; !propEnum.atEnd(); propEnum.moveNext())
        {
            var prop = propEnum.item();
            Cols[x] = GetValue(prop.Name, obj);
            x = x + 1;
        }
        Rows[v] = Cols;
        x = 0;
        v = v + 1;
    }
}
for(var a = 0;a < Names.Count; a++)
{
    txtstream.WriteLine("<tr><th align='left' nowrap>" + Names[a] + "</th>");
    for(var b = 0;b < Rows.Count; b++)
    {
        var C = Rows[b];
        txtstream.WriteLine("<td style='font-family:Calibri, Sans-Serif;font-size:
12px;color:navy;' align='left' nowrap='true'><input type=text value=""" + C[x] +
"""></input></td>");
    }
    txtstream.WriteLine("</tr>");
}
txtstream.WriteLine("</table>");
txtstream.WriteLine("</body>");
```

```javascript
txtstream.WriteLine("</html>");
txtstream.close();
function GetValue(Name, obj)
{
    var tempstr = new String();
    var tempstr1 = new String();
    var tName = new String();
    tempstr1 = obj.GetObjectText_();
    var re = /"/g;
    tempstr1 = tempstr1.replace(re , "");
    var pos;
    tName = Name + " = ";
    pos = tempstr1.indexOf(tName);
    if (pos > -1)
    {
        pos = pos + tName.length;
        tempstr = tempstr1.substring(pos, tempstr1.length);
        pos = tempstr.indexOf(";");
        tempstr = tempstr.substring(0, pos);
        tempstr = tempstr.replace("{", "");
        tempstr = tempstr.replace("}", "");
        if (tempstr.length > 13)
        {
            if (obj.Properties_(Name).CIMType == 101)
            {
                tempstr = tempstr.substr(4, 2) + "/"  + tempstr.substr(6, 2) + "/" +
tempstr.substr(0, 3) + " " + tempstr.substr(8, 2) + ":" + tempstr.substr(10, 2) + ":" +
tempstr.substr(12, 2);
            }
        }
        return tempstr;
    }
    else
    {
        return "";
    }
}
```

Stylesheets

Decorating your web pages

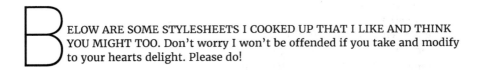ELOW ARE SOME STYLESHEETS I COOKED UP THAT I LIKE AND THINK YOU MIGHT TOO. Don't worry I won't be offended if you take and modify to your hearts delight. Please do!

NONE

```
txtstream.WriteLine("<style type='text/css'>");

txtstream.WriteLine("th");

txtstream.WriteLine("{");

txtstream.WriteLine("   COLOR: white;");

txtstream.WriteLine("}");

txtstream.WriteLine("td");

txtstream.WriteLine("{");

txtstream.WriteLine("   COLOR: white;");
```

```
txtstream.WriteLine("}");
txtstream.WriteLine("</style>");
```

BLACK AND WHITE TEXT

```
txtstream.WriteLine("<style type='text/css'>");
txtstream.WriteLine("th");
txtstream.WriteLine("{");
txtstream.WriteLine("   COLOR: white;");
txtstream.WriteLine("   BACKGROUND-COLOR: black;");
txtstream.WriteLine("   FONT-FAMILY:font-family: Cambria, serif;");
txtstream.WriteLine("   FONT-SIZE: 12px;");
txtstream.WriteLine("   text-align: left;");
txtstream.WriteLine("   white-Space: nowrap;");
txtstream.WriteLine("}");
txtstream.WriteLine("td");
txtstream.WriteLine("{");
txtstream.WriteLine("   COLOR: white;");
txtstream.WriteLine("   BACKGROUND-COLOR: black;");
txtstream.WriteLine("   FONT-FAMILY: font-family: Cambria, serif;");
txtstream.WriteLine("   FONT-SIZE: 12px;");
txtstream.WriteLine("   text-align: left;");
txtstream.WriteLine("   white-Space: nowrap;");
txtstream.WriteLine("}");
txtstream.WriteLine("div");
txtstream.WriteLine("{");
txtstream.WriteLine("   COLOR: white;");
```

```
txtstream.WriteLine("    BACKGROUND-COLOR: black;");
txtstream.WriteLine("    FONT-FAMILY: font-family: Cambria, serif;");
txtstream.WriteLine("    FONT-SIZE: 10px;");
txtstream.WriteLine("    text-align: left;");
txtstream.WriteLine("    white-Space: nowrap;");
txtstream.WriteLine("}");
txtstream.WriteLine("span");
txtstream.WriteLine("{");
txtstream.WriteLine("    COLOR: white;");
txtstream.WriteLine("    BACKGROUND-COLOR: black;");
txtstream.WriteLine("    FONT-FAMILY: font-family: Cambria, serif;");
txtstream.WriteLine("    FONT-SIZE: 10px;");
txtstream.WriteLine("    text-align: left;");
txtstream.WriteLine("    white-Space: nowrap;");
txtstream.WriteLine("    display:inline-block;");
txtstream.WriteLine("    width: 100%;");
txtstream.WriteLine("}");
txtstream.WriteLine("textarea");
txtstream.WriteLine("{");
txtstream.WriteLine("    COLOR: white;");
txtstream.WriteLine("    BACKGROUND-COLOR: black;");
txtstream.WriteLine("    FONT-FAMILY: font-family: Cambria, serif;");
txtstream.WriteLine("    FONT-SIZE: 10px;");
txtstream.WriteLine("    text-align: left;");
txtstream.WriteLine("    white-Space: nowrap;");
txtstream.WriteLine("    width: 100%;");
txtstream.WriteLine("}");
```

```
txtstream.WriteLine("select");
txtstream.WriteLine("{");
txtstream.WriteLine("    COLOR: white;");
txtstream.WriteLine("    BACKGROUND-COLOR: black;");
txtstream.WriteLine("    FONT-FAMILY: font-family: Cambria, serif;");
txtstream.WriteLine("    FONT-SIZE: 10px;");
txtstream.WriteLine("    text-align: left;");
txtstream.WriteLine("    white-Space: nowrap;");
txtstream.WriteLine("    width: 100%;");
txtstream.WriteLine("}");
txtstream.WriteLine("input");
txtstream.WriteLine("{");
txtstream.WriteLine("    COLOR: white;");
txtstream.WriteLine("    BACKGROUND-COLOR: black;");
txtstream.WriteLine("    FONT-FAMILY: font-family: Cambria, serif;");
txtstream.WriteLine("    FONT-SIZE: 12px;");
txtstream.WriteLine("    text-align: left;");
txtstream.WriteLine("    display:table-cell;");
txtstream.WriteLine("    white-Space: nowrap;");
txtstream.WriteLine("}");
txtstream.WriteLine("h1 {");
txtstream.WriteLine("color: antiquewhite;");
txtstream.WriteLine("text-shadow: 1px 1px 1px black;");
txtstream.WriteLine("padding: 3px;");
txtstream.WriteLine("text-align: center;");
txtstream.WriteLine("box-shadow: inset 2px 2px 5px rgba(0,0,0,0.5);, inset -2px -2px 5px rgba(255,255,255,0.5);;");
```

```
txtstream.WriteLine("}");
txtstream.WriteLine("</style>");
```

COLORED TEXT

```
txtstream.WriteLine("<style type='text/css'>");
txtstream.WriteLine("th");
txtstream.WriteLine("{");
txtstream.WriteLine("   COLOR: darkred;");
txtstream.WriteLine("   BACKGROUND-COLOR: #eeeeee;");
txtstream.WriteLine("   FONT-FAMILY:font-family: Cambria, serif;");
txtstream.WriteLine("   FONT-SIZE: 12px;");
txtstream.WriteLine("   text-align: left;");
txtstream.WriteLine("   white-Space: nowrap;");
txtstream.WriteLine("}");
txtstream.WriteLine("td");
txtstream.WriteLine("{");
txtstream.WriteLine("   COLOR: navy;");
txtstream.WriteLine("   BACKGROUND-COLOR: #eeeeee;");
txtstream.WriteLine("   FONT-FAMILY: font-family: Cambria, serif;");
txtstream.WriteLine("   FONT-SIZE: 12px;");
txtstream.WriteLine("   text-align: left;");
txtstream.WriteLine("   white-Space: nowrap;");
txtstream.WriteLine("}");
txtstream.WriteLine("div");
txtstream.WriteLine("{");
txtstream.WriteLine("   COLOR: white;");
```

```
txtstream.WriteLine("   BACKGROUND-COLOR: navy;");
txtstream.WriteLine("   FONT-FAMILY: font-family: Cambria, serif;");
txtstream.WriteLine("   FONT-SIZE: 10px;");
txtstream.WriteLine("   text-align: left;");
txtstream.WriteLine("   white-Space: nowrap;");
txtstream.WriteLine("}");
txtstream.WriteLine("span");
txtstream.WriteLine("{");
txtstream.WriteLine("   COLOR: white;");
txtstream.WriteLine("   BACKGROUND-COLOR: navy;");
txtstream.WriteLine("   FONT-FAMILY: font-family: Cambria, serif;");
txtstream.WriteLine("   FONT-SIZE: 10px;");
txtstream.WriteLine("   text-align: left;");
txtstream.WriteLine("   white-Space: nowrap;");
txtstream.WriteLine("   display:inline-block;");
txtstream.WriteLine("   width: 100%;");
txtstream.WriteLine("}");
txtstream.WriteLine("textarea");
txtstream.WriteLine("{");
txtstream.WriteLine("   COLOR: white;");
txtstream.WriteLine("   BACKGROUND-COLOR: navy;");
txtstream.WriteLine("   FONT-FAMILY: font-family: Cambria, serif;");
txtstream.WriteLine("   FONT-SIZE: 10px;");
txtstream.WriteLine("   text-align: left;");
txtstream.WriteLine("   white-Space: nowrap;");
txtstream.WriteLine("   width: 100%;");
txtstream.WriteLine("}");
```

```
txtstream.WriteLine("select");
txtstream.WriteLine("{");
txtstream.WriteLine("    COLOR: white;");
txtstream.WriteLine("    BACKGROUND-COLOR: navy;");
txtstream.WriteLine("    FONT-FAMILY: font-family: Cambria, serif;");
txtstream.WriteLine("    FONT-SIZE: 10px;");
txtstream.WriteLine("    text-align: left;");
txtstream.WriteLine("    white-Space: nowrap;");
txtstream.WriteLine("    width: 100%;");
txtstream.WriteLine("}");
txtstream.WriteLine("input");
txtstream.WriteLine("{");
txtstream.WriteLine("    COLOR: white;");
txtstream.WriteLine("    BACKGROUND-COLOR: navy;");
txtstream.WriteLine("    FONT-FAMILY: font-family: Cambria, serif;");
txtstream.WriteLine("    FONT-SIZE: 12px;");
txtstream.WriteLine("    text-align: left;");
txtstream.WriteLine("    display:table-cell;");
txtstream.WriteLine("    white-Space: nowrap;");
txtstream.WriteLine("}");
txtstream.WriteLine("h1 {");
txtstream.WriteLine("color: antiquewhite;");
txtstream.WriteLine("text-shadow: 1px 1px 1px black;");
txtstream.WriteLine("padding: 3px;");
txtstream.WriteLine("text-align: center;");
txtstream.WriteLine("box-shadow: inset 2px 2px 5px rgba(0,0,0,0.5);, inset -2px -2px 5px rgba(255,255,255,0.5);;");
```

```
txtstream.WriteLine("}");

txtstream.WriteLine("</style>");
```

OSCILLATING ROW COLORS

```
txtstream.WriteLine("<style>");

txtstream.WriteLine("th");

txtstream.WriteLine("{");

txtstream.WriteLine("   COLOR: white;");

txtstream.WriteLine("   BACKGROUND-COLOR: navy;");

txtstream.WriteLine("   FONT-FAMILY:font-family: Cambria, serif;");

txtstream.WriteLine("   FONT-SIZE: 12px;");

txtstream.WriteLine("   text-align: left;");

txtstream.WriteLine("   white-Space: nowrap;");

txtstream.WriteLine("}");

txtstream.WriteLine("td");

txtstream.WriteLine("{");

txtstream.WriteLine("   COLOR: navy;");

txtstream.WriteLine("   FONT-FAMILY: font-family: Cambria, serif;");

txtstream.WriteLine("   FONT-SIZE: 12px;");

txtstream.WriteLine("   text-align: left;");

txtstream.WriteLine("   white-Space: nowrap;");

txtstream.WriteLine("}");

txtstream.WriteLine("div");

txtstream.WriteLine("{");
```

```
txtstream.WriteLine("    COLOR: navy;");
txtstream.WriteLine("    FONT-FAMILY: font-family: Cambria, serif;");
txtstream.WriteLine("    FONT-SIZE: 12px;");
txtstream.WriteLine("    text-align: left;");
txtstream.WriteLine("    white-Space: nowrap;");
txtstream.WriteLine("}");
txtstream.WriteLine("span");
txtstream.WriteLine("{");
txtstream.WriteLine("    COLOR: navy;");
txtstream.WriteLine("    FONT-FAMILY: font-family: Cambria, serif;");
txtstream.WriteLine("    FONT-SIZE: 12px;");
txtstream.WriteLine("    text-align: left;");
txtstream.WriteLine("    white-Space: nowrap;");
txtstream.WriteLine("    width: 100%;");
txtstream.WriteLine("}");
txtstream.WriteLine("textarea");
txtstream.WriteLine("{");
txtstream.WriteLine("    COLOR: navy;");
txtstream.WriteLine("    FONT-FAMILY: font-family: Cambria, serif;");
txtstream.WriteLine("    FONT-SIZE: 12px;");
txtstream.WriteLine("    text-align: left;");
txtstream.WriteLine("    white-Space: nowrap;");
txtstream.WriteLine("    display:inline-block;");
txtstream.WriteLine("    width: 100%;");
txtstream.WriteLine("}");
txtstream.WriteLine("select");
txtstream.WriteLine("{");
```

```
txtstream.WriteLine("   COLOR: navy;");

txtstream.WriteLine("   FONT-FAMILY: font-family: Cambria, serif;");

txtstream.WriteLine("   FONT-SIZE: 10px;");

txtstream.WriteLine("   text-align: left;");

txtstream.WriteLine("   white-Space: nowrap;");

txtstream.WriteLine("   display:inline-block;");

txtstream.WriteLine("   width: 100%;");

txtstream.WriteLine("}");

txtstream.WriteLine("input");

txtstream.WriteLine("{");

txtstream.WriteLine("   COLOR: navy;");

txtstream.WriteLine("   FONT-FAMILY: font-family: Cambria, serif;");

txtstream.WriteLine("   FONT-SIZE: 12px;");

txtstream.WriteLine("   text-align: left;");

txtstream.WriteLine("   display:table-cell;");

txtstream.WriteLine("   white-Space: nowrap;");

txtstream.WriteLine("}");

txtstream.WriteLine("h1 {");

txtstream.WriteLine("color: antiquewhite;");

txtstream.WriteLine("text-shadow: 1px 1px 1px black;");

txtstream.WriteLine("padding: 3px;");

txtstream.WriteLine("text-align: center;");

txtstream.WriteLine("box-shadow: inset 2px 2px 5px rgba(0,0,0,0.5);, inset -2px -2px 5px rgba(255,255,255,0.5);;");

txtstream.WriteLine("}");

txtstream.WriteLine("tr:nth-child(even);{background-color:#f2f2f2;}");

txtstream.WriteLine("tr:nth-child(odd);{background-color:#cccccc; color:#f2f2f2;}");
```

```
txtstream.WriteLine("</style>");
```

GHOST DECORATED

```
txtstream.WriteLine("<style type='text/css'>");
txtstream.WriteLine("th");
txtstream.WriteLine("{");
txtstream.WriteLine("    COLOR: black;");
txtstream.WriteLine("    BACKGROUND-COLOR: white;");
txtstream.WriteLine("    FONT-FAMILY:font-family: Cambria, serif;");
txtstream.WriteLine("    FONT-SIZE: 12px;");
txtstream.WriteLine("    text-align: left;");
txtstream.WriteLine("    white-Space: nowrap;");
txtstream.WriteLine("}");
txtstream.WriteLine("td");
txtstream.WriteLine("{");
txtstream.WriteLine("    COLOR: black;");
txtstream.WriteLine("    BACKGROUND-COLOR: white;");
txtstream.WriteLine("    FONT-FAMILY: font-family: Cambria, serif;");
txtstream.WriteLine("    FONT-SIZE: 12px;");
txtstream.WriteLine("    text-align: left;");
txtstream.WriteLine("    white-Space: nowrap;");
txtstream.WriteLine("}");
txtstream.WriteLine("div");
txtstream.WriteLine("{");
txtstream.WriteLine("    COLOR: black;");
txtstream.WriteLine("    BACKGROUND-COLOR: white;");
```

```
txtstream.WriteLine("    FONT-FAMILY: font-family: Cambria, serif;");
txtstream.WriteLine("    FONT-SIZE: 10px;");
txtstream.WriteLine("    text-align: left;");
txtstream.WriteLine("    white-Space: nowrap;");
txtstream.WriteLine("}");
txtstream.WriteLine("span");
txtstream.WriteLine("{");
txtstream.WriteLine("    COLOR: black;");
txtstream.WriteLine("    BACKGROUND-COLOR: white;");
txtstream.WriteLine("    FONT-FAMILY: font-family: Cambria, serif;");
txtstream.WriteLine("    FONT-SIZE: 10px;");
txtstream.WriteLine("    text-align: left;");
txtstream.WriteLine("    white-Space: nowrap;");
txtstream.WriteLine("    display:inline-block;");
txtstream.WriteLine("    width: 100%;");
txtstream.WriteLine("}");
txtstream.WriteLine("textarea");
txtstream.WriteLine("{");
txtstream.WriteLine("    COLOR: black;");
txtstream.WriteLine("    BACKGROUND-COLOR: white;");
txtstream.WriteLine("    FONT-FAMILY: font-family: Cambria, serif;");
txtstream.WriteLine("    FONT-SIZE: 10px;");
txtstream.WriteLine("    text-align: left;");
txtstream.WriteLine("    white-Space: nowrap;");
txtstream.WriteLine("    width: 100%;");
txtstream.WriteLine("}");
txtstream.WriteLine("select");
```

```
txtstream.WriteLine("{");
txtstream.WriteLine("   COLOR: black;");
txtstream.WriteLine("   BACKGROUND-COLOR: white;");
txtstream.WriteLine("   FONT-FAMILY: font-family: Cambria, serif;");
txtstream.WriteLine("   FONT-SIZE: 10px;");
txtstream.WriteLine("   text-align: left;");
txtstream.WriteLine("   white-Space: nowrap;");
txtstream.WriteLine("   width: 100%;");
txtstream.WriteLine("}");
txtstream.WriteLine("input");
txtstream.WriteLine("{");
txtstream.WriteLine("   COLOR: black;");
txtstream.WriteLine("   BACKGROUND-COLOR: white;");
txtstream.WriteLine("   FONT-FAMILY: font-family: Cambria, serif;");
txtstream.WriteLine("   FONT-SIZE: 12px;");
txtstream.WriteLine("   text-align: left;");
txtstream.WriteLine("   display:table-cell;");
txtstream.WriteLine("   white-Space: nowrap;");
txtstream.WriteLine("}");
txtstream.WriteLine("h1 {");
txtstream.WriteLine("color: antiquewhite;");
txtstream.WriteLine("text-shadow: 1px 1px 1px black;");
txtstream.WriteLine("padding: 3px;");
txtstream.WriteLine("text-align: center;");
txtstream.WriteLine("box-shadow: inset 2px 2px 5px rgba(0,0,0,0.5);, inset -2px -2px 5px rgba(255,255,255,0.5);;");
txtstream.WriteLine("}");
```

```
txtstream.WriteLine("</style>");
```

3D

```
txtstream.WriteLine("<style type='text/css'>");
txtstream.WriteLine("body");
txtstream.WriteLine("{");
txtstream.WriteLine("   PADDING-RIGHT: 0px;");
txtstream.WriteLine("   PADDING-LEFT: 0px;");
txtstream.WriteLine("   PADDING-BOTTOM: 0px;");
txtstream.WriteLine("   MARGIN: 0px;");
txtstream.WriteLine("   COLOR: #333;");
txtstream.WriteLine("   PADDING-TOP: 0px;");
txtstream.WriteLine("   FONT-FAMILY: verdana, arial, helvetica, sans-serif;");
txtstream.WriteLine("}");
txtstream.WriteLine("table");
txtstream.WriteLine("{");
txtstream.WriteLine("   BORDER-RIGHT: #999999 3px solid;");
txtstream.WriteLine("   PADDING-RIGHT: 6px;");
txtstream.WriteLine("   PADDING-LEFT: 6px;");
txtstream.WriteLine("   FONT-WEIGHT: Bold;");
txtstream.WriteLine("   FONT-SIZE: 14px;");
txtstream.WriteLine("   PADDING-BOTTOM: 6px;");
txtstream.WriteLine("   COLOR: Peru;");
txtstream.WriteLine("   LINE-HEIGHT: 14px;");
txtstream.WriteLine("   PADDING-TOP: 6px;");
```

```
txtstream.WriteLine("    BORDER-BOTTOM: #999 1px solid;");

txtstream.WriteLine("    BACKGROUND-COLOR: #eeeeee;");

txtstream.WriteLine("    FONT-FAMILY: verdana, arial, helvetica, sans-serif;");

txtstream.WriteLine("    FONT-SIZE: 12px;");

txtstream.WriteLine("}");

txtstream.WriteLine("th");

txtstream.WriteLine("{");

txtstream.WriteLine("    BORDER-RIGHT: #999999 3px solid;");

txtstream.WriteLine("    PADDING-RIGHT: 6px;");

txtstream.WriteLine("    PADDING-LEFT: 6px;");

txtstream.WriteLine("    FONT-WEIGHT: Bold;");

txtstream.WriteLine("    FONT-SIZE: 14px;");

txtstream.WriteLine("    PADDING-BOTTOM: 6px;");

txtstream.WriteLine("    COLOR: darkred;");

txtstream.WriteLine("    LINE-HEIGHT: 14px;");

txtstream.WriteLine("    PADDING-TOP: 6px;");

txtstream.WriteLine("    BORDER-BOTTOM: #999 1px solid;");

txtstream.WriteLine("    BACKGROUND-COLOR: #eeeeee;");

txtstream.WriteLine("    FONT-FAMILY:font-family: Cambria, serif;");

txtstream.WriteLine("    FONT-SIZE: 12px;");

txtstream.WriteLine("    text-align: left;");

txtstream.WriteLine("    white-Space: nowrap;");

txtstream.WriteLine("}");

txtstream.WriteLine(".th");

txtstream.WriteLine("{");

txtstream.WriteLine("    BORDER-RIGHT: #999999 2px solid;");

txtstream.WriteLine("    PADDING-RIGHT: 6px;");
```

```
txtstream.WriteLine("    PADDING-LEFT: 6px;");

txtstream.WriteLine("    FONT-WEIGHT: Bold;");

txtstream.WriteLine("    PADDING-BOTTOM: 6px;");

txtstream.WriteLine("    COLOR: black;");

txtstream.WriteLine("    PADDING-TOP: 6px;");

txtstream.WriteLine("    BORDER-BOTTOM: #999 2px solid;");

txtstream.WriteLine("    BACKGROUND-COLOR: #eeeeee;");

txtstream.WriteLine("    FONT-FAMILY: font-family: Cambria, serif;");

txtstream.WriteLine("    FONT-SIZE: 10px;");

txtstream.WriteLine("    text-align: right;");

txtstream.WriteLine("    white-Space: nowrap;");

txtstream.WriteLine("}");

txtstream.WriteLine("td");

txtstream.WriteLine("{");

txtstream.WriteLine("    BORDER-RIGHT: #999999 3px solid;");

txtstream.WriteLine("    PADDING-RIGHT: 6px;");

txtstream.WriteLine("    PADDING-LEFT: 6px;");

txtstream.WriteLine("    FONT-WEIGHT: Normal;");

txtstream.WriteLine("    PADDING-BOTTOM: 6px;");

txtstream.WriteLine("    COLOR: navy;");

txtstream.WriteLine("    LINE-HEIGHT: 14px;");

txtstream.WriteLine("    PADDING-TOP: 6px;");

txtstream.WriteLine("    BORDER-BOTTOM: #999 1px solid;");

txtstream.WriteLine("    BACKGROUND-COLOR: #eeeeee;");

txtstream.WriteLine("    FONT-FAMILY: font-family: Cambria, serif;");

txtstream.WriteLine("    FONT-SIZE: 12px;");

txtstream.WriteLine("    text-align: left;");
```

```
txtstream.WriteLine("    white-Space: nowrap;");
txtstream.WriteLine("}");
txtstream.WriteLine("div");
txtstream.WriteLine("{");
txtstream.WriteLine("    BORDER-RIGHT: #999999 3px solid;");
txtstream.WriteLine("    PADDING-RIGHT: 6px;");
txtstream.WriteLine("    PADDING-LEFT: 6px;");
txtstream.WriteLine("    FONT-WEIGHT: Normal;");
txtstream.WriteLine("    PADDING-BOTTOM: 6px;");
txtstream.WriteLine("    COLOR: white;");
txtstream.WriteLine("    PADDING-TOP: 6px;");
txtstream.WriteLine("    BORDER-BOTTOM: #999 1px solid;");
txtstream.WriteLine("    BACKGROUND-COLOR: navy;");
txtstream.WriteLine("    FONT-FAMILY: font-family: Cambria, serif;");
txtstream.WriteLine("    FONT-SIZE: 10px;");
txtstream.WriteLine("    text-align: left;");
txtstream.WriteLine("    white-Space: nowrap;");
txtstream.WriteLine("}");
txtstream.WriteLine("span");
txtstream.WriteLine("{");
txtstream.WriteLine("    BORDER-RIGHT: #999999 3px solid;");
txtstream.WriteLine("    PADDING-RIGHT: 3px;");
txtstream.WriteLine("    PADDING-LEFT: 3px;");
txtstream.WriteLine("    FONT-WEIGHT: Normal;");
txtstream.WriteLine("    PADDING-BOTTOM: 3px;");
txtstream.WriteLine("    COLOR: white;");
txtstream.WriteLine("    PADDING-TOP: 3px;");
```

```
txtstream.WriteLine("    BORDER-BOTTOM: #999 1px solid;");
txtstream.WriteLine("    BACKGROUND-COLOR: navy;");
txtstream.WriteLine("    FONT-FAMILY: font-family: Cambria, serif;");
txtstream.WriteLine("    FONT-SIZE: 10px;");
txtstream.WriteLine("    text-align: left;");
txtstream.WriteLine("    white-Space: nowrap;");
txtstream.WriteLine("    display:inline-block;");
txtstream.WriteLine("    width: 100%;");
txtstream.WriteLine("}");
txtstream.WriteLine("textarea");
txtstream.WriteLine("{");
txtstream.WriteLine("    BORDER-RIGHT: #999999 3px solid;");
txtstream.WriteLine("    PADDING-RIGHT: 3px;");
txtstream.WriteLine("    PADDING-LEFT: 3px;");
txtstream.WriteLine("    FONT-WEIGHT: Normal;");
txtstream.WriteLine("    PADDING-BOTTOM: 3px;");
txtstream.WriteLine("    COLOR: white;");
txtstream.WriteLine("    PADDING-TOP: 3px;");
txtstream.WriteLine("    BORDER-BOTTOM: #999 1px solid;");
txtstream.WriteLine("    BACKGROUND-COLOR: navy;");
txtstream.WriteLine("    FONT-FAMILY: font-family: Cambria, serif;");
txtstream.WriteLine("    FONT-SIZE: 10px;");
txtstream.WriteLine("    text-align: left;");
txtstream.WriteLine("    white-Space: nowrap;");
txtstream.WriteLine("    width: 100%;");
txtstream.WriteLine("}");
txtstream.WriteLine("select");
```

```
txtstream.WriteLine("{");
txtstream.WriteLine("   BORDER-RIGHT: #999999 3px solid;");
txtstream.WriteLine("   PADDING-RIGHT: 6px;");
txtstream.WriteLine("   PADDING-LEFT: 6px;");
txtstream.WriteLine("   FONT-WEIGHT: Normal;");
txtstream.WriteLine("   PADDING-BOTTOM: 6px;");
txtstream.WriteLine("   COLOR: white;");
txtstream.WriteLine("   PADDING-TOP: 6px;");
txtstream.WriteLine("   BORDER-BOTTOM: #999 1px solid;");
txtstream.WriteLine("   BACKGROUND-COLOR: navy;");
txtstream.WriteLine("   FONT-FAMILY: font-family: Cambria, serif;");
txtstream.WriteLine("   FONT-SIZE: 10px;");
txtstream.WriteLine("   text-align: left;");
txtstream.WriteLine("   white-Space: nowrap;");
txtstream.WriteLine("   width: 100%;");
txtstream.WriteLine("}");
txtstream.WriteLine("input");
txtstream.WriteLine("{");
txtstream.WriteLine("   BORDER-RIGHT: #999999 3px solid;");
txtstream.WriteLine("   PADDING-RIGHT: 3px;");
txtstream.WriteLine("   PADDING-LEFT: 3px;");
txtstream.WriteLine("   FONT-WEIGHT: Bold;");
txtstream.WriteLine("   PADDING-BOTTOM: 3px;");
txtstream.WriteLine("   COLOR: white;");
txtstream.WriteLine("   PADDING-TOP: 3px;");
txtstream.WriteLine("   BORDER-BOTTOM: #999 1px solid;");
txtstream.WriteLine("   BACKGROUND-COLOR: navy;");
```

txtstream.WriteLine("   FONT-FAMILY: font-family: Cambria, serif;");

txtstream.WriteLine("   FONT-SIZE: 12px;");

txtstream.WriteLine("   text-align: left;");

txtstream.WriteLine("   display:table-cell;");

txtstream.WriteLine("   white-Space: nowrap;");

txtstream.WriteLine("   width: 100%;");

txtstream.WriteLine("}");

txtstream.WriteLine("h1 {");

txtstream.WriteLine("color: antiquewhite;");

txtstream.WriteLine("text-shadow: 1px 1px 1px black;");

txtstream.WriteLine("padding: 3px;");

txtstream.WriteLine("text-align: center;");

txtstream.WriteLine("box-shadow: inset 2px 2px 5px rgba(0,0,0,0.5);, inset -2px -2px 5px rgba(255,255,255,0.5);;");

txtstream.WriteLine("}");

txtstream.WriteLine("</style>");

SHADOW BOX

txtstream.WriteLine("<style type='text/css'>");

txtstream.WriteLine("body");

txtstream.WriteLine("{");

txtstream.WriteLine("   PADDING-RIGHT: 0px;");

txtstream.WriteLine("   PADDING-LEFT: 0px;");

txtstream.WriteLine("   PADDING-BOTTOM: 0px;");

txtstream.WriteLine("   MARGIN: 0px;");

txtstream.WriteLine("   COLOR: #333;");

```
txtstream.WriteLine("    PADDING-TOP: 0px;");

txtstream.WriteLine("    FONT-FAMILY: verdana, arial, helvetica, sans-serif;");

txtstream.WriteLine("}");

txtstream.WriteLine("table");

txtstream.WriteLine("{");

txtstream.WriteLine("    BORDER-RIGHT: #999999 1px solid;");

txtstream.WriteLine("    PADDING-RIGHT: 1px;");

txtstream.WriteLine("    PADDING-LEFT: 1px;");

txtstream.WriteLine("    PADDING-BOTTOM: 1px;");

txtstream.WriteLine("    LINE-HEIGHT: 8px;");

txtstream.WriteLine("    PADDING-TOP: 1px;");

txtstream.WriteLine("    BORDER-BOTTOM: #999 1px solid;");

txtstream.WriteLine("    BACKGROUND-COLOR: #eeeeee;");

txtstream.WriteLine("
filter:progid:DXImageTransform.Microsoft.Shadow(color='silver', Direction=135,
Strength=16");

txtstream.WriteLine("}");

txtstream.WriteLine("th");

txtstream.WriteLine("{");

txtstream.WriteLine("    BORDER-RIGHT: #999999 3px solid;");

txtstream.WriteLine("    PADDING-RIGHT: 6px;");

txtstream.WriteLine("    PADDING-LEFT: 6px;");

txtstream.WriteLine("    FONT-WEIGHT: Bold;");

txtstream.WriteLine("    FONT-SIZE: 14px;");

txtstream.WriteLine("    PADDING-BOTTOM: 6px;");

txtstream.WriteLine("    COLOR: darkred;");

txtstream.WriteLine("    LINE-HEIGHT: 14px;");

txtstream.WriteLine("    PADDING-TOP: 6px;");
```

```
txtstream.WriteLine("   BORDER-BOTTOM: #999 1px solid;");
txtstream.WriteLine("   BACKGROUND-COLOR: #eeeeee;");
txtstream.WriteLine("   FONT-FAMILY: font-family: Cambria, serif;");
txtstream.WriteLine("   FONT-SIZE: 12px;");
txtstream.WriteLine("   text-align: left;");
txtstream.WriteLine("   white-Space: nowrap;");
txtstream.WriteLine("}");
txtstream.WriteLine(".th");
txtstream.WriteLine("{");
txtstream.WriteLine("   BORDER-RIGHT: #999999 2px solid;");
txtstream.WriteLine("   PADDING-RIGHT: 6px;");
txtstream.WriteLine("   PADDING-LEFT: 6px;");
txtstream.WriteLine("   FONT-WEIGHT: Bold;");
txtstream.WriteLine("   PADDING-BOTTOM: 6px;");
txtstream.WriteLine("   COLOR: black;");
txtstream.WriteLine("   PADDING-TOP: 6px;");
txtstream.WriteLine("   BORDER-BOTTOM: #999 2px solid;");
txtstream.WriteLine("   BACKGROUND-COLOR: #eeeeee;");
txtstream.WriteLine("   FONT-FAMILY: font-family: Cambria, serif;");
txtstream.WriteLine("   FONT-SIZE: 10px;");
txtstream.WriteLine("   text-align: right;");
txtstream.WriteLine("   white-Space: nowrap;");
txtstream.WriteLine("}");
txtstream.WriteLine("td");
txtstream.WriteLine("{");
txtstream.WriteLine("   BORDER-RIGHT: #999999 3px solid;");
txtstream.WriteLine("   PADDING-RIGHT: 6px;");
```

```
txtstream.WriteLine("    PADDING-LEFT: 6px;");
txtstream.WriteLine("    FONT-WEIGHT: Normal;");
txtstream.WriteLine("    PADDING-BOTTOM: 6px;");
txtstream.WriteLine("    COLOR: navy;");
txtstream.WriteLine("    LINE-HEIGHT: 14px;");
txtstream.WriteLine("    PADDING-TOP: 6px;");
txtstream.WriteLine("    BORDER-BOTTOM: #999 1px solid;");
txtstream.WriteLine("    BACKGROUND-COLOR: #eeeeee;");
txtstream.WriteLine("    FONT-FAMILY: font-family: Cambria, serif;");
txtstream.WriteLine("    FONT-SIZE: 12px;");
txtstream.WriteLine("    text-align: left;");
txtstream.WriteLine("    white-Space: nowrap;");
txtstream.WriteLine("}");
txtstream.WriteLine("div");
txtstream.WriteLine("{");
txtstream.WriteLine("    BORDER-RIGHT: #999999 3px solid;");
txtstream.WriteLine("    PADDING-RIGHT: 6px;");
txtstream.WriteLine("    PADDING-LEFT: 6px;");
txtstream.WriteLine("    FONT-WEIGHT: Normal;");
txtstream.WriteLine("    PADDING-BOTTOM: 6px;");
txtstream.WriteLine("    COLOR: white;");
txtstream.WriteLine("    PADDING-TOP: 6px;");
txtstream.WriteLine("    BORDER-BOTTOM: #999 1px solid;");
txtstream.WriteLine("    BACKGROUND-COLOR: navy;");
txtstream.WriteLine("    FONT-FAMILY: font-family: Cambria, serif;");
txtstream.WriteLine("    FONT-SIZE: 10px;");
txtstream.WriteLine("    text-align: left;");
```

```
txtstream.WriteLine("    white-Space: nowrap;");

txtstream.WriteLine("}");

txtstream.WriteLine("span");

txtstream.WriteLine("{");

txtstream.WriteLine("    BORDER-RIGHT: #999999 3px solid;");

txtstream.WriteLine("    PADDING-RIGHT: 3px;");

txtstream.WriteLine("    PADDING-LEFT: 3px;");

txtstream.WriteLine("    FONT-WEIGHT: Normal;");

txtstream.WriteLine("    PADDING-BOTTOM: 3px;");

txtstream.WriteLine("    COLOR: white;");

txtstream.WriteLine("    PADDING-TOP: 3px;");

txtstream.WriteLine("    BORDER-BOTTOM: #999 1px solid;");

txtstream.WriteLine("    BACKGROUND-COLOR: navy;");

txtstream.WriteLine("    FONT-FAMILY: font-family: Cambria, serif;");

txtstream.WriteLine("    FONT-SIZE: 10px;");

txtstream.WriteLine("    text-align: left;");

txtstream.WriteLine("    white-Space: nowrap;");

txtstream.WriteLine("    display: inline-block;");

txtstream.WriteLine("    width: 100%;");

txtstream.WriteLine("}");

txtstream.WriteLine("textarea");

txtstream.WriteLine("{");

txtstream.WriteLine("    BORDER-RIGHT: #999999 3px solid;");

txtstream.WriteLine("    PADDING-RIGHT: 3px;");

txtstream.WriteLine("    PADDING-LEFT: 3px;");

txtstream.WriteLine("    FONT-WEIGHT: Normal;");

txtstream.WriteLine("    PADDING-BOTTOM: 3px;");
```

```
txtstream.WriteLine("    COLOR: white;");
txtstream.WriteLine("    PADDING-TOP: 3px;");
txtstream.WriteLine("    BORDER-BOTTOM: #999 1px solid;");
txtstream.WriteLine("    BACKGROUND-COLOR: navy;");
txtstream.WriteLine("    FONT-FAMILY: font-family: Cambria, serif;");
txtstream.WriteLine("    FONT-SIZE: 10px;");
txtstream.WriteLine("    text-align: left;");
txtstream.WriteLine("    white-Space: nowrap;");
txtstream.WriteLine("    width: 100%;");
txtstream.WriteLine("}");
txtstream.WriteLine("select");
txtstream.WriteLine("{");
txtstream.WriteLine("    BORDER-RIGHT: #999999 3px solid;");
txtstream.WriteLine("    PADDING-RIGHT: 6px;");
txtstream.WriteLine("    PADDING-LEFT: 6px;");
txtstream.WriteLine("    FONT-WEIGHT: Normal;");
txtstream.WriteLine("    PADDING-BOTTOM: 6px;");
txtstream.WriteLine("    COLOR: white;");
txtstream.WriteLine("    PADDING-TOP: 6px;");
txtstream.WriteLine("    BORDER-BOTTOM: #999 1px solid;");
txtstream.WriteLine("    BACKGROUND-COLOR: navy;");
txtstream.WriteLine("    FONT-FAMILY: font-family: Cambria, serif;");
txtstream.WriteLine("    FONT-SIZE: 10px;");
txtstream.WriteLine("    text-align: left;");
txtstream.WriteLine("    white-Space: nowrap;");
txtstream.WriteLine("    width: 100%;");
txtstream.WriteLine("}");
```

```
txtstream.WriteLine("input");

txtstream.WriteLine("{");

txtstream.WriteLine("    BORDER-RIGHT: #999999 3px solid;");

txtstream.WriteLine("    PADDING-RIGHT: 3px;");

txtstream.WriteLine("    PADDING-LEFT: 3px;");

txtstream.WriteLine("    FONT-WEIGHT: Bold;");

txtstream.WriteLine("    PADDING-BOTTOM: 3px;");

txtstream.WriteLine("    COLOR: white;");

txtstream.WriteLine("    PADDING-TOP: 3px;");

txtstream.WriteLine("    BORDER-BOTTOM: #999 1px solid;");

txtstream.WriteLine("    BACKGROUND-COLOR: navy;");

txtstream.WriteLine("    FONT-FAMILY: font-family: Cambria, serif;");

txtstream.WriteLine("    FONT-SIZE: 12px;");

txtstream.WriteLine("    text-align: left;");

txtstream.WriteLine("    display: table-cell;");

txtstream.WriteLine("    white-Space: nowrap;");

txtstream.WriteLine("    width: 100%;");

txtstream.WriteLine("}");

txtstream.WriteLine("h1 {");

txtstream.WriteLine("color: antiquewhite;");

txtstream.WriteLine("text-shadow: 1px 1px 1px black;");

txtstream.WriteLine("padding: 3px;");

txtstream.WriteLine("text-align: center;");

txtstream.WriteLine("box-shadow: inset 2px 2px 5px rgba(0,0,0,0.5);, inset -2px -2px 5px rgba(255,255,255,0.5);;");

txtstream.WriteLine("}");

txtstream.WriteLine("</style>");
```